USAAF

FIGHTER STORIES

Other books by Ian McLachlan:

Night of the Intruders
First-hand accounts chronicling the
slaughter of homeward bound USAAF
Mission 311.

Final Flights
Dramatic wartime incidents revealed by
aviation archaeology.

Eighth Air Force Bomber Stories
(with Russell J. Zorn)
Eye-witness accounts from American
airmen and British civilians of the
perils of war.

USAAF
FIGHTER STORIES

Dramatic accounts of US fighter pilots in training
and combat over Europe in the Second World War

IAN McLACHLAN

Haynes Publishing

DEDICATION

For Sue

My Mustang MK III. Two crashed, this one has the endurance.

First published in hardback in October 1997
This hardback edition published in March 2012

British Library Cataloguing in Publication Data:
A catalogue record for this book is available from the British Library

ISBN 978 0 85733 227 1

Library of Congress catalog card no. 2100937155

Published by Haynes Publishing,
Sparkford, Yeovil, Somerset BA22 7JJ, UK
Tel: 01963 442030 Fax: 01963 440001
Int. tel: +44 1963 442030 Fax: +44 1963 440001
E-mail: sales@haynes.co.uk
Website: www.haynes.co.uk

Haynes North America Inc.,
861 Lawrence Drive, Newbury Park, California 91320

Printed and bound in the USA by Odcombe Press LP,
1299 Bridgestone Parkway, La Vergne, TN 37086

Contents

Preface

THE HOLLYWOOD IMAGE of American fighter pilots of the Second World War shows young heroes, flamboyant, romantic, silken-scarved knights of the skies. Flashes of such caricatures may emerge in some of the following personalities, but these stories are not celluloid. Young once, the survivors are now elderly, and have many comrades who remain forever young in their hearts and minds. To them all, I offer this book as a tribute. Together, they shared a love of flying that permeates these pages, but it is against a backdrop of gruelling air combat and many unforgiving enemies: fate, flak, human failings, mechanical malfunction, weather, and adversaries who fought from icy heights to deadly duels amongst the tree-tops. Such realism may dent images of chivalry offered elsewhere, but I offer no apology for iconoclasm. I simply ask the reader to remember young Americans who flew single-seat fighters, to think not only of aces but also of the total contribution made by many pilots who shared the same risks, and to recognise the contribution made by ground personnel.

Ian McLachlan
Beccles, Suffolk
1997

Acknowledgements

FIGHTER PILOTS flew solo. This author did not. Without the unstinting support given by former fighter pilots and their families there would be no book. Nor would it exist without the generosity of other authors, historians and friends who shared information and photographs – so much so that I am already planning a second volume, because not all would fit within these pages.

This book would also have been impossible without the love, support and 'stretched tolerance' of my wife Sue, to whom it is dedicated. She has had to endure the endless hours involved and then, on top of it all, type the entire manuscript.

My thanks also go to the children – Rowan, Jake, Maddie and Bethan – for sacrificing time and events we might have attended. My hope is that they and their generation will read of the young men from a former generation who fought for the legacy of freedom we now share.

Finally, my special thanks to the following:

A. Abendroth; H. C. Addy; S. Ananian; J. Balding; Char Baldridge; Brian Baldwin; Geoff Barker; N. Beckett; B. Billings; C. Bishop; S. Bishop; J. O. Bleidner; Theo Boiten; Martin Boswell; G. D. Bratley; Eugene F. Britton; Audree Buxton; Ron Buxton; Don Caldwell; Jeff Carless; CD Centre, Norwich; Tony Chardella; Rémy Chuinard; P. Claydon; Forrest S. Clark; M. Coffman; Bob Collis; Harry R. Corey; M. J. Cotter; Graham Cross; Jack T. Curtis; J. Deacon; Joe De Shay; Phyliss DuBois; S. Dunham; Colin Dunwell; *East Anglian Daily Times*; *Eastern Daily Press*; Dan Engle; Jeff Ethell; Roy W. Evans; Stewart P. Evans; Pat Everson; F. Fillet; R. R. Forbes-Morgan; Claude Foucher; N. Franks; R. A. Freeman; Garry L. Fry; the late Bill Gadd; Terry Gander; Chris Gardner; Tom Glenn, 36FG; Steve Gotts; John B. Guy; D. Hammond; C. Hall; George Hampson; Jeremy Hands, Anglia Television; J. Harris; Sid Harvey; Andy Height; Tom Hetherington; John Hey; J. Hogendyk; Harry F. Howard; Mrs Delmer F. Hubbell Jr; Jack Ilfrey; A. B. A. Jansen; O. W. Joiner; Osce R. Jones; A. A. C. Jordan; E. King; F. Kozaczka, Col USAF (Ret); D. Knight; Joseph A. Kuhn, Editor of *Lightning Strikes*; H. C. Kwik, Bulletin Air War; Leo D. Lester; R. M. Littlefield; Carol Lochhead; J. Mankie; T. Mann; Miss I. Marshall; John F. McAlevey; Jack E. McCoskey; Noel McDonald; D. McKenzie; D. McKibben; J. Measures; G. Meuzel; B. Meys; I. Miles; P. Miles; Ervin 'Dusty' Miller; F. Miller; Kent D. Miller; J. Mills; Jack Mitchell; Bill Moore; Mrs Helen Moore; Danny Morris; Bob Mynn, BOTNA; Clive Norman; Merle Olmsted; B. C. Orland; Duane W. Owens; B. Paul; Dick Penrose; Babs and Russ Pleasance; Bob Powell; Ron W. M. A. Putz; Dennis B. Rawls; C. Robinson; P. A. Rounce; Albert Scott; M. Sheldrick; Ross Smart; Pete Snowling; Lucien O. Sonnier; Sam Sox Jr; P. Stanley; Jim Starnes; Ed Stern; Frank M. Stillwell; Richard G. Thieme; Paul Thrower; B. Tyson; P. Tyson; Ken Underwood Jr; Donna Rae (Wetmore) Van Dyke; David Wade; R. T. Warboys;

D. Ward; Peter West; Col Robert V Weller USAF (Ret); P. Wilson; S. Woods; Major J. L. Wright, USAF (Ret); Ed Zellner; 100BG MAM; 390BG MAM; 93BG MAM HQ Air Force Inspection & Safety Centre Norton AFB; Norfolk & Suffolk Aviation Museum; and the Imperial War Museum.

Finally, there is special appreciation for the team at Haynes. My anchor editor, Flora Myer, guides the style and provides encouragement. To copy editor Will Adams my thanks for nabbing the mistakes, while Darryl Reach steers the project overall, ably supported by Alison Roelich and others whose efforts will hopefully make *USAAF Fighter Stories* as successful as its 'Bomber Stories' companion.

1: The iron-assed Eagle

MANY AMERICAN FIGHTER PILOTS saw combat before their own nation became embroiled in the Second World War. Young men, adventurers, idealists, the politically astute, those with a sense of justice, or boys who simply loved flying, volunteered to fight for the Allied cause. They were the plinth upon which many later achievements could be built.

An unsung and modest pilot whose own story encapsulates and represents many others is Ervin L. Miller, whom the author met following a chance meeting with two members of Duxford's famous Fighter Collection. Sitting bored in a departure lounge at London Heathrow in September 1995, I spotted a young man wearing a leather flying jacket bearing the Fighter Collection's Indian Head motif. Introducing myself, he turned out to be Chris Gardner, bound for America with Colin Dunwell. Enviously, I heard they were attending the Confederate Air Force Airshow in Texas before attending the Eagle Squadron/4FG reunion in San Diego, California. Also bound for San Diego, my own trip was purely business for my company, Wavetek. As fellow enthusiasts, we nattered about aircraft and I coveted the opportunities they had to fly in some famous warbirds.

Outlining to Chris my search for USAAF fighter pilot stories, he suggested I contact a friend of his, a genuine ex-Eagle, Ervin L. 'Dusty' Miller, who was still living in the UK. Addresses exchanged, we parted at Fort Worth, arranging to meet up on our return, when Chris would introduce me to Dusty. But it was not to be. Less than a week later both Chris and Colin died when the last airworthy B-26 Marauder crashed. By agreement with Dusty, this chapter is dedicated not only to him but to young Chris and his friend Colin, whose spirited enthusiasm for flying was reminiscent of Dusty's own those many years ago.

California back in 1926 had an inspiring atmosphere for any air-minded youngster – cloudless skies and a nation agog with the achievements of pioneering pilots. Twelve-year-old Ervin used to skinny-dip in San Francisco Bay as aircraft puttered into nearby Oakland Airport. One day he saw joy-rides advertised for $5.00, but could only stand wistfully aside, such a sum being well beyond his means. In later years Dusty recalled, 'I started to haunt the hangar. I was finally recognised as keen and was offered rides if I helped sweep out the hangar and wash down aircraft'.

Young Ervin eagerly joined crowds thronging to see idols such as Kingsford-Smith and Lindbergh. He spent hours crafting a solid wood scale model of the 'Spirit of St Louis' to win first prize in a school competition. Sadly his aspirations to attend the Boeing School of Aeronautics and study for a degree in aeronautical engineering, as well as working for his wings, were not supported by either friends or family. His parents strongly disapproved and would offer support only for the stifling environment of an Arts & Letters Course. Rebellion eventually overwhelmed him and he enlisted in the United States Navy in 1934, hoping for a route towards becoming a naval aviator.

Ervin was too good. Passing an Aviation Ordnance Course on torpedoes with 100 per cent, he found himself designated as a Torpedoman Striker! No amount of bucking could break the system, and the ship's Executive Officer rejected every request for a transfer. Instead of sulking, however, Ervin studied, passed further exams and gained promotion.

His real ambitions were assuaged by enrolling at a San Diego civilian flying school and being taught to fly in a Kinner side-by-side open-cockpit trainer. By now 23 years old, he was a gifted, natural pilot and soloed in only 5 hours 40 minutes. He flew at every opportunity in anything capable of defying gravity and, on one memorable occasion, in a Taylor Cub that was not. Having passed his Private Pilot's Test, he was accumulating hours in the Cub when his engine cut out during take-off. As the little 40hp continental engine quit, Ervin was confronted by power lines and the perimeter fence. Dodging both, he selected the only space available and tucked the little monoplane neatly between the volley-ball courts in the US Marine base next door. A few years later this experience helped him out of a predicament in an RAF Spitfire.

Leaving the Navy, Ervin found himself a job at Sacramento Airport and kept up his hours and experience by flying a variety of aircraft. In December 1940 a notice pinned in the flight shack attracted his attention – it would change his life. Giving an Oakland number, it asked for anyone interested in joining the British Royal Air Force to get in touch. Intrigued, Ervin phoned, outlined his experience, and was told to go to the Leamington Hotel, Oakland. Mysteriously he had to avoid reception and report to a specific room where he was ushered in for a cloak-and-daggerish interview by some civilians. He had, in fact, made contact with the Clayton Knight Organisation.

Prior to America entering the war, influential supporters of the Allied cause sought ways of aiding a by now beleaguered Britain and its courageous RAF. The concept of a squadron, perhaps more, of American pilots originated with a prominent anglophile and London resident, Charles Sweeney. His feelings were shared by other members of his prestigious family, also with British connections. They were, of necessity, diplomatically prudent to avoid breaching US neutrality laws, but in time their initially surreptitious activities became more open.

An early figure providing support was Air Vice Marshall Billy Bishop VC, a Canadian First World War ace and Royal Flying Corps hero. Bishop contacted an American friend, Clayton Knight, who had also flown in the RFC, and they formulated the ideal recruitment route – pass the pilots discreetly across the US border into Canada. Before long Clayton Knight committees were actively vetting applicants throughout America, and Ervin left his meeting confident that he would soon be flying Spitfires.

Weeks passed, then, around May 1941, he was asked to take a flight test. 'It was an aeroplane I'd never flown in before, a Waco 450 or Waco F1, I think they called it. I went up with a Britisher, he was a Squadron Leader, except he was in civilian clothes… I did all right, but I scared the hell out of him, and me, because he asked me to do a roll off the top. I asked him at what speed should I go into it with this airplane because I wasn't familiar with it, and he replied over the mouthpiece but I didn't understand it. I went into the manoeuvre at what I thought he said, but I came off the top and I flicked and ended up going in the same direction as we started. He asked what the hell had happened and said to try again, but a bit faster, which was all right.'

Dusty's first flight in a Hurricane 'scared the living hell' out of him. An example of the British fighter is pictured here later in the war. (W. Stanley)

Having passed, Ervin found himself with 30 other pupils at the Spartan School of Aeronautics in Tulsa, Oklahoma, flying US Army Trainers with civilian instructors. On completion of the course they were told how to leave the country. Ervin, like others, was registered for the draft, so was advised to inform his Draft Board that he was going to Canada 'on holiday'. Some holiday. As soon as he crossed the Canadian border he would be in the RAF and on its payroll; his 'holiday' would be protracted.

Crossing into Canada, he quickly found himself with 12 others on the *Letitia*, which convoyed into Liverpool under darkness. Disembarking, the bemused Americans were shepherded on a bus journey through the blitzed city, then on to a train for London. Arrival at the Strand Palace Hotel was rapidly followed by another nocturnal outing to Moss Bros. Entering in civvies, they were swiftly issued with uniforms and emerged in RAF blue as Pilot Officers. For political and practical reasons the pace continued onwards to Bournemouth, where the selection process, Ervin recalls, was, 'Those on the left, you're fighter pilots – those on the right, you're bomber pilots'.

Ervin was thankful he was on the left, and next found himself at RAF Ternhill for familiarisation training on Miles Masters, both the in-line Kestrel-engined and radial-engined variants. He then graduated to Hurricanes. The day of his first Hurricane flight remains vivid, unlike the weather that soggy Shropshire morning. Conditions were so poor that pilots assumed there would be no flying. Wrong! A tannoy disturbed the clack of snooker balls and gently rustling newspapers. All pilots were ordered to the flight line where stood the intimidating figure of their instructor, his handle-bar moustache still bristling. Where had they been? They were flying that day. He seemed impervious to the fact that the runway's perspective was truncated by heavy mist and the horizon an indistinct blending of grey into grey.

Ervin, now christened 'Dusty' by his chums, was one of the first scheduled to fly, and voiced the feelings of them all when, peering down the mist-enshrouded runway, he said, 'You can't be serious.'

They were. A brief introductory cockpit check on the Hurricane, a summary of the 'dos and don'ts' and, with the Merlin crackling characteristically, Dusty shimmied out behind the first two Hurricanes. He watched them power up and disappear into the mist still attached to the runway. Now it was his turn, and he prayed that no misfortune had caused a crack-up hidden on the runway ahead. Although accustomed to flying in sunnier California climes, Dusty was good on instruments. He needed to be, for this was his first solo over British soil in a combat aircraft, and 'it just scared the living hell' out of him.

Immediately after take-off Dusty concentrated on his instruments, flew a neat pattern and emerged from cloud less than 12 minutes later to find the runway exactly where expected. Sighing with relief, he touched down and taxied in. Others were less fortunate, and one pilot, lost and out of fuel, eventually crash-landed in Devon.

From Ternhill, Dusty travelled to 53 Operational Training Unit at Llandow in Wales, and there met an RAF legend. No sooner had the new arrivals unpacked when they were ordered to one of the aerodrome's more remote buildings. Pushing open the door, they were greeted by silence. Filing in, some 12 bewildered Americans stood glancing uneasily around the room, curious about the purpose behind this treatment. Gazing at the walls, their discomfort intensified as they moved forward to study the many pictures. No glamorous pin-ups, no recognition charts. In neat ranks were photographs of funerals, coffins draped, each and every one, with the Stars and Stripes. Minutes passed as they contemplated what had befallen some of their predecessors, then the door swung briskly open and in strode Group Captain Ira 'Taffy' Jones, a First World War ace with 40 victories to his credit, whose deeds were legendary to airmen in those days.

Leaping to attention, the Americans stood, poker-faced, while Taffy surveyed the scene and surrounding decor. Then, in his famous stutter, he said, 'I j-j-just w-w-want to tell you ch-chaps that I don't want to see any of you like that!' and walked out. His point had been made and he endeared himself to them during the coming weeks, especially in the bar where his capacity earned great respect. Taffy also knew how serious the situation was for the country, and welcomed the Americans wholeheartedly.

Britain's parlous position came home to Dusty from the weapon given to him for defence in case of a German paratroop attack: 'Pikes! Honestly. Had no guns. The airport defence people called us together and said, "This is your weapon in the event of a paratroop attack. You will proceed inside the perimeter fence and protect yourself with a pike." Well, can you imagine protecting yourself with a pike with a German paratrooper coming up with a tommy-gun! But that's a fact. I had mine sitting over in the corner of my billet – a damn stick with a knife on it!'

During those training days there were many escapades as pilots learned their art. There were 14 accidents in the first week, but none added to the picture gallery. Dusty remembers how instructors always urged wheels up early after take-off, and one trainee, George Middleton, was over-enthusiastic. Tucking the wheels up too soon, he overlooked his Spitfire's tendency to settle slightly, so chewed the propeller and bent his undercarriage. With its somewhat modified propeller, the only way to keep airborne was full throttle, and the hapless pilot screeched around his circuit with an agonised Merlin sounding like a banshee with toothache. Even worse, the aircraft shook so much that it vibrated the throttle shut, and poor George was obliged to contort one knee as a wedge while porpoising around the airfield attempting to hand-pump the undercarriage into place. Staggering back for a crash-landing, he emerged a wiser airman.

Other skirmishes occurred with the British weather, and Dusty also tangled with one of the RAF's mythical gremlins. Nipping along on a low-level sortie, he realised that his engine temperature was suddenly climbing and the Merlin wheezed out its growing discomfort in puffs of glycol and smoke. Too low to jump, Dusty decided he might just make the airfield at St Eval, but then found the runway obstructed by what looked like old bombers in storage. As before in California, he faced another nowhere-else-to-go choice. Avoiding trees, he found a field like the proverbial postage stamp, cut his throttle and slipped the Spitfire down on the grass with its wheels up. Sliding to a standstill, Dusty quickly vacated his machine in case the dangerously hot engine ignited, but both pilot and plane were allowed to cool off while a recovery crew spent 2 hours trying to find them.

His training complete, Dusty was posted to 130 Spitfire Squadron at Perranporth for a frustrating few winter weeks of anti-shipping patrols. Elsewhere in the RAF, American casualties had been mounting, and Dusty's days of boredom vanished with a vengeance when he found himself transferred to 133 'Eagle' Squadron at the premier station of Biggin Hill.

It was June 1942 and the RAF was baiting the Luftwaffe over its own territory. Such operations were costly and, with hindsight, largely unproductive. The RAF's Spitfire Vs were outclassed, especially by the Focke-Wulf 190, which was faster and more manoeuvrable, except in turns. Dusty's recollections of this period involve eager young American pilots and other RAF comrades challenging highly skilled enemies and suffering grievous losses. The German chisel was still sharp and cut deeply, but even though German losses were lower, every one eroded that edge.

'They were always above us – they had the advantage because we were sweeping France. That was their home base and we used to fly over on the deck and start climbing about mid-Channel to try and surprise them. But they were always up there, waiting… That was their tactic. They'd hit, dive out of the sun and go right through us. My first mission, we lost four and I didn't even see a Jerry.'

Dusty was wingman for Don Blakeslee, whose terse command had been simply 'Don't lose me, Miller', and Dusty dared not. 'I was holding on his tail and, as he flew, all I could see was his tail-wheel.'

Retrospectively still proud of their achievements, Dusty is saddened when he remembers the many lads lost whose sacrifice made no significant strategic contribution to the war's outcome.

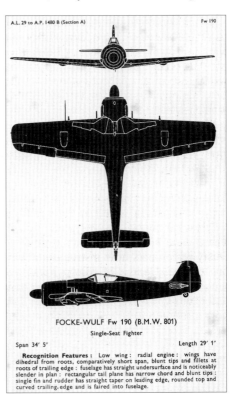

FOCKE-WULF Fw 190 (B.M.W. 801)
Single-Seat Fighter

Span 34' 5"   Length 29' 1"

Recognition Features : Low wing : radial engine : wings have dihedral from roots, comparatively short span, blunt tips and fillets at roots of trailing edge : fuselage has straight undersurface and is noticeably slender in plan : rectangular tail plane has narrow chord and blunt tips : single fin and rudder has straight taper on leading edge, rounded top and curved trailing edge and is faired into fuselage.

A recognition chart for the Fw 190, which outclassed the Spitfire V and, through various marks, proved a tough opponent for Allied pilots throughout the war.

Eagles all: Spitfire days at Debden as pilots and personnel of the 336FS, 4FG, await briefing for a sortie in 1943. Seated on the hood (or bonnet!) is Bob Messenger. Dusty is rear left, then (from left to right) Major Jim DuFour, Squadron Commander; unknown; the Medic; unknown. Lt Bob Mirsch is in the driving seat while Lt Bishop enjoys a cigar. (E. Miller)

'We'd just be a nuisance – nuisance raids because we didn't have any endurance. One and a half hours was about the peak and, if you got into combat, it was less than that – you had to allow for return to base.'

Dusty's adored Spitfire, beautiful to fly and a deadly defensive interceptor, lacked the range required. The long-legged Mustang was over a year away from entering combat, and these pioneer American pilots duelled and died bravely alongside their Allied brothers-in-arms. They contributed to an erosion in the balance of fighter-pilot quality that their successors would expand upon over the next three years.

'It affected us,' Dusty remembers, 'but you never thought about pranging really. I never did. I was apprehensive sometimes, when it was a long raid and we knew we were going to fly into heavy flak. It was pretty painful. We used to escort Bostons to bomb Abbeville and St Omer, which were the two main fighter squadrons in France, and the Boston was a fast aircraft. We'd fly close formation with 'em… The Jerries were all around but they wouldn't come in because of the flak – it was right up your butt! In some cases it would get somebody… We always hated those areas as far as the flak was concerned.'

Away from flak and enemy fighters, the Eagles sought to enjoy life like any other young men. Recognising the need for the correct type of female companionship, various clubs had emerged where officers from overseas could meet young women of suitable character. One winter's night, a foray into London took Dusty and a companion up some stairs to a small club off Leicester Square. A roaring fire and comfortable armchairs compensated for the early evening emptiness, then, hastening in from the cold, came two very attractive young women. One, Pat, made an immediate impression on Dusty. Persuaded by her friend to go, Pat had been very reluctant, but Dusty soon established diplomatic relations. Introductions made, the four chatted easily, but, to Pat's annoyance, Dusty seemed more interested in her friend. Now, after over five decades of marriage, she feels it was a deliberate ploy, and admits that it worked!

Soon Dusty, returning from raids, was regularly buzzing Hampstead Garden Suburb, often to the consternation of other residents and the local authorities. While Pat and her sister energetically waved bath towels from their back garden, others became quite alarmed. On one occasion Dusty even triggered an air-raid alert and suddenly found his Spitfire being hemmed in by rapidly rising barrage balloons. Thankfully he spiralled upwards unscathed, having sent one woman into labour. Pat and her sister never let on, and Dusty's flying career continued unblemished.

On 26 September 1942 disaster struck 133 Squadron when a planned escort for B-17 'Flying Fortresses' went tragically wrong. Dusty was scheduled to fly the mission in one of the squadron's recently acquired Spitfire IXs and had already placed his parachute and helmet on board when a slight change of plan set him and Don Gentile aside as spares. Dusty's room-mate went instead, and died over France.

Of the 12 Spitfires that took off, only one came back: Pilot Officer R. N. Beaty had engine trouble and turned back to crash-land near Kingsbridge, fortunately suffering only slight injuries. Commanded by a British Officer, Flight Lieutenant E. G. Brettell, the remaining 11 aircraft, unable to find the bombers, searched onwards over an unrelenting brilliance of unbroken clouds. They believed the bombers were ahead and hoped to catch up, but a combination of cloud and unpredictably strong winds now sealed their fate. With all landmarks obscured, they lost any visual reference to their true ground speed, while tail-winds forecasted for 40mph were exceeding 100mph and pushing the Spitfires unwittingly beyond their point of no return. When they eventually turned for home it was already too late – none had the range to get back. A descent over heavily defended Brest only compounded matters as flak, fighters and, finally, lack of fuel took down every single Spitfire.

Dusty was stunned. Had it not been for that adjustment in orders, his name would have been one of the 11 missing pilots. It was an inauspicious background to the squadron's transfer to the USAAF – 133 Squadron had virtually ceased to exist. Within hours movement orders drew in other Americans scattered throughout Fighter Command, and the official handover occurred on 29 September.

Speaking at the parade, the words of Air Marshall Sir Sholto Douglas represented the feelings of many: 'It is with great personal regret that I today say "Goodbye" to all you boys whom it has been my privilege to command. You joined us readily and of your own free will when our need was greatest and before your country was actually at war with our common enemy. You were the vanguard of the great host of your compatriots who are now helping to make these Islands a base from which to launch that great offensive which we all desire. You have proved yourself great fighters and good companions, and we shall watch your future with confidence. There are those of your number who are not here today – those sons of the United

A Spitfire of 336FS receives attention after a mishap at Martlesham Heath. (E. Miller)

States who were the first to give their lives for their country. We of the RAF, no less than yourselves, will always remember them with pride…'

The smartness of their turn-out that day contrasted with the mixed garb normally worn by this still-hybrid unit. Dusty flew attired in British uniform trousers and an American flying jacket, but the forthcoming weeks saw the three former RAF squadrons, 71, 121 and 133, blend into the USAAF's 334, 335 and 336 Squadrons, 4th Fighter Group. Dusty, like other original Eagles, never relinquished the proudest part of his RAF uniform, his wings. Special dispensation was afforded, allowing Eagles to wear both their RAF wings and the new silver wings of the USAAF.

However, another aspect of their origins would soon pass into history – their much-loved Spitfires were to go. Early in 1943 the Spitfire's stunning shape faded from Debden in favour of the large, chubby Republic P-47C Thunderbolt.

Like others, Dusty lamented the loss of his Spitfire: 'It was beautiful … beautiful. I sat in that Spitfire and felt a part of it… You just can't explain the ecstasy… You'd put on that airplane and get up amongst the clouds, it was just be-au-ti-ful. A Spitfire was fun to fly, but a Thunderbolt you had to watch. It didn't take kindly to people who didn't have their wits about 'em. You could stall a Spitfire, put the power on and she'd just keep on going, wobble on out and keep going. Do that with a Thunderbolt and you were in! That damn wing on a Thunderbolt was as high as a Spitfire cockpit – it was a monster. Seven tons! We were all apprehensive … but it proved to be a good bird – it was big, safe. But we lost four Thunderbolts initially for the simple reason that they tried to out-turn the Spitfire at low altitude. They failed, and when a Thunderbolt flicks at under 8,000 feet, you're dead. It'd just go, and go right in, so they had to warn everybody, "No unusual attitudes under 8,000 feet".'

Gradually the great beast earned grudging respect from many 4FG pilots for the attributes it had, but it never settled with them as it did elsewhere, most famously with the 56FG.

Dusty continued his combat career through 1943 as the balance of air superiority continued to tilt in favour of the Allies, but even so he never underestimated his enemy: 'We respected those German pilots, you damn betcha. They weren't amateurs you know – ended up amateurs.' He was no amateur himself, and it was realised that his knowledge could benefit the enthusiastic neophytes now arriving from America.

The Control Tower at Atcham, Shropshire, home of the 495 Fighter Training Group, on a summer's day. (E. Miller)

Dusty selected this natural-metal-finish P-47 to be his personal aircraft when he became a one-man 'Luftwaffe' and earned his reputation as 'Iron-ass' Miller. (E. Miller)

In September 1943 he was therefore posted, protesting vigorously, to the head of training for what became the 495 Fighter Training Group at Atcham, Shropshire. Dusty was married, somewhat older than the average combat pilot, and Pat had just given birth to a son. It was felt that he had earned a respite, although there is no doubt that the training programme he introduced could hardly be described as restful. He knew that he could save lives by imparting his combat experience to the increasing flow of eager young birdmen now arriving from America. For training to be valuable it had to be realistic, so Dusty soon became a one-man 'Luftwaffe'. Selecting an all-silver P-47 modified with a water injection system that increased engine power and climb, he played 'Jerry' and soon the reputation of 'Iron-Ass Miller' became renowned. Hurtling down like a harrier, he would strike and soar away from startled trainees who were 'dead' before they knew it, a tragic occurrence Dusty had so often seen for real.

Inwardly he admitted that he was lucky to have his modified P-47:

'Those young pilots were keen as mustard and they could beat the hell out of me, so I'd just hit and run, show 'em what it was like to be attacked by a German.'

Dusty has no doubt that those he caught and taught took their training experiences into combat, but, as in all flying tuition, there were casualties. Some were caused by inexperience, some by over-confidence, others by mechanical malfunction and many by that perpetual enemy, the British weather.

'I grounded pilots because they just didn't have it,' Dusty recalls. 'A chap wrapped up Thunderbolts twice in two weeks. One was at Shawbury – said his engine quit and he rolled it up in a ball – the next was at Boscombe Down, which had about 4 miles of runway. I had to ground him and he was pleased I did. I lost a pilot because he was too cocky. I was warning him about flat spins and unusual attitudes under 8,000 feet and he said, "Thunderbolt! It can't flat spin." He went up and he did it and he got killed. Another pilot boasted, "Aw, the old feller don't know what the hell he's talkin' about", and he killed himself.'

Dusty cared for the men under his command and helped whenever he could. He even talked down one terrified rookie after six nerve-racking landing attempts had failed. Speaking gently but firmly from the tower, he guided the lad through every inch of his approach and was later rewarded when that same youngster made the grade as a successful fighter pilot.

A scene at Atcham. Dusty had several aircraft at his disposal, ranging from P-47s to the AT-6 and C-64 Norseman on the right. (E. Miller)

'We had every type of accident you could possibly have at Atcham. I had my private air force and could go out at any time and fly one of those aircraft. I was Chief Investigating Officer, and every time we had an accident, I was there. If it was a small field I took my Cub, and if I had to take an engineer or photographer, I took a bigger plane. I had an inch-to-the-mile map of our flying area on the wall. Every day we had 48 Thunderbolts airborne. The Wrekin was only 2½ miles from us – we didn't ever have a Thunderbolt hit the Wrekin, but we had other mountains. Boy! We clobbered 'em. Atcham was initially a reception centre for all the fighter squadrons, then it became a training group when I went up there. I had to start from scratch, more or less.'

The casualty rate was too high and Dusty suspected some fundamental problems with the quality of pilots being passed across from training establishments in America.

'We were losing pilots on sector reconnaissance… The squadron instructors

'Every day we had 48 Thunderbolts airborne.' P-47 pilots return from a training flight. (E. Miller)

Atcham's role diminished towards the end of 1944 and scenes like this soon became history. Ground crew are busy on a 495FG Thunderbolt. (E. Miller)

would take up a group of pilots and just fly around Shropshire to show 'em the lay of the land, Welsh hills, and we started losing pilots on these flights – flying into the ground. Then we started losing them spinning out of cloud. Silly accidents.'

This alarming accident rate prompted questions from higher command in the USA, who seemed not to appreciate that the higher the number of hours flown, the higher the accident rate. However, Dusty himself became suspicious of a more fundamental problem and began to investigate. Setting aside an interview room, he took newly arrived pilots and went in detail through the categories of flying time they had accrued according to their Form 5: 'Instruments, formation, cloud, low-flying, the lot'. It soon became evident that some creative accounting had occurred to embellish records and enhance figures for achieving trainee throughput. This also avoided the political and public relations embarrassment of reporting a higher domestic accident rate, and such requirements encouraged shifting the problem overseas. Immediately instigating some back-to-basics training, Dusty saw the accident rate reduce.

Atcham's role diminished towards the end of 1944 and Dusty found that his days as 'Iron-ass Miller' were over. Post-war he retired from the Air Force, was recalled for Korea but found himself back in England with the Third Air Force. Eventually he and Pat settled to a happy retirement in a cosy Norfolk cottage. This Eagle had landed, content in the country he fought to protect before teaching others the skills necessary to continue the task.

2: An unlucky Lockheed

RELEASING HIS SEAT HARNESS, First Lieutenant Tom Hetherington fell heavily on his back into the inverted canopy of his crashing fighter. Struggling to get free, he realised that his seat-pack parachute had wedged behind the hinged section of the canopy structure. Upside down and hurtling earthwards, Tom was trapped in a doomed and disintegrating aircraft.

The exigencies of war sometimes urged aircraft into combat when consideration of known flaws became outweighed by stronger advantages, or the risks were not fully understood. There might also be the drive to replace current types outmoded by the performance of their adversaries. In the technological arms race encouraged by war, designers encountered aerodynamic phenomena about which little knowledge existed and, in the demand for ever-increasing performance, risks had to be taken. Lockheed's P-38 Lightning, like its contemporaries, was nearing the limitations of piston-engined performance and was bedevilled by problems with its twin Allison engines and a spectre of aerodynamic malevolence known then as 'compressibility'. The P-38 undoubtedly deserves its reputation as one of the premier fighters of the Second World War, but these difficulties curtailed its potential in the European Theatre of Operations and killed many young pilots.

First Lieutenant Thomas F. Hetherington Jr stood on the tarmac cynically surveying the recently arrived Lockheed P-38J-10-LO, Army Air Force serial number 42-67498. Built in Burbank only weeks earlier, the $120,000 aircraft had just 22 hours flying time and was one of the first of this variant to reach the 55th Fighter Squadron, 20FG. With over 1,223 flying hours to his credit, Tom had flown many previous models including the P-38D, E, F, G and H, together with some earlier J series. To Tom, each succession seemed more complex, less manoeuvrable and suffered from more minor malfunctions than its predecessor.

Lieutenant Thomas F. Hetherington Jr was determined to 'wring out' Lockheed's latest offering. (T. Hetherington)

Above *Tom had flown many variants of the Lightning, including the P-38F seen here.* (C. Norman)

Right *An example of the P-38J series. To Tom, each succession seemed more complex and less manoeuvrable than its predecessor.* (Lockheed/ J. K. Huhn)

Critical to the survival of any fighter pilot was his machine's ability to turn. Having sampled the nimble Spitfire, and flown a P-47, Tom was admittedly very doubtful about the P-38 in comparison, and was determined to 'wring out' Lockheed's latest offering during this test flight. Staff Sergeant Carpenter and his team had checked the new machine and, after exterior inspection, Tom duly signed the flight forms before climbing aboard and stowing them in the documents case. Feeling somewhat superstitious, he did not welcome the appearance of a photographer, but rather than behave churlishly he allowed the man to continue. He never saw those photographs.

Settling in his seat, Tom verified the status of the electrical fuel pump, set the ignition switches, then turned the starter switch for the port engine. A familiar whine from the inertia starter soon followed. Engaging the port engine, he felt the airframe shake as the propeller juddered into life, protested a little, then blended its blades into a blur as the Allison sent its ritual blast of blue-grey smoke writhing along the tail boom. Invigorating the starboard engine, Tom carefully continued his pre-flight checks: oil pressures; engine temperatures; magnetos; propeller pitch; hydraulics; free movement of the flight controls. Nothing amiss. Before taxiing, he boosted both engines to take-off power and checked the superchargers. His earlier inspection had registered some visual differences on this variant because alterations had been made to improve performance of the supercharger intercoolers, but all seemed well.

After clearance from Wittering Control, Tom taxied out. The burble of each engine was broken when he gunned on power to help the turn, finally swivelling the olive drab aircraft on to the runway. Rolling forwards a few feet he straightened the nose wheel. Permission received, his take-off began.

No wise pilot ever takes for granted his departure from terra firma, and the Lightning had some notoriety for engine failure. In this marriage of destinies, the P-38 could be an unfaithful wife, and Tom tensed himself to react should either Allison fail, a frequently fatal situation if the aircraft's sudden yaw was not instantly countered. Passing 70mph, he eased back the yoke, the nose lifted and at over 100mph she transitioned smoothly into the air. Gear up, mixture to auto rich, intercooler flaps open and airspeed over 160mph, the new Lockheed ascended steadily to Tom's trial altitude.

Initially, Tom tested the aircraft's behaviour by performing several routine checks and obtaining a 'feel' for this fighter. Now for a more rigorous evaluation. At 35,000 feet he commenced a series of fast, level runs, mentally noting the speeds at which a characteristic known as 'buffeting' occurred. The P-38's innovative design and performance enabled altitudes and airspeeds that put it into then relatively unknown realms of aerodynamic behaviour. Buffeting was created by air, disturbed when flowing over the forward wing section and gondola, tumbling aft to slap or 'buffet' the empennage, sometimes with disastrous consequences.

Satisfied with his speed tests, Tom next tried a crucial manoeuvre called the 'break'. If an alarm call was received – for example 'Break right, Blue Two!' – any pilot anxious to live would whip into the tightest turn possible to evade the assailant making a bounce. Simulating this, Tom ran the P-38 to maximum speed then, imagining an enemy bounce, he broke sharply to starboard. In fractions of a second the Lightning snapped out of control and lunged earthwards.

Sensing serious structural failure, Tom still tried to recover, but the Lightning fell with increasing speed. Frantically he throttled back, adjusted the propeller pitch and quickly re-trimmed using elevator trim tabs as advised in the pilot's manual. Anticipating recovery, he waited a few moments. Nothing happened. Further cranking of the trim-tab handle. Still no result. Tom's P-38 was descending like a demon late for the devil's wedding.

Having cranked it some 15 degrees one way, he stared in disbelief at the trim tab scale, then, in desperation, tried to reverse it – anything to stop his headlong plunge towards oblivion. No response. In fear and exasperation he even dropped flap, but his aircraft stubbornly ignored any coercion. Applying power was not recommended, but Tom was beyond the book and, in a final gesture, he threw power into the engines, praying that it might pull the P-38 from its locked-in enthusiasm to crash. But the Lightning ignored him and had now tucked its nose beyond the vertical; airspeed had passed the red zone of 420mph, and violent vibrations warned of complete disintegration. Time to go … if he could.

Cutting power, Tom released his seat harness and promptly dropped into the inverted canopy, his seat pack pinning itself in the tapering space between structure and streamlined perspex. Reaching with his right hand for the emergency canopy release, he tucked one index finger round and pulled. No response. The ground, eager to devour both him and the Lightning, seemed to be surging towards him. Grasping the stubborn release with his left hand, then bracing his left wrist with his right hand, Tom tugged hard. Everything went blank.

Coming to, he found himself seemingly in darkness, his chin forced down on his chest and no strength in him to resist. He was blind. Falling. A terrifying dream? Reality? His senses strove to pull his ripcord but his right arm would not move. All was silent, peaceful. No screeching engines or sounds of tortured aluminium tearing apart, just a distant, almost soothing, rush of air. Without worry or fear, he felt he was dead, not falling but floating upwards into Valhalla. Relaxing completely, he realised that this journey needed no effort. Then, with a tremendous jolt, he was shocked back into the cold, painful hard-frozen reality of winter farmland. Somehow the impact instantly restored his vision, but his pain-racked body was unable to move. Wind, billowing cruelly into his parachute, now tormented him by jerking his body from crest to crest on frozen-waved furrows of farmland. Every dip and peak renewed and strengthened the bursts of agony stabbing into his mind, cursed and prolonged by the paralysis that locked his limbs into immobility.

During a pause in this excruciating process, Tom saw two farmworkers warily approaching, pitchforks poised but clearly lacking the wit to realise that he was no threat, nor a German. Ignoring his pleas for them to take the hunting knife in his harness and cut him free, the reluctant rustics simply stood, perplexed, watching him. Shock now set in, and Tom's body trembled, but still they would not help.

Then, lurching towards them Tom saw the salvation of a jeep. An American sergeant leapt out, ran across and quickly cut the cords of the grateful pilot's parachute. A syringe of morphine emerged, perhaps from Tom's first aid kit, and he was given a shot. Gently covering him with a blanket, the sergeant lit a cigarette before easing it between Tom's lips. Only then did his Samaritan speak, but Tom's fading senses failed to register any introduction, only pain and the prolonged wait for an ambulance. More medication, perhaps morphine, then another darkness, but softer and without fear of falling.

Close to death, Tom was taken to the 231st Station Hospital where doctors began to investigate the extent of his injuries. Fractured fibulas and tibias on both sides were but a beginning. His fourth and fifth lumber vertebrae were also fractured, and he had a dislocated left shoulder and humerus. Stretched 9 inches like some grotesque cartoon character, his pelvis had separated. This 'bone' is actually in two parts, the left and right pelvic halves, with the thigh bones attached. Joints here are strengthened by muscle but, if torn open, there is a severe risk of internal damage to the bladder, bowel and arteries. Tom was a medical miracle to be still alive, and the 231st intended keeping him that way.

Fortunately Tom's general fitness helped as he began his long struggle towards recovery. Less serious but outwardly more alarming, his appearance shocked early visitors including friend and fellow pilot Carl Jackson. Tom looked like a pugilistic nightmare. As if repeatedly punched by a giant, his nose had retreated into a swollen, purple-blue face with both eyes blackened and, where white should have been, there was only vampire red from ruptured blood vessels. Carl had brought him a souvenir panel from his parachute and revealed how the 'D' ring had been found still seated in its pocket – Tom had never pulled his parachute ripcord.

Together the two pilots conjectured the sequence of events. When Tom had yanked open the release, he had popped out of the aircraft like a champagne cork because of the pressure differential. The cockpit gondola in the wing centre section was styled like an aerofoil and, travelling at high speed, it produced low pressure over the canopy, which, when ejected, had caused Tom to be wrenched out of the cockpit, causing damage to his left arm and shoulder. The blast of air tore off his helmet, goggles, oxygen mask and three pairs of flying gloves – silk, chamois and leather gauntlets – plus his watch. The pummelling from a 420mph slipstream knocked him out. Instead of being conscious for deceleration to a terminal velocity of some 125mph, then opening his parachute, he was falling to his death.

Luckily, his snagged parachute pack may have torn during his violent exit and air had then forced free the remaining folds. Snapping open, the canopy had acted like a sudden brake, literally stretching and twisting his torso in its harness. The parachute had then either burst under the pressure of air as it opened, or some panels had been torn by pieces of his disintegrating aircraft. Either way, with his parachute now preserving only partial functionality, he had plummeted to earth, where the impact had added further injuries by reversing the stretching sustained earlier into a crushing concertina causing compression fractures in his vertebrae.

Such varied injuries were beyond the resources of the 231st, and after initial care plus a failed attempt to force his pelvis into place, they put him in a double-hipped spica cast and transferred him to the 30th General Hospital at Mansfield near Nottingham. Staffed by top US doctors and surgeons, the 30th embarked on a comprehensive reconstruction and rehabilitation process. Tom found himself in a 'Rube Goldberg' contraption comprising two horizonal bars about 4 feet above his bed, parallel to the sides and attached to the bed both head and foot. Central in each bar arrangement was a pulley wheel and ropes linked to a bag of heavy lead balls with the ropes then secured to a sling in which Tom lay suspended about an inch off the mattress. This was normal orthopaedic procedure, because finely tuned traction proved essential to link the ends of fractured bones, aid healing and resist the risk of muscle movement distorting bone alignment.

Adding to Tom's woes, his right leg was plaster-cast from his pelvis to his foot, which was then wedged against a wooden stop to keep it straight. Operating on his left leg, surgeons pinned through his left tibia, below the knee, and a 'U'-shaped rod was fitted to each end of the pin and ropes rigged from this through another wheel-and-lead-ball arrangement at the foot of the bed. His left arm was similarly furnished from elbow to fingertips by attachment to another rope and pulley system that kept it perpendicular. This meant that his right arm was the only limb with any mobility.

For ten weeks Tom hung in this contrivance. Then further complications occurred when thrombophlebitis (blood clots) developed, resulting from his injuries and prolonged inactivity. During emergency surgery doctors ligated the femoral vein in his left leg to eliminate the risk of blood clots reaching his heart or brain. Happily this danger passed and Tom survived, but it was April 1944 before he could be assisted into standing for the first time. Later that month he was sent home on a hospital ship and continued his treatment at Brooke Hospital in San Antonio. In November he was transferred to a USAAF rehabilitation centre at Fort Logan, Colorado. At first mobile on crutches, then only a cane, it was nonetheless evident that his career as a fighter pilot was over, and he officially retired from the USAAF in December 1944.

In the spring of 1945, the war he helped win ended. Like many veterans, Tom had a new life to develop: a bachelor's degree at UT Austin, then to the prestigious Yale for a law degree before a successful business career. His encounter with that unlucky Lockheed failed to dampen his pleasure in piloting, and he eventually purchased his own aircraft to enjoy a more docile form of aviating.

Lockheed's troubled beauty continued to encounter problems in the European climate and, during the summer of 1944, faded from front-line inventory as an Eighth Air Force fighter. However, an admirable performance elsewhere, particularly in the Pacific Theatre, earned many accolades for the P-38 and ensured its place in the history of wartime aviation.

During 1974 local aviation archaeologists found the crash site of Tom's troublesome fighter and eventually contacted him. Early indications were that a lot of the Lightning lay still buried, but recovery was thwarted when the digger exhausted its reach at 14 feet after finding engine fragments, an oil cooler and one propeller blade. Fifteen years later, on 11 March 1989, another group, including the author, gathered to complete the task.

Our activities attracted several local inhabitants as the digger snorted noisily into position atop the roadside embankment near Walsham le Willows in Suffolk. Some spectators remembered the dramatic events of December 1943. Teddy Hubbard, then aged 12, had been playing soccer that afternoon, but took his eye off the ball to watch the fighter 'doing aerobatics' high above. Next second the engine sounds changed, intensifying alarmingly as the aircraft came screeching earthwards minus its tail section and continuing to disintegrate. The sound terrified Teddy's sister, Barbara, playing nearby. She saw a propeller whirl away from the falling fighter to embed itself in a nearby field, leaving a 'vee' of blades visible. Two farmworkers dived for cover as the P-38 exploded nearby, while the pilot's parachute was seen falling in the direction of Wyverstone.

A report submitted by Police Constable Sykes states that Tom landed at 3.30 pm near Westhorpe Church. Later, local children gathered ammunition littering surrounding farmland but, unhappily for the present-day enthusiasts, the erstwhile youngsters also remembered how a USAAF recovery team had dragged away the engines and lifted the nose out of the roadside crater with all the guns dangling from the debris. This was confirmed when strong detector readings faded after clearing several chunks of aluminium.

Cutting below the drainage ditch into virgin clay, we caught the reek from entrapped pockets of aviation fuel, but the wreckage terminated in a layer of burnt detritus barely 2 feet beneath the embankment's turf. Mingled amidst this shale were bullets, fragments of engine, several spark plugs and, best of all, the remains of the aircraft's clock. After slicing a series of very deep channels across the crash site and encountering nothing else, our disappointed team closed the dig.

'Mingled amidst this shale were bullets, fragments of engine…' The scene at a roadside embankment near Walsham le Willows on 11 March 1989. Left to right are David Wade, Jeff Carless, Geoff Barker and Clint Cansdale. (John Measures)

3: Wendell's wallet

SOME TIME AGO, in mysterious circumstances, I was given a wallet that had belonged to Second Lieutenant Roy E. Wendell of the 78th Fighter Group from Duxford. Its contents typified the official and personal paraphernalia of a USAAF flier: pictures of a girlfriend; officer's identity card; medical records; and salary allotment forms for $50.00, increasing later to $100.00 per month to his mother in Sioux Falls, South Dakota. His service in the UK was denoted by a ration card and stamps for the Officers' Mess, together with a ticket stub from a recent orchestral performance at the Howard Athenaeum.

In time, such minutiae of life is often discarded, but circumstances had seemingly encapsulated and preserved this fascinating insight into the life of its owner. But what were those circumstances? The wallet clearly came from a dig and still reeked of aviation fuel, but the regular digging fraternity knew nothing of it. All my informant knew was that it had been in the possession of the USAF, who had planned

*This portrait of sweetheart Norma Jean Bishop (**below left**) reminds us that war is not heroics or the speed and glamour of fighters. Like so many she faced the cruel personal loss of love promised but denied by fate. The second photograph is another snapshot to warm the heart of a homesick flier.*

Left   Sister? Another picture from the lost airman's wallet.

Above   After being buried for decades this picture survived to record happy moments for three fliers before they sailed overseas into the uncertainties of war. Roy (centre) never returned.

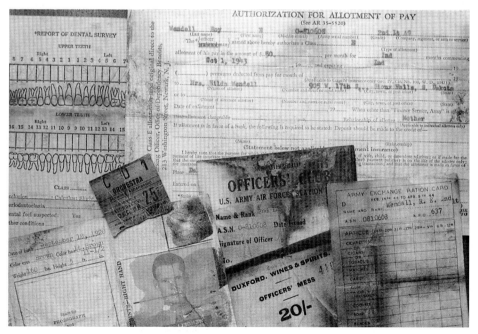

The personal and official contents of Wendell's wallet provide an insight into his life.

to incinerate it, but that someone had recognised its potential and facilitated its 'escape' in my direction. Early enquiries into its origins proved fruitless, but then investigations by fighter crash specialist David Wade, supported by my research, unravelled a wartime tragedy.

The weather and material malfunctions on 13 March 1944 handicapped the USAAF's potential striking power although a series of attacks on V weapons sites were accomplished. Missing from the day's cast was the Mustang, because all P-51s were grounded pending inspection and modification to the wing and engine mounting bolts after a series of failures, some fatal. For the P-47 groups not operational, the need for training continued, and by mid-afternoon the clouds over Cambridgeshire were only one-tenth small cumulus, the progress of which was hastened by a 26mph wind from the west-north-west. Wrapped and gloved as best they could, Technical Sergeant Falkenburg and his men had prepared Roy Wendell's P-47C, serial 41-6223, for a local gun-camera training sortie. With him would be his Flight Leader, another experienced pilot whom we will call Second Lieutenant 'X'.

Twenty-three years old, Roy had some 401 hours of flying experience, almost half of them on Thunderbolts, so Republic's portly product was familiar to him. However, sense saw discipline dictating the initiation of any flight, and Roy carefully checked the aircraft's exterior before climbing into the cockpit. Being almost 6 feet tall, he benefited from the P-47's comparatively spacious cockpit as he shuffled his parachute, adjusted his seat and thanked his Crew Chief for helping with the harness.

Instinctively he began the familiar ritual of a cockpit check – landing gear 'down', flaps 'up', flap equaliser 'closed' – a litany that proceeded clockwise around the cockpit through ignition and propeller switches, intercooler and oil shutter settings, fuel booster pump position and fuel pressure, then, importantly, confirmation that the gun switch was 'off'. As part of their pre-flight duties, Falkenburg and his men had

An early P-47 pictured at Duxford. (C. Norman)

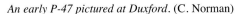

already 'pulled through' the Curtis Electric propeller, 12 feet 2 inches in diameter. A feature and potential fire hazard of the Pratt & Whitney R-2800 radial engine, like other piston engines, was for oil to accumulate in the lower cylinders when they were stationary. To disperse any residual oil, the ground crew had to grasp the lower propeller blade, pull it round, greet its replacement and continue the process. Resistance from the complexity of push rods and pistons made this an arduous task, even dangerous if an ignition switch had been left on. Roy had already confirmed that the ignition was off as part of his own check-list.

The master battery was turned on, the supercharger positioned 'off' while the fuel selector valve was placed to feed from the main tank concealed beneath his seat, extending upwards between himself and the engine. Nudging the throttle lever forwards, Roy 'cracked' it slightly and set the fuel mixture, boost pump and propeller controls. As yet the P-47 had no life, but Roy was now ready to initiate that infusion. Priming the engine, he quickly flicked on the ignition and energised the dormant motor. As if startled, the propeller blades stumbled jerkily into motion. For a few seconds each could be seen staggering then, as the engine caught, they took up a rhythm that blurred as a blast of smoke haloed aft around the rear fuselage.

Roy's first action was to confirm that the oil pressure was climbing resolutely beyond the 25lb minimum while engine rpm rose steadily, vibrating life into the airframe. The thrum changed to a snarl as he gunned it and checked the propeller, both magnetos and the supercharger. After fussing around their charge, his groundcrew, stepped aside as Roy released his parking brake, unlocked the tail-wheel and exchanged signals clearing the P-47 to move.

Meanwhile the Thunderbolt flown by 'X' was already snaking over the turf towards the grass strip selected as their runway. Like all tail-wheeled fighters, the P-47's ground posture gave no forward visibility, so taxiing involved 'essing' from side to side to the take-off position.

Soon both P-47s sat awaiting clearance from flying control. Roy had set trim tabs, checked his fuel and propeller settings, confirmed flaps were set for take-off and opened the engine cowling gills to prevent overheating. All was ready. A burst of power nudged the P-47 forwards to straighten the tail-wheel, which he then locked. Seconds later the duo were permitted to go, and a smooth application of throttle saw Roy's P-47 thrusting over the grass, building up speed. Then, in that moment of almost magic, over 6 tons of fighter transformed itself from an earth-bonded alien into a power projection of technology using man's understanding of air pressure combined with skills in aeronautical engineering developed by Alexander Kartveli and his team at Republic Aviation.

Climbing westwards, Roy switched to draw fuel from his belly tank as he and 'X' gained altitude before the training commenced. Arriving in the vicinity of the 92nd BG airfield at Podington, Bedfordshire, Roy assumed the role of target while 'X' simulated a series of 'attacks', taking gun-camera film to be analysed later. For several minutes the two Thunderbolts snapped like puppies in mock combat until 'X' had fulfilled his part of their sortie. On his final attack 'X' had also swept after a B-24 that had lumbered into the area. Dummying an assault on the bomber, 'X' used the momentum of his dive to zoom past, and climbing away he radioed for Roy to begin his part of their original plan.

However, not wishing to be outdone, Roy was also making passes at the B-24 and, while acknowledging his leader's call, continued to simulate attacks on the Liberator. Rejoining the fray, 'X' swooped to 'protect' the bomber, not realising that he had not returned his gun switch guard to safety after using the camera. The next unwitting

Duxford, home of the 78FG. (C. Norman)

step to tragedy occurred when he inadvertently caught, perhaps with his sleeve, the gun switch when closing his intercooler, the controls for which were close to the gun switch toggle, which had now clicked from 'camera only' through 'off' to 'gun and camera'. Closing swiftly on Wendell, the P-47 piloted by 'X' was now fully armed.

Peering through the gunsight, 'X' followed the evasive manoeuvres made by Roy's P-47. As Roy curved away, 'X' anticipated his friend's course, allowed 30 degrees angle and a two-radii lead through the N-3A gunsight. Now! Pressing the trigger, 'X' was startled by the unexpected burst from his eight .5 calibre machine-guns. Instantly he ceased, but each Browning fired some 750 rounds per minute, and his burst, lasting only four-tenths of a second, released six from each weapon. Forty-eight bullets with a velocity of 2,850 feet per second converged on Wendell's P-47.

'X' had no time to shout a warning. As part of their 'game', Wendell was already trying to evade. In those heart-freezing moments, 'X' prayed that his marksmanship was off, that Wendell's P-47 might twist away from destiny, that any blow struck would be ineffective – a few shards of torn aluminum, some dented armour plating – embarrassment at the bar. Horrified, 'X' saw strikes registering on Wendell's aircraft. Stunned by the unexpected assault, Wendell's P-47 nosed up, pleading towards the firmament. A partial stall summoned hope, suddenly thwarted as the P-47 nosed into another dive. Desperate pleas from 'X' for Wendell to pull out went unanswered. Then his P-47 recovered, soaring steeply, perhaps imbued with life, perhaps mocking a pilot already dead. For a few agonising seconds the P-47 climbed, but hope slipped away as airspeed, like life, ebbed into a final stall. Hanging momentarily, the fighter's nose then pitched into a steepening dive and the now frantic appeals from 'X' broadcast unanswered on the airwaves of eternity.

Wendell apparently made no attempt to bale out and, at 3,000 feet, the belly tank tore away as the P-47 screeched earthwards announcing its agony over miles of countryside. Seconds later it exploded in a field near the headquarters building at Podington. The impact buried the engine nearly 15 feet, ripping through a water main. A burst of blazing fuel spurted on to haystacks some 50 feet away and Corporal William J. Turcotte of the 407th Bombardment Squadron was knocked unconscious

Roy Wendell, victim of a ghastly accident, rests with many comrades at Cambridge.

by an earth clod blasted about 250 feet from the crash.

Responding swiftly, the 2042nd Engineering Aviation Fire Fighting Platoon dealt with the fires. Wendell's remains were recovered for burial at Cambridge, where this victim of a ghastly accident rests today.

'X' had a successful career with the 78th Fighter Group and survived the war. Contacted by the author, he understandably wished to retain his anonymity, but confirmed the tragic sequence of events. Others, too, retained memories of the crash and one, Douglas Ward, then a schoolboy, harboured thoughts about the lost fighter for many years. Convinced that parts of the plane had been left buried, Douglas was encouraged by the discovery of fragments when walking over the site. In 1979 he was a JCB driver, and one job provided an opportunity to investigate the crash site with his machine. Gaining the landowner's consent but unaware of the other formalities for excavation, Douglas became alarmed when his activities unearthed an enormous amount of the P-47, including some grim reminders of its young pilot, one a fuel-soaked wallet.

Worried by his findings, Douglas contacted Peter Miles, an ex-RAF Officer, and soon the authorities took charge. The wallet commenced its uncertain journey into my possession, while Douglas donated the engine to the Imperial War Museum collection at Duxford, where it lay in storage for many years. Following the investigations by David Wade and myself, another aviation archaeologist, Pete Stanley, completed the recovery of P-47C-2-RE 41-6223 during the summer of 1995. Carefully avoiding the water mains, Pete's team cut deep into blue clay and retrieved all eight of the fighter's machines-guns.

The culmination of all these activities occurred at Duxford in 1997. Discussions between myself and Martin Boswell of the IWM drew attention to the wallet's existence and the engine still in storage. Conscious of our nation's debt to American airmen, the IWM had long planned an American Air Museum to house its prestigious collection of US warplanes. Martin's role as exhibition project co-ordinator was to support the display of complete aircraft with memorabilia related to the men who flew them and, recognising the Duxford provenance of both engine and wallet, Martin agreed with my convictions that smaller exhibits often carry a more powerful aura of human interest than complete aircraft. The items associated with Roy Wendell tell a poignant tale that cut short one life and scarred another in tragic circumstances during intensive combat training.

In time for the opening on 1 August 1997, my wife Sue and I presented the wallet to Duxford for display in the American Aviation Museum, and we are pleased with the small part we have played in ensuring its preservation.

4: One hundred to one

STILL IN HIS EARLY TWENTIES during 1944–5, First Lieutenant Ray Shuey Wetmore was the epitome of an air ace. Sandy-haired, athletic and handsome, the former student was blessed with vision that became legendary within his 359FG. At first fellow pilots thought him rather arrogant, as George 'Pop' Doersch, himself an ace, later recalled: 'I first met him in the 370th Fighter Squadron. Self-assured and somewhat vocal about it, I was initially turned off by someone so obviously sure of himself. I learned later that he was as good as he said he was. A mutual respect later turned to friendship of the deep and lasting kind forged in the heat of combat and tempered over years.'

In keeping with his image, Ray was also fond of the girls, but here we have a tender departure from the scarf-in-the-slipstream, ladykiller cliché. True, Ray had women in his life, and two predominated, his wife Carmelina and their baby daughter, Diane. Blending a love of flying with thoughts of the family he missed,

Major Ray Shuey Wetmore epitomises the air ace in this late-war portrait. (Donna Rae [Wetmore] Van Dyke)

'Daddy's Girl': Ray named each of his aircraft after his daughter, Diane, a vivacious little charmer back home. (Donna Rae [Wetmore] Van Dyke)

Ray adorned his aircraft with a flourishing nose art proclaiming 'Daddy's Girl' as a reminder of his vivacious little charmer back home. Perhaps, also, the name represented even deeper reasons for fighting this war.

Ray's first step on the road to acedom occurred on 10 February 1944 when some 20 Me 109s bounced the 359FG. As Thunderbolts and Messerschmitts scattered across the sky, Ray grasped an opportunity, half rolled and nipped in behind an Me 109. Opening fire from 350 yards, he thrashed his victim, closing up until a collision seemed inevitable. At that instant the enemy pilot leapt clear, but Ray still pursued the abandoned fighter until it exploded on impact. Curving his P-47 victoriously skywards, Ray Wetmore, 'Smack' to his fellow pilots, had made his debut.

Recognising always that bomber protection was paramount, Ray was no glory hunter, nor did he selfishly seek credit on his own. His next victory on 4 March was an Me 109 shared with three other pilots. There were also occasions when even the most valiant efforts by escorting fighters proved unable to prevent the Luftwaffe from reaching the bombers. On 16 March 1944 the 370FS intercepted a batch of Fw 190s diving from 30,000 feet into a B-17 formation, and Ray's encounter report vividly describes events at 13.45 hours near Paris:

'I was leading Blue Flight when I sighted two Fw 190s at 1 o'clock low in a diving attack on the bomber formation. I called White Leader and told him I was attacking. Closing on one enemy aircraft, I fired with 20° deflection from 500 yards. Continuing to close, to 200 yards, I kept firing and gradually reduced my deflection to 0°. When my controls began to buffet, I broke off the attack to avoid compressibility. I observed no flashes but the enemy aircraft exploded violently immediately thereafter. Having broken off at 10,000 feet, I reformed the flight and started to regain altitude. While we were climbing, I saw two Fw 190s come out of the overcast at 3 o'clock, flying line astern, about 1,000 yards away. I called the flight for attack and turned into the enemy aircraft. They apparently didn't see us since they took no immediate evasive action. I tagged on to the last enemy aircraft at 800 yards. At this point they must have seen me for they went into a steep dive toward the cloud layer below. I commenced firing at 400 yards with 40° deflection, but saw no strikes. Closing to 250 yards, I fired again. We were then about 500 feet above the overcast. I fired continually as I closed to within 75 yards, and we went into the overcast. As he was still visible, I fired one long burst before breaking in an upward direction. As I cleared my tail, I saw the enemy aircraft explode, and pieces were blown above the overcast. As my flight was still with me, I assembled them into combat formation and we began climbing. We had to turn to avoid two parachutes. I observed one B-17 slightly below us at 12 o'clock on fire. As we turned in that direction to investigate, Blue 2 called "Blue Flight, break!" We broke abruptly to the left and I saw one Fw 190 attacking my wingman. He broke off the attack without scoring any hits, and pressed the attack on the burning bomber whose crew was baling out. We attacked the enemy aircraft but he dived into the overcast before we could get within range. Our gas supply was low so we turned to go home when I saw the enemy aircraft come back out of the overcast. I turned toward him but he dived again into the cloud layer and we came home. I believe the bomber crew had all baled out from the burning aircraft. I claim two (2) Fw 190s destroyed. Serial number of aircraft 75068… Ammunition expended 1,015 rounds of incendiary.'

During the spring of 1944 USAAF fighter pilots forayed for the enemy from over 4 miles high down to 40 feet or even less. Ray's remarkable vision helped on numerous

Ray Wetmore's P-47 CS-P 42-75068. (C. Baldridge/E. De Graves)

occasions, such as 11 April 1944 when, homeward bound at 17,000 feet, he not only picked out a camouflaged enemy aerodrome but also counted the '15 plus bandits' trying to hide around it. Positioning themselves in classic style, the P-47s came hurtling out of the sun. Ray built up so much speed that even his keen eyesight could not compensate for the shuddering pull-out, and the first parked aircraft blurring into his gunsight was unidentified but soon despatched.

Zooming upwards on power-waves of momentum, the American fighters banked steeply and came swooping back to risk a second run. Selecting a twin-engined Junkers 88 squatting at dispersal, Ray's bullets strode destructively into its airframe and the bomber began to smoke like overdone toast. Similar treatment on another Ju 88 produced a more satisfyingly spectacular explosion, and Ray was aiming for victim number three when the bulb in his gunsight blew. Unable to aim properly, his next two passes raked buildings, aircraft and facilities at random until the 370FS felt satisfied and came home to claim five Ju 88s destroyed plus others damaged along with many airfield installations.

Eleven days later Ray made a mistake that could have concluded his career. Following a dogfight over Hamm (as described in my previous book, *Night of the Intruders*), Ray strafed some locomotives but became separated from his squadron. Sighting two aircraft nearby, he slid into formation assuming that they were his lost comrades and, looking over to wave a greeting, found himself face-to-face with Leutnant Herbert-Konrad Eh of 3 Staffel Jagdegeschwader 1. Startled, the German veered away while Ray, cursing his own complacency, cut quickly in behind the Fw 190, now weaving away from him. They were so low that Ray could not get his gunsight to bear on his erratically manoeuvring enemy, but a well-judged burst hit Eh's silvery-grey machine. The Fw 190's fate was sealed when a pair of P-47s appeared, cutting off its escape route. Eh's steeply climbing aircraft suffered further hits from 1st Lieutenant Harry L. Matthew, and the German wisely baled out. A somewhat abashed Wetmore would never repeat that mistake.

Early in May the 359FG converted to Mustangs and Ray's first claims from this new mount were flak towers and gun emplacements during another airfield strafing session on the 11th. Recognition of his prowess occurred three days later when he received the Distinguished Flying Cross, and he celebrated on 19 May by achieving his fourth and fifth kills for the coveted 'ace' status. The 359FG were escorting bombers near Berlin and became embroiled in fierce combat. Three Mustangs fell amid the towering cumulus as the aircraft fought over 100 Me 109s, claiming 10½ kills.

Wall-art for an ace in Ray's quarters at East Wretham. (C. Baldridge/T. P. Smith)

Ray's Yellow Flight charged into the German swarm. Firing on an Me 109 as he closed to 100 yards, Ray saw it flick over and burn its way into a spin. Banking away, he spotted a P-51 having problems with a more aggressive Messerschmitt and chased it off in a steep dive. For some time he and the German played tag as the '109 scuttled between clouds, hunted by brief bursts from Ray's guns. There and gone. There and gone. Finally the Me 109 sought sanctuary in a great comforting cumulus. Hoping to outwit the American, its pilot was unlucky. Hopping over the cloud crest, Ray calculated his enemy's exit point and the Messerschmitt emerged to a greeting of machine-gun bullets. Rolling over, the pilot gave up and baled out.

During the 'Chattanooga' assault on 21 May, Ray shared in the destruction of two locomotives plus damage to railroad installations and a radar tower. Such attacks were, however, unsuitable for his talents, and the 29th saw him expend 919 rounds to far greater effect. An early briefing gave the 359FG orders to rendezvous with B-24s near Stettin in Poland. At 1.15 pm they saw three waves of 20-plus Me 109s and Fw 190s converging on the bombers, and swung to engage. Gaining on the last wave of '190s, Ray fired from 400 yards to distract his opponent from the bombers, but saw no hits. Closing in, he held the trigger longer and saw strikes shredding the '190, which spun away on fire.

Selecting another, Ray's finger was poised when he received a radio warning of an Fw 190 on his own tail. Glancing back, Ray saw the deadly silhouette some 2,000 yards behind but gaining. Any error in judgement courted death, but he still wanted to destroy or at least deter the Fw 190 ahead. Combat boost urged it nearer, into his gunsight. Aiming, Ray spat an angry burst but saw no hits. Too late to get him now. The assassin astern must almost be in range, eager to pulverize Ray's P-51. Turning too soon would not shake off his assailant, judge it too late and he would be torn apart.

Now! Shoving the control column hard left, Ray broke into a fierce, climbing turn. The Fw 190 pilot found only air ahead, but reacted rapidly enough to cut into Ray's curve, still closing in. Ray forced the joystick back and skidded some rudder, stretching every sinew of airframe and body alike. 'G' force crushed him into his seat as the Mustang shuddered through the high-speed turn. His manoeuvre prevented the Fw 190 from getting a good shot, but Ray realised that the man across that aerial arena was also an expert. Jousting from the stratosphere, the two fighters spiralled earthwards in a deadly duel of technical performance and human skill. Neither pilot out-matched the other as they descended right over a German airfield; perhaps Ray's opponent was performing for a home crowd.

Instinctively, Ray drew on every comparison he knew between his Mustang and the Fw 190. The Focke-Wulf outclassed his rate of roll but left little to chose in turning circles and, held in a fast, constantly circling combat, Ray was confident that he had the initiative, although one report commented that 'Dog-fighting is not altogether recommended'. But Ray had no choice. Probing for every weakness, he dragged his adversary to tree-top level, then, in one split second, a chance.

Pulling the trigger at 40° deflection, Ray was rewarded by a sprinkling of hits along the Fw 190's fuselage. An instant later its canopy whipped away and the undercarriage came down. Damaged and desperate to land, the German pilot dropped towards the airfield. Ruthlessly Ray closed for the kill, but, guessing his intentions, the German suddenly pulled up, half-rolled and fell clear. His body tumbled a second or two, his parachute popped open and he was down in the middle of the airfield. Honour satisfied, superiority asserted, Ray had no intention of giving target practise to the aerodrome defences, and sped homewards.

Following D-Day, the 359FG frequently deployed to support the Normandy landings, and Ray added a quota of trucks and tanks to his increasingly impressive tally. Promotion to Captain came shortly before he went Stateside for a well-earned 30-day furlough. Ray was the first 370FS pilot to complete a full tour of 300 combat hours. Public relations released several pictures and stories about the 359FG ace, and he even found himself making a radio broadcast on 8 July before boarding a C-54 and flying home to the real 'Daddy's Girl'.

In America, his celebrity status continued and family commitments were interrupted to address the local Lions Club and other organisations about his experiences. A contemporary newspaper account describes him as 'an interesting and capable speaker', a compliment soon endorsed elsewhere. His travels introduced him

to a wide audience and, like many combatants, he deplored the 'gold-brickers' back home profiteering from the war.

Returning to Europe on the *Aquitania,* he was briefly assigned to the 16th Replacement Control Depot at Stone, Staffordshire, before working his way back to East Wretham on 10 October. Within minutes of arriving he felt again that satisfying surge of power as his Mustang crested the clouds. Ray Wetmore was back in his element.

Catching up on events, changes in combat techniques and new equipment took a few days, but, a week later, he led the entire 359FG on an uneventful escort mission to Cologne. Allied airpower had diluted Hitler's Luftwaffe and the early missions of his second tour provided no opportunity to announce his return until

Ray's increasing tally-board on the port side of Mustang 42-106894 – a public relations pose. (C. Baldridge/Mrs E. Palicka)

2 November, when he was escorting B-17s to bomb oil industry targets near Merseberg.

'I was leading Red Section,' Ray reported, 'when approximately 30 Me 109s attacked our bombers. We were on the box ahead. I called my section and told them to drop their tanks, then split-essed from the bomber formation. We caught them [the Me 109s] at 12,000 feet. I took my section right through their formation but our speed was so great that we didn't have a chance to fire. This split the Jerries up so I singled out one Me 109 and closed to about 400 yards before opening fire. I was using the new K-14 sight and my deflection was about 30°. I placed the pip on the portion where the wing joined the fuselage. As soon as I pulled the trigger I saw many strikes right where I was sighting. I got in one more good burst before overrunning him. He went down in a barrel roll straight through the overcast with me following at very close range. His roll developed into a spin and he never pulled out.

'By this time my wingman had engaged another Me 109 who was on his tail, so I was alone below the overcast. Before I had a chance to climb back up through the overcast at 6,000 feet, 15 to 20 Me 109s bounced me. I immediately went into a tight turn and started calling for help. The German pilots seemed very aggressive but ignorant about fighter tactics, for they never did take advantage of their positions. During the Lufberry I fired at a Jerry at about 70° deflection – the pip was located on his cockpit. I noticed about three or four strikes around the cockpit. It surprised me as much as it did the Jerry. Evidently I hit the pilot for the ship went into a stall and tumbled into the ground.

'The K-14 seems positive. When making a pass with a great amount of deflection I would advise either a diving or a climbing pass for if you make a level one your pip will go below your nose. I claim two Me 109s destroyed. Serial number of aircraft 4733... CS-L. Ammo expended: 294 rounds of API [Armour Piercing Incendiary].'

The K-14 gunsight to which Ray refers was a gyro-computing development of a British design and provided greater accuracy.

On 4 November Ray received the Distinguished Flying Cross from Lt Gen Spaatz during a ceremony at Eighth Air Force Headquarters. Media attention found him and eight other pilots facing flashbulbs almost as unnerving as enemy fighters, while

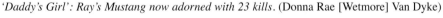

'Daddy's Girl': Ray's Mustang now adorned with 23 kills. (Donna Rae [Wetmore] Van Dyke)

The K-14 gunsight enhanced Ray's abilities. (S. Sox)

newsreel and radio propaganda broadcasts augmented the image of American fighter pilots for enthusiastic audiences at home. Reports tended to exaggerate those exploits, but on 27 November Ray and First Lieutenant Robert M. York provided a story that needed no embellishment.

Heavy flak and evasive action over Munster separated Ray's Red Flight from the 359FG and the four P-51s found themselves cruising alone in hostile airspace. Searching for the Group, Ray's keen eyesight spotted two large formations lower down in the distance. However, their identity made him swallow hard. One formation comprised some 100 Me 109s, while the other was a similar quantity of Fw 190s! Judging from their attitude, loose formation and retained drop tanks, Ray knew that they were mustering for a massive assault on American bombers attacking German marshalling yards. Records reveal that the enemy formations were Fw 190s from II/ Assault JG300 with Me 109s of III and IV JG300. Gathering from bases west of Berlin, they were joined by Fw 190s of I and II JG301 aloft from Salzwedal and Sachau. This enormous formation was part of the largest retaliation yet gathered by 1 Jagkorps, and here were only four Mustangs to hold the line. A disaster threatened for US bombers if the enemy broke through.

Seeking to become as inconspicuous as possible, the P-51s tried to pretend that they were innocent stray Germans and loosely attached themselves above and behind the enemy formations. Despite their exterior nonchalance, inside his cockpit Ray was frantically radioing for help and relaying their position, altitude and course. Contacting the rest of the group, the four interlopers waited for the cavalry. Minutes passed. Five. Ten. Fifteen. Making matters worse, the Germans kept unpredictably altering course and, like spies marching in the wrong army, the four P-51s kept finding themselves out of step. Ray knew that they must have been seen several times, but their audacity remained undiscovered. Then Red Four called in to say that his engine was losing power. Ray had no choice but to order Red Three to escort his ailing chum home and, avoiding attention, the two slid away undisturbed, leaving Ray and Rudy York still tailing 200 German fighters and feeling very, very lonely.

Finally the Germans became even more suspicious, and Ray observed several flights ease sideways from the main formations and begin to ascend to box in the strangers. The seconds were getting explosive. Soon the two Americans would be surrounded – their bluff had been called. Radioing his group, Ray acknowledged that the enemy were 'wise to what's going on', then, in what might have become famous last words, he called York: 'You take the hundred on the left and I'll take the hundred on the right. We're attacking, *now*!'

Enemy fighters were already above the two Mustangs and beginning their bounce, while dozens more swarmed below. Throttles slammed forward, Ray and Rudy sprang suicidally into the German formation. A blizzard of drop tanks from the aerial armada achieved one objective – it reduced their range. Ray added to the confusion by firing on his first Me 109 from 600 yards. The K-14 gunsight worked its magic and the Messerschmitt exploded before writhing earthwards in flames. Cutting in on the tail of another, York smothered it in bullets and it spun down on fire. Latching on to a second, a long burst from his guns savaged pieces off its airframe and sent it tumbling across the sky in crazy cartwheels, its death throes traced by a ragged banner of black smoke. More Me 109s were diving on the Mustangs and Ray's P-51 snarled round to meet them head on. Firing, his bullets lit up an Me 109, which whipped upside down and spun away burning fiercely.

Rudy York blew another one to pieces, then banked steeply to confront an Me 109 as it turned to meet him, perhaps intending a head-on charge when its nose-mounted cannon would have the advantage. His P-51 cut inside the '109's turn and he fired from 50 yards at 90° deflection. Holding down the trigger, Rudy hosed the '109 until his own engine obscured the view. Dabbing the stick forwards, he saw strikes on the enemy's centre section.

Suddenly, tracers were zipping over his own wing, 'like little base-balls of fire'. Snatching a glimpse over his shoulder, he saw the snout of another Me 109 closing in. Quarter-snapping the P-51, he flicked over and spun down, almost colliding with the Me 109 at which he had been firing only moments before. In those crazy, whirling seconds, Rudy glimpsed the German pilot baling out as he flashed past, twisting desperately to get the other Me 109 off his tail. Chased by another angry stream of tracer, Rudy dived into the welcoming concealment of a large, fat cloud, levelled off and headed home.

Meanwhile, Ray found himself on the wrong end of an aggressive, adeptly flown Me 109. Clashing at 30,000 feet, they began an intense duel that spiralled earthwards as each sought to latch on to the tail of the other. Down and down, both pilots tormenting the most from airframe and body, men and machines equally matched. Fate slid the advantage one way, then the other like a malevolent croupier in death's own casino. Realising that the German was slowly gaining, Ray worked his Mustang as never before, but nothing shook off his relentless pursuer. Even in these desperate seconds, Ray respected his enemy's skill.

Expertly using his flaps, the German encouraged every margin of manoeuvrability from his fighter and slowly gained the advantage of a firing position. Ray was caught. Two cannon shells ripped through the gun bay of his port wing and the shock almost snatched away his control but, catching it, Ray tugged even tighter into the turn. His life depended on his own ability and the structural strength of his damaged P-51. He was dead if he straightened out, so it did not matter if stress tore away his damaged wing as he hauled the protesting P-51 shuddering through its circle.

Maybe the German had become over-confident, maybe he slackened for one, vital instant. Perhaps the fierceness of Ray's manoeuvre surprised him, but here, momentarily, was a chance. Ray grabbed it. One short burst. Some strikes flickered on the Me 109's fuselage. Another burst. More strikes. The Messerschmitt wearied just a fraction. Vortexing in tight circles, almost at ground level, neither pilot had anywhere else to go, but Ray now had his opponent. Squeezing the trigger he was greeted only by the mocking hiss of air. He was out of ammunition! The croupier had pushed the chips to Ray's opponent, but, challenging fate, Ray feinted a final attack. To his utter astonishment, the Me 109 pilot promptly pulled up and baled out. A few frames on his gun-camera were a brief celebration, then Ray found himself surrounded by Fw 190s. Perhaps holding back pending the duel's outcome, some ten Focke-Wulfs now sought revenge.

Ray's only armament was no more than some powerful American invective. Even if the wolves at his heels could not hear the abuse hurled in their direction, Ray felt better knowing that he would go down still cursing them and all that they represented. For 10 minutes the lone Mustang bristled like an animal at bay. For 10 lifetimes Ray's tenacity kept him alive until, suddenly, a gap occurred in the ranks of encircling killers. Hurling himself through, Ray fled like a Pony Express rider racing for the fort.

Courageously tackling odds of 100 to 1, Ray and Rudy claimed seven kills, delayed the German formation and reduced its endurance by forcing fuel tanks to be jettisoned. Elsewhere that day, German intentions were similarly thwarted as American air and skill superiority asserted itself over a weakening Luftwaffe. JG300 and JG301 suffered 35 of over 50 German losses. While American claims of 98 were excessive, the battle's outcome was an overwhelming success because no bombers fell to German fighters, whose efforts were dissipated by marauding Mustangs and Thunderbolts. Undoubtedly the Americans generally benefited from numerical superiority and better training, but the two 359FG pilots demonstrated a foundation of courage whatever the odds.

Ray Wetmore had become an articulate advocate of his profession and found himself increasingly in demand to address a variety of audiences. Particular pleasure was taken on 14 December when he joined other pilots speaking to an enthusiastic gathering of enlisted men in the Squadron Alert Room. The 370FS diarist felt that the talks were 'informal yet vivid and forceful for all their humour'.

Proving his prowess again on the last day of December 1944, Ray shot down an Me 109 and chased another over the rooftops in Hanover to share its destruction with Lt Werner J. Rauschenberg. Two weeks later Ray and Rauschenberg really got into their stride as Ray's encounter report reveals:

'I was leading Red Section going to rendezvous east of Hanover when I noticed a bogie [unidentified aircraft] in front of me doing lazy eights and chandelles. I turned into the plane and he started climbing, going on a 270° heading. I called my flight

An informal picture of Ray in the ready-jeep. Note the parachutes up front. (C. Baldridge/P. Smith)

and told them to drop their tanks and started after him at full power. He ran away from us as if we were standing still. I followed him all the way to Dummer Lake, then gave up the chase. At this time Nuthouse called and said bandits were taking off from an airdrome 25 miles north-west of Dummer Lake. I took my flight up that way, but couldn't find anything. I then turned back towards Dummer Lake, and at this time Nuthouse said bandits were in the near vicinity. I saw a Lufberry low at 2 o'clock. Just then four Fw 190s went below me in trail, and we made the bounce. I caught the Jerries on the deck and picked my target. I closed to about 300 yards with 20° deflection and fired a long burst with excellent results. One landing gear came down, and the Hun tried to belly in and succeeded in creaming himself and the airplane too. I claim this enemy aircraft destroyed. I chose another 190 and gave him a short burst from dead astern at very close range. He tried to break, but snapped into the ground, exploding. I claim this enemy aircraft destroyed. There were still two Fw 190s in formation, and I called my wingman to take the one on the port side and I would take the other one. I made a pass at my Jerry from dead astern. I fired from about 300 yards, getting many strikes. He went into a spin and spun straight into the ground. I claim this enemy aircraft destroyed. Just then I saw my wingman making a pass on his target, but his windshield was all frosted up and he couldn't see his gunsight. I cut the Jerry off and we had him in a cross fire, both of us getting a lot of strikes. The German bellied his airplane in an open snow-covered field. At this time I told my wingman to strafe the German. He called back and said he couldn't see out of his canopy; so I strafed the Hun, killing the pilot and setting his plane on fire. I claim this enemy aircraft destroyed shared with Lt Rauschenberg. We then joined up and started climbing to altitude. Just then I saw two more Fw 190s. As I started to make my pass, a red-checkered-nose P-51 made a pass on the first Jerry and got good results in his firing because the German had to bale out. I fired at the second German from about 400 yards 30° deflection. I got several strikes, and the Jerry jettisoned his canopy and baled out. I claim this enemy aircraft destroyed.

'I claim four (4) Fw 190s Dest. in air and one (1) Fw 190 Dest. in air shared with Lt Rauschenberg. Ser. No of aircraft 4733… CS-L. Ammo expended: 1,324 rounds of API.'

The unit that Ray and the other US pilots savaged that crisp winter's day was the remnants of the once proud IV/JG54 aloft with other elements of JG54 from Vorden, Bramsche and Hesepe. Eight pilots were killed and two wounded, an accumulating climax of losses that closed its operational effectiveness.

Early in February Ray once again found himself on the airwaves, and a transcript of this broadcast has survived. Interviewed by Lt Col Ben Lyon, Head of Radio Department of Public Relations, USAAF, the question-and-answer broadcast contains some elements of scripted-in propaganda, but still provides an insight into Ray's opinions and experiences:

Q We are here tonight to ask you essentially this – after flying 440 combat hours and approximately 125 missions, what do you think are the requirements for success as a combat fighter pilot in this war?

A Average flying ability and a hell of a lot of luck.

Q Exactly what do you think average flying ability comprises?

A Ninety per cent of the American fighter pilots flying combat today have it.

Q You surely don't mean you get it at OTU [Operational Training Unit] or RTU [Replacement Training Unit]? Were you ready for combat after finishing OTU?

A No, but I should say I was more ready for combat than replacement pilots are today.

Q Was that because you had more time or because you had better instruction?

A Call it a little of both.

Q Do you think you have a particular advantage because you went through OTU with a unit rather than RTU as a replacement?

A Absolutely. In OTU you knew who you were flying with and who you were going to fly with during combat. You were used to one another's capabilities.

Q What ideas do you have about combat now that differ from ideas you had on 19 December 1943?

A I have so many.

Q How do the ideas you acquired in the preceding three years about combat differ? Since then there have been 440 combat hours – what notions have changed in your mind?

A The inferior skill of the German pilots.

Q What did you expect to find?

A I expected then to find that they had the same flying spirit we have – looking for fights instead of running away. I expected them to have better planes – conventional types – than they did have as compared with ours.

Q Does that go for the models of the Thunderbolt you were flying in December 1943?

A Right.

Q You have said that at least two particular differences were lack of spirit and ability on the part of the German pilot, and the inferiority of his equipment, his aircraft. How about your own doctrine and technique before entering combat?

A I was not so aggressive then as I am now.

Q Had you been trained to use more evasive action?

A Right. Due to the type of aircraft we were flying then – the P-47 – we were told never to go down to altitudes lower than 20,000. Soon after we started flying combat we learned that we could combat Germans at any altitude.

Q Did you learn this yourselves?

A I should say most of our combat experience came the hard way – from ourselves and our own experience.

Q You learned first you could attack the German at altitude?

A We attacked Germans flying 109s at 25,000 feet.

Q What date?

A About 10 February 1944, 10 miles east of the Zuider Zee. But when I shot him down we were at 2,000 feet.

Q What happened?

A Captain Bill Hodges was leading the flight and I was flying number 3. We jumped a 109 at 25,000 and he split-essed away from the attack. He levelled out at about 5,000 feet then two 360-degree turns down to 2,000 feet, that is turning inside of him all the time. We believed he baled out without ever getting hit.

Q Whose decision was it to go down, yours or Hodges?

A I believe I called the Jerries to him and he led the attack.

Q To go back to 13 December 1943, what differences in doctrine (aside from this increase in aggressiveness) do you have now than were in your mind that day? All you knew then was what you had read or had been told to you?

A That day we were all a lot more frightened than we have ever been since. A dog-fight over Germany is not what you might expect to see in the movies, due to the fact that it is scattered out all over the sky. Also we saw that our battlefield in the sky does not resemble battle on the ground at all. There is none of that crashing and banging, and you feel it is less glamorous than you expected it to be.

Q How closely does actual air fighting resemble mock combat?

A I believe there is a vast difference between it and mock combat. If you do lose you have just had it. You will do things in combat that you would never dream of doing in mock battle or on a joy ride.

Q What are the limits you have reached as to speeds and stalls?

A 29 May 1944, in a P-51, I reached an indicated air speed of 650mph going into a vertical dive. We split-essed at 31,000 feet and levelled off at 6,000 feet. I began to pull out about 8,000 feet. The Jerry never did pull out.

Q Do you think it was speed or simply fright of an American in the aircraft?

A Well, a little of both. I believe in my mind, from the way they fight, the Germans fear our aircraft more than they should.

Q Don't you think it takes enormous guts to attack one of our bomber formations?

A For you and me, yes, but not for them. Because they are told and briefed that a bomber is an easy thing to knock down. We say beware of our bombers, because of their massed firepower.

Q Is there anything that you proposed to do, that you were willing to do on 13 December 1943, that you would not do now? Are there any don'ts?

A I can think of a lot of 'don'ts', but they were still effective then.

Q Run through them and see how many play a wide part in your thinking

A I think the thing to stress like hell is: during manoeuvres never reverse your turn, when you are in a *tight* turn, due to an enemy's tendency to shoot behind you. If you reversed your turn you would come right through his line of fire.

Q Any examples?

A 27 November 1944.

Q Was that with Rudy York?

A Yes, in a run-in with a 109 at 30,000 feet. I won then because we went round and round and neither of us ever reversed our turns in the procedure.

Q What happened?

A I knocked his coolant out and his engine froze. He baled out.

Q Was he the hottest rock you ever fought? Was that demonstrated in his ability to keep turning with you?

A Yes, he could handle his ship, which was inferior to mine, well enough to make me look sick several times.

Q On the turns?

A On the turns and in acceleration and deceleration and use of his dive flaps.

Q He managed to get shots at you?

A He shot at me several times and hit me two different times.

Q How many times were you in firing position on him and he on you?

A The combat itself lasted 20–25 minutes and he was only in position to fire about four times and I was on him at least 10 or 12 times. I hit him eight or nine out of 11 or 12.

Q What would you think that involved – 25 turns?

A No, about 20 turns.

Q Losing about 1,000 feet per minute?

A No, losing varying amounts at different times. Sometimes you were not losing any and sometimes 10,000 per minute.

Q If that is Rule 1, what is Rule 2? If Rule 1 is not to make any reverse turns?

A Be very, very aggressive in the air.

Q Why?

A Because the best possible defence is a very strong offence.

Q Does that arise inevitably in any single-seater combat?

A Right – fixed guns. Your best method of attack in the world is using the element of surprise. Don't hesitate to attack regardless of the position of the sun. The sun does not play enough of a part in it to worry about.

Q Were you extremely sun-conscious when you came over?

A Yes, of course. That was all I had ever been briefed, to watch and attack out of the sun. I have never recalled any time when I have used it.

Q Is that because the possibility of being seen while you get in the sun position is greater?

A That is correct. Do not waste your time getting in the sun when you could have had one or two shots down by the time you get into the sun.

Q If you do not care about the sun, how about contrails?

A They are important only as a means of identification. No, I do not make an effort to stay out of the contrails except to gain altitude, but everyone knows altitude is more to your advantage than being out of the contrails.

Q Do you just ignore contrails?

A Other than means of identification. When you see the contrails you see their type of formation, also by that and the type of contrail you can identify them as friend or foe. Whenever you see a gaggle of contrails coming from the direction that you suspect the German to be coming from, and also see the contrails darting as though they were a bunch of bees, you can bet your last dollar they are Germans.

Q Don't Americans fly in gaggles?

A Americans fly in formations that may at times be considered sloppy, but they always fly in a straight line. Also the German aircraft have a different colour and size contrail than our aircraft do.

Q Can you describe it?

A Their conventional-type fighters usually have a light bluish contrail whereas ours have a dense white contrail.

Q What do you suppose is the cause? More efficient superchargers?

A I cannot answer that. I do not know.

Q What is the farthest you have ever identified a German?

A As far as I can see the contrails, which I estimate at 50 miles. That was not positive identification, but in our minds they were Germans until proven otherwise.

Q You have been reported as being a recognition shark. Was that due to study or was it instinct?

A That is due to instinct, for I have not studied any more than the other pilots. It is knowing what to look for.

Q What do you look for?

A You do not look for any special feature in the German plane, but look at the German plane as a whole.

Q Apart from the formation, does the 'sit' of the aircraft in the air tell you anything?

A No, just looking at the airplane and taking the whole aircraft into view tells you rather more than looking for small details.

Q Right, now you have told us to be aggressive, to ignore the sun, ignore the contrails level and watch the formation and behaviour of other aircraft in the vicinity?

A That is strictly all offensive work. Do not ignore the sun on the defensive because
   you are likely to get an attack.

Q How about bouncing?

A I think three or four different times I was by myself, and when you are by yourself
   you are more alert than when the formation is with you. Most times being
   bounced by myself was my own stupidity. Once after shooting down a German I
   went down to take pictures after he had crashed, and before I know it the Jerries
   were bouncing me.

Q How often do you look behind?

A I should say you never stop taking in the whole sky. You never fix your eyes on
   one certain point until you pick up something there.

Q You look at your instruments?

A That's right. You give a quick glance at your instrument panel as you are turning
   your head.

Q Do you mean for hours you are constantly turning your head?

A Right. Constantly turning your head looking from one side to the other side,
   because in such a short time something can pop up. Pilots get chafed necks when
   they fail to wear a scarf, because they must keep twisting their heads.

Q What do you tell the new men in your flight?

A Well, we go through our procedure of combat tactics.

Q What is your procedure in the attack?

A My method is using the element of surprise. Finding him and shooting him before
   he has a chance to see you, and attack without hesitation.

Q Do they go down in a string after you leading or does the man who sees the
   enemy go down first and the rest follow him?

A In my flight I go down, but the boys are as near abreast as possible.

Q Do you make an attempt to use the Navy technique of boxing or do you go
   straight for his tail?

A It depends altogether on the number of aircraft you are attacking.

Q Single aircraft or two – you box them in?

A Yes. The new pilot going out on my wing has only one requirement I ask of him.
   That is, 'Do not lose me'. I figure on his first mission I can keep both our tails
   clear. As he becomes more accustomed to combat I expect more, but on his first
   few missions I don't even expect him to shoot at Germans.

Q When you commence talking to a new wingman about protecting your tail, I
   assume you tell him that you do not want anyone on your tail, including him.

A That is correct. I do not at any time want any one on my tail. I ask them to stay
   as far abreast as possible. When I go into attack I go in full throttle. Sometimes
   it is awfully hard for the men to keep up.

Q The point I am trying to make is, if you do go in at full throttle, do you want him
   to stay far out so you can see him?

A The further behind the wingman falls, the further out he must fly so I can still see
   him.

Q Is there anything else?

A Not for the first few missions. After that if an enemy plane comes in on my tail
   and the wingman does not warn me I shall probably tell him about it when he gets
   back. After all, that is his job.

Q You break into the attack?

A I always break into the attack. Another hard thing to do but good policy when
   being attacked – wait until the enemy gets within 1,000 yards, otherwise if you

break too soon you will probably be facing a head-on attack, which is not very good.

Q Do you have any rule about never breaking away from head-on attack or making the German break before you do?

A No, I would close in to a distance where you still have a reasonable chance of being able to break without colliding. On the other hand some of the German aircraft's fire power is much greater than ours and they have no reason for breaking. We do.

Q In that situation, breaking head-on into 190s that have two 30mm and two 20mm cannons, would you go into a fire fight with them head-on?

A No, I do not believe in head-on attacks.

Q What would your instinct be? Break down?

A No, break to the side and wait for his next move. It depends on the superior turning speed. In a P-51 that is absolutely your best defensive weapon. You have the best rate of turn.

Q Do you approve of aerobatics?

A No, I get violent, but no aerobatics.

Q Do you disapprove of them as a waste of time?

A Right. It cuts down your air speed and disrupts your sense of co-ordinated flight. I want to know where I am at all times.

Q Do you make an attempt never to split the controls?

A No, you are wrong there. I get very violent with the aeroplane, but there are probably only two aeronautical terms of flight that I use. One is the tight turn and the other is the half roll. Other than that I lay off aerobatics.

Q Using the half roll in preference to the split-ess?

A Right, absolutely. Because during the half roll you can see the enemy a lot better than in a split-ess, and you do not gain too much speed.

Q I used to see a lot of combat pictures of Germans doing rolls under fire. What good could they be?

A There are different methods of turn for different types. For instance, a P-47 turns much sharper in violent skids than it does in a co-ordinated turn, so in flying them you skid all over the sky. Whereas the P-51 turns its best in a co-ordinated turn on the verge of stalling, regardless of speed.

Q At what altitude in the P-51 aircraft do you begin to think about your high-speed stall?

A I high-speed stall this aeroplane at any altitude above 500 feet, whereas in a P-47 I high-speed stall at any altitude above 50 feet.

Q Have you seen people go in?

A I have.

Q What do you think is the usual error – in the pilots or in the aircraft?

A Do you mean German or Allied? In Germans because they are usually taking evasive action, and when they are trying to save their lives I think they feel nervous and take a chance on certain things where they normally would not. In Allied aircraft I think the boys put their attention on something else other than flying the aircraft.

Q They concentrate too much on the target?

A Yes, especially when trying to destroy a ground target. Then they get their mind fixed all on this target and forget their high speed and type of turn that they are trying to make.

Q When you are in combat do you attempt to keep the aircraft trimmed or do you hastily trim before firing?

A With the old sight we tried to keep it in trim, whereas with the new gyro-sight we do not pay any attention to it. It compensates for all skids and slips. We do over-boost the engine in combat, also over-stress the wings of the aeroplane.

Q You do that on the theory that the aircraft will stand more than you? Or don't you have a theory?

A No. We do that because our sole purpose is to destroy the enemy. You forget the rules. Whereas in normal flight a pilot won't go into compressibility, when trying to save his life he will take a chance on anything. It hurts fighter pilots more to have a German get away than anything else.

Q Did you come over here with that feeling of ferocity or did you acquire it?

A I acquired it after flying for a while. When I came over here all this was a complete blank to us. We were eager to learn.

Q What was your interest, academic or did you want to shoot down Germans?

A My greatest desire even in lower grades at High School was to acquire the American Air Force Wings. Immediately after war broke out it was to shoot down five enemy planes.

Q That was glamour.

A Right, that was glamour.

Q When did glamour change in you to bloodthirstiness?

A When you start packing a boy's things to send home after he has gone down. The more you think the more bloodthirsty you get. On the other hand, the more fights you are in I should say possibly the more aggressive you get, and in all probability you will eventually be a little more cautious as a pilot (as distinct from fighting) too.

Q What do you think the optimum point is? At some point a pilot's experience and caution will become balanced with his increasing desire for action?

A Right. I do not know if I can answer exactly what point. I can say this much, at the beginning of operations I would hesitate before attacking a large group of enemy fighters, whereas now with a flight I trusted I wouldn't hesitate to attack any number.

Q Was that because you despised them as opponents or because you are convinced that only a certain number can shoot at any one time?

A I did not exactly despise them as opponents; on the other hand past experience shows that a flight of ours can handle any force they meet.

Q Is that because a given volume of air can only hold so many aircraft? Do you agree or do you think that is a wrong idea?

A Immediately upon attacking your aircraft, you get them spread around the area and work as a team. You can be doing all the firing.

Q Give us an example of that. You say that if four well-schooled pilots work as a flight attacking say 20 opponents, none of the four need be exposed to fire?

A The two wingmen have for their job flying formation and keeping the tail clear. Immediately on seeing anyone coming in on your tail he will call and if the element leader is on the ball he will break at the proper time. Before making an attack you will have superior altitude for superior speed. Make sure you have them: speed and altitude. One works hand in hand with the other.

Q When do you make a planned attack, against large numbers?

A Against large numbers in all probability, yes. Against small numbers, never hesitate.

Q Right, that is the attack procedure you have instructed your new flight member in. Let's run over it: 1 First is the element of surprise. 2 Ignore the sun. 3 Don't hesitate – attack. 4 Keep my tail clear. 5 Stay up where I can see you. 6 Keep the speed that superior altitude gives you. 7 Don't break too quickly. 8 If you do not have gyro sight, keep your airplane in trim. 9 Aerobatics waste speed. You need only ability to turn tightly and understanding of the possibilities of the half roll.

Q Is there anything else to tell them?

A Except that this applies to P-47 and P-51 aeroplanes. Any other type I have not dealt with. And against 109s and 190s.

Q What would you tell them about jets?

A To acquire all these methods and procedures I've already talked about, it takes a lot of experience in flying combat.

Q Now, except for the abnormal stress and abnormal boost that occurs only in real fighting, is it possible for you to give this new boy this experience in mock combat?

A No. It is not possible because every time he fights the enemy he will learn something new.

Q How about jets?

A As of yet we know very little about them other than some of their capabilities. They have far superior speed on us.

Q Does that frighten you?

A It does not frighten me as long as I know there is a German flying them. If I thought an American was flying them I should be scared to death.

Q That is a question again of this aggressiveness.

A Right, I believe the German sees the wrong method of attack: we still can out-manoeuvre them very easily by turning. His firing power is probably the greatest we have ever run up against.

Q Let us reverse the situation and say that you and your doctrine and training are flying against German heavy bomber formations that are escorted by 51s and 47s comparable to ours, and you are one of the 30, 40 or 50 jets detailed to harass these formations. What would you do?

A I would probably send out four or five pilots in the jets to harass, shoot up and scare hell out of the escort and make them turn back, more or less dispersing them, with the rest of the remaining force at high altitude above the formation. When the time prevailed that there was no immediate escort I would begin my attack on the bombers.

Q Assume the Germans did that, what would be your answer?

A My answer would be that if they did that they would probably shoot down a lot more of our planes.

Q Do you think their failure in the air war is primarily a failure to solve the problem of our fighters?

A Absolutely. Another reason for that is the German method of credit as they accomplish more by shooting down a bomber than a fighter in the minds of the German people.

Q Let us go back to your new pilot. You have talked to him about combat, and now what about formation? Will you describe the formation you want him to fly, the distance to maintain and the rules to follow?

A In going to and from rendezvous you will fly number 1 formation or instrument formation, that is wing-tip to wing-tip, in a 'V'. Assuming that you are echeloned to starboard, then the Flight Leader will be number 2 from left, that is, wingman. Number 1 from left on the Flight Leader's port wing and the Flight Leader is element leader on his starboard wing and number 4 on the starboard of the element leader. From left to right, except that going to and from rendezvous the element will fly on the down-sun side.

Q Briefly why? Just for a moment talk to us about the influence of the sun on your mind as you fly to and from rendezvous.

A Number 1 Flight leading the squadron will be in the lead. Number 2 or Blue Flight will be on the up-sun side to protect from any attacks on the down-sun side. Normally the Germans attack down-sun, so consequently you put the next two flights on the down-sun side to counteract any attacks out of the sun.

Q How about the respective altitudes?

A Number 2 Flight will be slightly lower than number 1 or White Flight; that is for manoeuvrability of the squadron. Number 3 or Red Flight will be slightly higher than White flight. Number 4 or Yellow Flight will be slightly higher than Red Flight. Differences of altitude are strictly for manoeuvrability of the squadron. Cross over in 90-degree turns is best.

Q You want all elements in the squadron down-sun?

A All elements will be down-sun going to and from rendezvous.

Q How about this formation from the standard of anti-flak?

A That is one of the reasons for flying this type of formation. Each flight can take its evasive action without breaking up the flight.

Q How much interval between flights?

A Going out over rendezvous not more than 1,000 yards. This is for control. This formation will get a squadron over a flak-defended area as fast as any other. After making rendezvous we spread out into combat formation. It is the same type of formation except that the interval between aeroplanes is three wing-spans, 120 feet. Interval between flights is about 300 to 500 yards and you disregard the sun.

Q What do you think is the best position for the squadron in relation to the bomber formation? Should the escort flights be careful to be up-sun or not?

A No, you still retain flights 1 and 2 on the one side and flights 3 and 4 on the other side, but in respect of the bombers, you escort back and forth on both sides. You usually spend most of your time on the side you normally expect the German to be coming from. That involves bases, not the sun. Sometimes we get as far as 15–20 miles to one side or the other of them.

Q This is to break up the enemy before they reach the bombers?

A Very much, because each German formation is of 50 aeroplanes, and with a mere eight to 16 ships it is impossible to stop them if you are too close to the bombers. We work to whittle them down say 15 or 20 miles from the bombers, and by the time they get to the bombers there is nothing left. Because if you are too close to the bomber stream you only get a chance to knock down four or five and the Germans will disregard the loss and continue to make the attack. Out of a group I approve very thoroughly of flying one freelance squadron to try to catch the Germans as far away from the bombers as possible.

Q Now assume we don't have any efficiently run control. Assume that your problem is to escort a single box of bombers 200 miles inside enemy territory. How would you disperse the group?

A I would let one squadron remain with the bombers and there could be one squadron or two flights on one side, and the other flights on the other, approximately 3,000 feet above the bombers, and the other squadrons are then free to freelance out in front and two of the sides, one taking one side and the other the other side. The attacks from the rear are not probable except on withdrawal.

Q   You have had a lot of success in immediately going about 10,000 feet below the bomber box during an attack.

A   That is correct – you have no chance sometimes to stop an attack before it is too late. The German method of evasive action is generally split-ess after the attack. If you can get down there the same time as they get down, we have enough gasoline to fight them to their bases, knock them down and get home safely.

Q   In that situation you would be closing at about 400mph?

A   That is correct. If you were doing that speed, you would be in excess of his speed and if he did not recognise you, you had better check throttle and drop a little flap to avoid over-shooting him.

Q   I want to ask you two things. What about this use of flap in excessive speed? And if you should see a gaggle of Germans and you are both closing in a dive, should you latch on the nearest German or will the next German latch on you?

A   That is a danger. But in their minds, after their attack, they are through. They are heading for home. You should latch on to the rear of their formation and work up.

Q   How about this use of flap?

A   That is to avoid over-running your German. He has a great technique of chopping his throttle and dropping flaps as soon as you are in firing range to cause you to over-run him. To avoid this you do the same. In the P-51 we drop 10 at any speed. At any speed below 250mph I would drop 20. I would never drop more than 20.

Q   Never?

A   Never, because you are liable to tear off your flaps to begin with, and in the second place you do not want to lose too much of your speed, but you can always pull training school methods on him, which is going in for one short burst and pulling out. Half roll, and continue to do this until you shoot him down. This is a great method of attacking with jets.

Q   Do you think that their combat potentiality is as dangerous as ours?

A   It can be if you lose your head.

Q   What rules would you give the new pilot on weather flying?

A   First to get his formation down to letter perfect. If he can fly excellent formation he can fly instruments.

Q   Do you subscribe to the school of the whole flight spinning in together?

A   Absolutely correct. You have got to trust your leaders or you will end up on the short end of the deal. Don't be over-confident in weather for you are liable to slip up. As long as you are a little cautious you will be all right.

Q   Do you do this thing of tensing up every 10 or 15 minutes on instruments?

A   No. I would say that you can be alert and still relaxed, and you have to be relaxed regardless of whether you are in weather or fighting.

Q   You have seen the pilots go through here. What mistakes are most common?

A   Over-confidence. In the respect that you disregard a few minor points that may turn out to be very major ones.

Q   As example?

A   One of our best and most outstanding pilots spun in a P-51 and killed himself just because he forgot to chop throttle in a spin. Never take the attitude that you can become a one-man air force.

Q   What do you mean by that?

A   You can beat the German at any place, at any altitude, against any numbers, as long as there is a team. Individually, they will knock you off as quickly as you can say it.

Q   Will you describe what the situation is if you lose your partner?

A If you lose your partner the first thing to do is to look for another companion and join up. If this is not successful in a matter of minutes, turn around and go home. Another reason for our losses is that pilots disregard certain information we have about enemy gun positions. In other words you have got to know your aeroplane, you have got to think on your own.

Q In the States the standard advice to the new pilot was to select one or two methods of attack he liked and practice them until perfect. Do you do that?

A No. Absolutely not, because with every situation a new method of attack may prevail. As the war goes along tactics will change. For every new offensive we get, they get a new defensive and vice versa.

Q What is your policy on opening fire? Do you open fire at extreme range?

A My approved method of opening fire is not exactly how I do it. Do what I say, not what I do. Do not open fire above 700 yards with the gyro sight. With the old-type gun sight do not open fire above 400 yards.

Q What happens in combat? Are you so anxious to get in that you open fire?

A I do have a great tendency to open fire at too long range. I have a bad habit of not letting up until he has gone down. I have not had any trouble with guns; the only trouble I have had was running out of ammunition.

Q Do you think you sacrifice manoeuvrability by carrying maximum ammunition?

A I do not, though I have heard other pilots claim that. My plane has lots of extra equipment – 500 to 600 lb heavier than the others – and yet the boys complain of not being able to keep up with me.

Q A similar point – what is the maximum amount of gas you have in your fuselage tank in combat?

A Forty gallons. I have experimented with more and found the aircraft snapped out differently and spun differently. With the P-51, the controls work so easily that you must be on your guard. With the P-47 there is a vast difference – you just put two feet on the instrument panel and heave on the stick.

Q Have you ever been in compressibility?

A I have never been in compressibility, but I have been on the verge of it several times.

Q Do you get buffeting in a P-47?

A In a 47, yes. In a 51, the controls tend to freeze. With a little back pressure the little Mustang takes it OK.

Q Have you ever had to trim the airplane out?

A Although I have done great speeds in both, I am on my guard against violent pull-outs and try to ease out, altitude permitting. Another thing, in combat proper your greatest interest should be in your airplane and your maintenance men. You cannot know too much about them.

The 'extra equipment' to which Ray referred almost proved his undoing on Saturday 10 March 1945. By then Hitler's vaunted Reich was rapidly shrivelling into a history of bitter taste. A self-inflicted puncture to infuriate the Fuhrer had occurred on 7 March when retreating engineers had severely damaged but failed to destroy the Ludendorff Bridge over the Rhine at Remagen. Seizing the opportunity, General Omar Bradley's 12th Army Group had streamed over the tottering structure to gain a swift toe-hold on the eastern bank. Supplying his soldiers through this steel umbilical cord was essential until pontoon crossings could be established, and, realising this, the Germans ferociously counter-attacked and drew upon a depleted Luftwaffe for desperate sacrifices to cut the oxygen of Allied materials. Resisting

First Lieutenant John F. McAlevey was wingman for Wetmore when Allied anti-aircraft gunners at Remagan set the ace's aircraft on fire. (J. F. McAlevey)

these efforts, the US Army amassed a formidable array of anti-aircraft guns and the skies above Remagen became a cauldron of flak whose gunners distrusted any approaching aircraft.

That Saturday saw the 359FG released from escort to provide protection over the valuable bridgehead. Ray Wetmore's wingman was First Lieutenant John F. McAlevey, who later wrote of their 'Encounter at Remagen':

'While the bombers were engaged in their work, "Chairman" – code name for our fighter group leader – received a call from the 8th Air Force's new ground controller at Aachen, Germany, asking if we were in a position to be diverted from escort to take out German dive-bombers attempting to knock out a bridge over the Rhine.

The 370th Squadron CO Lt Col Daniel D. McKee was leading our group that day. He reported no German aerial activity. The bombers could proceed alone. We were hungry for action and would be delighted to be vectored to a place where Germans were aloft. We heard Col McKee attach one condition: ground control must check with the ground commanders and receive assurance that their anti-aircraft guns would be stood down when he arrived with his fighters. The bane of Allied fighters was the Allied flak that failed to distinguish a friendly plane in hot pursuit from the foe being pursued, and often shot down the Yank or RAF pilot instead.

Our loosely scattered group was reformed and, receiving the requisite assurances and other data, began its descent. Halfway back in the 370th Squadron formation, Captain Ray Wetmore, the top-ranking US fighter ace in the ETO, was leading his flight of four ships.

Wetmore was under peculiar restraints. He had recently been the subject of a special directive that prohibited him and certain other top aces from any low-level activity in the combat zone except in the course of actual serial engagement. The purpose was to scotch the prevalent notion that all of the top aces "got it" eventually by keeping them away from that impersonal and purely chance hit by ground fire, which can kill an ace as easily as a neophyte and all too often had.

If Wetmore was supposed to leave when the group began its descent that day, he did not. The temptation was too great. We were being vectored to Germans that no one could see from above, not even Wetmore, who was credited with "X-ray eyes" by the other pilots.

The cloud cover blanketed Western Europe like a comforter 7,000 feet thick. The 359th Group entered it at about 9,000 feet. It was pea soup immediately. The Colonel had ordered the tightest formation possible before the ships entered. The leaders of each squadron were on instruments and all others were on them.

Captain Wetmore's eyes were fixed on the tail of the ship ahead and inches above him. His element leader was Captain Jimmy Shoffit, a seasoned pilot whose tour was almost done. Shoffit was having radio trouble. He could neither transmit nor receive and did not know what was going on. Shortly after the group went on instruments, he decided to pull up out of formation and, with his wingman, left for home. Wetmore caught peripherally the motion of Shoffit leaving and turned his head for an instant. When he turned back, the tail of the ship he had been following through the soup had disappeared. Afraid that he might cut the tail off the ship ahead before he could see it again, he went completely on instruments and, still continuing his descent, executed a turn to starboard to take a new course away from the now invisible tails of the four ships immediately in front.

Wetmore was hard on his wingmen. He was a quick, wordless and erratic mover. An instinctive hunter. The few times he led the squadron he managed to scatter it all over the sky. His wingmen were often left far behind also. This was only my tenth mission, but I had now flown as his wingman several times. He couldn't lose me and I became his almost regular wingman for the rest of the war.

I stayed with him now in the manoeuvre in the clouds. The leader of the flight behind, having no forewarning of the course change, was not prepared to follow and consequently lost visual contact with us. The following flights continued to descend on the original group heading, a course chosen by the Colonel so as to break through the overcast upstream of the bridge. The group would then turn north and fly down the river in the clear looking for Jerries.

All did except Captain Wetmore and Lieutenant McAlevey. Wetmore's course change early in the descent put him miles north of the group. We were unwittingly descending on a course that broke us out right over the bridgehead at Remagen.

The ground gunners heard our ships descending and pumped everything they had into the clouds at the "Germans" attacking the bridge. While we were still in the overcast, I was startled to see flames erupt from the underside of Wetmore's ship. Still engrossed with his instruments, Wetmore did not know he was afire. The thumping of the hits in the clouds with no visual evidence of flak could be indistinguishable from turbulence.

When I radioed that he was on fire, Wetmore took one fast look out of the cockpit and then back to the instruments – we were dangerously low now and loss of control could be death by spiralling out the bottom with no room for recovery, but almost that instant we broke out. The Eiffel hills around Bonn and Remagen are about 1,500 feet high. The bottom of the overcast was at about 2,000 feet – the bridge, the river and the flak were all there. The air was alive with flak. All around flew hundreds of lobbing tracer shells, the flaming backside of every fifth or tenth shell that visually tells the gunner roughly where the other invisible slugs are going.

Now Wetmore eluded his new wingman for the first and last time. Still saying nothing, he decided that this flak-filled area at low altitude in the hills over a river was no place to bale out. One might as well stand upright in an artillery impact range as descend in a parachute at that point. He abruptly poured on full power and began a steep climb in his still-burning plane back into the clouds from whence the two had just emerged. The tight formation is not the way to fly in combat, and I started to pull an appropriate distance away as soon as we broke out. Now I was not close enough to close up tightly before the re-entry. I remained the only ship over the bridge, my Mustang looking for all the world like a Messerschmitt out to do it harm. Whether from lack of co-ordination, disregard of orders or as a result of the unscheduled appearance of our two planes over the bridge, one will never know, but the guns were certainly not stood down. And there were plenty of them.

Being all alone with no function to perform and the sole target of every gun, I decided to get out of there. I have never been able to understand how the guns failed to bring my ship down also. I was only inches from Wetmore when he was hit. Now I was the sole aerial target for every gun defending the Remagen bridge. It is the illogical kind of escape that tempts one to think fate is saving him for something else.

I pushed "all balls to the firewall" – full power that is – and headed down a valley between the hills. Away from the bridge I switched on my radio from combat frequency to the rescue channel to follow a frightful new drama unfolding on the R/T.

Wetmore was calling for help. He had pulled up into the overcast to acquire safe altitude for a bale out, but when he pulled the jettison handle, the canopy snapped up about 2 inches after it flew loose and stopped there – jammed.

Wetmore was paying a second price for his keen vision and alertness. He was the darling of our group's intelligence officers. Many times at debriefing he reported seeing things of significance on the ground that others had not seen. A special camera had therefore been fitted to the back of his armour plate and aimed off one of the wing-tips so that he could bring home photos for S-2 if he thought the subject worth recording. The cross support for the bubble canopy of the P-51 was right behind the pilot's armour plate when closed. Bubble canopies are normally closed when jettisoned. But the one in Captain Wetmore's plane needed to be rolled partly open first because of the camera. No one had warned him of that. The canopy when released had snapped into the slipstream only to ram its cross-arm into the bottom side of the camera, thus seizing the bubble securely so that it could move no further.

Trapped in a plane set afire by our own anti-aircraft, the man who had been prohibited from strafing so as to spare him this very fate was now calling for a homing to a field, any friendly field where he could put down.

He was vectored to a field – no good – bulldozers were still making it. No room to land. Minutes went like hours until a second field further away seemed OK. He was going in and then went off the air.

After Wetmore was reported on the ground, I asked Aachen for a homing to the same field. In the ever-worsening weather, I could not find it and set down instead at an advanced cargo strip near Liège. Regardless of my desire to follow Wetmore down, I needed to land anyway. For a long time after leaving the bridge at high speed I had been so engrossed in the life-and-death drama on the R/T that I had forgotten to throttle back. I consequently had little fuel left. The hour was now 1630. On the original mission flight plan the 359th Group was due back at its base in England at 1520 hours.

After the ship was fuelled and I was fed, I took off for home, landing at East Wretham at 1840, but not without some trouble finding my own field in the bad weather and darkness.

Staff Sergeant Paczkowski, my chief crew, was waiting at the ship's revetment, the only man on the line at that hour – waiting, as crew chiefs always do. I had asked "Cannibal" – the Liège field – to let my outfit know I was safe.

Back at the pilot's quarters, I learned the score. No Germans racked up, but three of our ships and two pilots lost. Wetmore was safe. The fire had burned out before he reached the second field, and with his hydraulic system shot out he bellied in safely without wheels or flaps. They said it took about 20 minutes to pry the canopy off after he was down.

Headquarters was right. Even top aces have no skill that protects against flak. This time, however, the pilot cheated death.'

The other two casualties were Second Lieutenant George H. Blackburn and Second Lieutenant James McCormack, both of whom perished. Initially it was thought that they had also fallen to 'friendly fire', but German researcher Heinz Jirousek has recovered wreckage of both machines and believes that they were victims of German light flak.

The war's end was a few weeks away and the Luftwaffe had strength only for occasional appearances, so Ray was unable to enhance his score until 15 March. Near Wittenberg he saw two of the distinctively shaped Messerschmitt 163 rocket-fighters circling at 20,000 feet and some 20 miles distant. Leading Red section towards them at 25,000 feet, Ray started to attack the nearest Me 163, but was seen at a range of 3,000 yards. Applying power, the enemy fighter soared effortlessly away from Ray's Mustang, but the rocket had one major disadvantage – its endurance was only some 6–12 minutes. After leaping to 26,000 feet, the Walter bi-fuel engine cut out, its supply of chemical fuels 'T Stoff and C Stoff' exhausted.

Split-essing into a steep dive, the Me 163 hurtled earthwards with Red Flight pounding pistons in pursuit. Ray's altimeter unwound from 25,000 feet while his airspeed indicator trembled to 500mph … 550mph … 600mph as he risked disintegration. Clinging to the Me 163, Ray knew that it had to level off and his own momentum could close the gap. At 2,000 feet it flattened from its dive and Ray caught up, firing from 200 yards. A flurry of fragments ripped off the rocket craft and it banked steeply to starboard, seeking to shake off Ray, but another snap from his guns tore away half of its port wing and set the aircraft alight. Ray saw the pilot bale out moments before his aircraft exploded on impact.

It was Ray's last victory and left him as the highest scoring American ace still on active duty in Europe. His personality contained the arrogance and self-confidence essential for the successful ace, but beneath them were traits that mocked his own image and, in a profound sense, kept his feet on the ground.

The 370FS diarist said of him in March 1945: 'But few enemy aircraft were even seen on these routine runs, and of those few, Capt Wetmore – not surprisingly –

Ray's final victim, an Me 163 rocket-fighter. (J. McLachlan)

bagged one, an Me 163 to add to his collection of aeronautical trophies. This remained our sole victory for the month… Capt Wetmore continued his flying record extraordinary by being shot up by flak which proved to have come from our own guns at Remagen bridge; Capt Wetmore was forced to belly-land his plane, a feat which he successfully accomplished, and then, safely dismounting, he proceeded to give a quizzical ear to the explanations and apologies. Men of all ranks in the Squadron, so closely associated with Capt Wetmore as they have been during his two tours of duty, are apt not to realise how outstanding a figure he is, far beyond our Squadron and Group, far beyond our Air Force. Squadron enlisted men have received letters from buddies on the Continent saying: "Tell me about Wetmore". Besides, at home, newspapers and photographs have been published far and wide that we in the ETO have had our attention called to but fitfully, write-ups such as the half-column affair in the *Los Angeles Times* of 30 January 1945 headed by a large picture entitled "X-Ray Eyes" and the headlines: "New Air Ace Scoffs at his Battle Feats". At present with our news-reading limited largely to the *Stars and Stripes*, we shall doubtless not know for a long time how noted a flier Capt Wetmore has become to the great American reading public. Nor is this all. Capt Raines reports an article soon to appear about Capt Wetmore in the De Gaulle French press; with this of course will come fame for Capt Wetmore in two languages…'

On 19 March Ray took temporary command of the 370FS and led a strafing sortie south-east of Hamm five days later. Firing in anger for the last time, Ray shared damage claims for locomotives, trucks and staff cars. It was also fitting that their most successful ace should lead the 359FG for its final sortie on 25 April. No enemy fighters were seen. During May Ray was promoted to Major, effective 1 June, and kept a sense of discipline in the air and on the ground as rumours of their future abounded and Pacific orientation instruction ensued. However, plans for this

redeployment vanished in mushroom clouds over Japan, and the 359FG continued winding down in England until November, when it sailed from Southampton on the *Queen Mary* to disband at Camp Kilmer, New Jersey.

Ray returned to his family and the next few years saw the arrival of two more 'Daddy's Girls' and a son. He loved his family and still loved flying. On St Valentine's Day 1951 Ray took off in an F-86 from Westover Field on a routine flight. His jet went down near Otis Air Force Base, Massachusetts, and USAF investigators found a crater 12 feet deep and 20 feet in diameter ringed with tiny metal fragments. Of Ray, all that could be discerned were his helmet and one shoe.

Ray Shuey Wetmore was deservedly

Another victory for the ace earns jubilant treatment from his groundcrew. (C. Baldridge/ E. De Graves)

The 359FG sailed home on the Queen Mary *in November 1945. Converted into a troopship, the great Cunarder carried many Americans to and from the war.* (H. Quinton)

one of the most decorated American fighter pilots. He was also an 'ace'. But, perhaps more than these achievements, he was a family man who loved and was loved in return. Ray's family shared him with their nation when needed, but then the publicity passed and his aerial achievements slipped from headlines into history. For this story, the family proudly blew dust off old documents and shared with us again that spirit that made Ray Shuey Wetmore, officially credited with 22½ aerial victories, an 'Ace'.

Ray's family shared him with their nation when needed, but then the publicity passed. Now they share again the spirit that made Ray Shuey Wetmore an 'Ace'. (C. Baldridge/E. Palicka)

5: Lost Lightning

SECOND LIEUTENANT Duane W. Owens was puzzled by the peculiar behaviour of Green 3, but had little time to dwell as the four 385FS Lightnings slid upwards into cloud like grey sharks in a murky sea. Flying as Green 2, Owens's concentration was on Green 1, Lieutenant Linn, just ahead and to starboard. As Flight Leader, Linn would act as instruments man for all four aircraft. Green 3, Second Lieutenant Curtis A. Smith, also formated on Linn but just behind and to Linn's right, while Green 4, Lt James F. Vann, used Smith for reference, again astern and off-set right. This procedure normally meant that a cohesive flight of four would ascend safely through cloud, breaching its grey barrier into the crystal-cut realms above.

Fifty 364FG Lightnings had been launched as part of the escort protecting bombers attacking Brunswick on 29 March 1944, and Linn's flight had taken off normally from Honington at 1317 hours. Gathering his chicks beneath the lowering gloom at 1300 feet, Linn observed that the meteorological officer's predictions were proving accurate. Thick clouds now confronting them would taper to drizzle at 9–10,000 feet. Fortunately, the dismal conditions were devoid of strong winds; the 8mph north-easterly breeze nudging the formation posed no threat, nor provided any reason for Smith's continued drifting, which also disrupted Vann's ability to maintain

Second Lieutenant Duane W. Owens, flying as Green 2 on 29 March 1944. (USAF Official)

James F. Vann and Curtis A. Smith, who had disappeared when the formation emerged from the cloud. (Both USAF Official)

JAMES F. VANN

CURTIS A. SMITH

formation. Safety in their ascent meant each matching his leader's speed, and Owens had tuned his own P-38 to 2,300rpm, 25 inches of mercury and a steady 190mph climb.

Smith continued to wander. After levelling off in rain at 4,000 feet, his aircraft slid left until it was immediately behind Linn, an undesirable position because of propwash and the risk of collision. Trailing Linn for some moments, Smith then slipped beneath the formation to its port side. The shadow of his aircraft became more indistinct then faded from reality.

Untethered from his leader, Smith was now alone in a world with no horizon other than that on the gyro in his cockpit. Senses could, and did, deceive, instruments could

Pete Snowling (right) ponders the use of the digger bucket as Paul Thrower, David Wade and Jeff Carless disentangle smaller items from the wreckage.

Remains of the dinghy and its sail are recovered.

fail, and the confusing search for one's true flight attitude might become a panic. Although inexperienced, Smith was no neophyte and had over 244 flying hours, but only 19 during the last six months had been specifically on instruments. Both he and Vann would have to climb though the clouds alone.

At 10,000 feet, Linn slithered into sharp sunlight to discover only Owens still with him. Radio appeals for both Green 3 and 4 went unanswered. Smith and Vann had vanished…

Kicking clusters of unbaled barley amidst the stubble was fun, but our activities had a serious purpose: the area cleared marked the extent of metal detector readings and created an operating arena for the mechanical digger. Sunlight burning off the early morning mist promised a fine day, but we had only one weekend before the land was required for crop, so we would continue whatever the conditions. Hopefully 22 July 1989 would see the culmination of research by the East Anglian Aircraft Recovery Group. Detector readings confirmed local stories of the fighter whose shards had shown evidence to the plough for over 45 years.

Pat Ramm powered his Massey Ferguson into action, lowered the bucket and bulldozed aside the first strip of top soil. Diggers descending in his wake like excited seagulls jubilantly gathered the first fragments of aluminium and an exploded 20mm cannon shell casing. Soon the routine of sifting soil was in full swing, and more signs

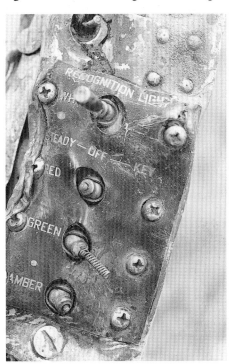

of the lost Lightning were gathered. Chunks of armoured glass; pieces of perspex; earth-encrusted items that only cleaning could decipher. Within an hour Pat had cleared the area of top soil, which would be reset on completion of the dig because earth at the centre of our workings now reeked heavily with the stench of high-octane aviation fuel. Sifting through emerging debris enabled orientation of the crash to be established, and our attention focused on clearing remains of the cockpit pod.

A radical design in its day, the twin-engined P-38 departed from a traditional fuselage to create a superbly handsome configuration, housing the cockpit and weapons in the wing centre-section. Then, streaming twin booms aft nearly 38 feet to the integral tail fins, Lockheed's concept contained the powerplants; radiators; superchargers; main undercarriage; oxygen bottles; and ancillary equipment. This styling established a classic fighter, but also

Above right The recognition light panel removed from the cockpit wreckage.

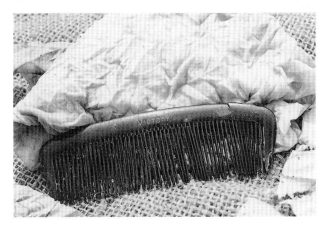

Right Manufactured by the 'Victory' company, Smith's comb and handkerchief – everyday items carried by the unlucky airman.

engendered difficulties of aerodynamics, as related elsewhere, which handicapped the aircraft's potential and created risks for the unwary aviator. Whether such factors had contributed to the demise of our discovery was unknown, but the impact had concertina'd the cupola into the light brown soil and we were now picking carefully into the cockpit.

Using the machine risked further damage to potential museum exhibits, so Paul Thrower, David Wade and Jeff Carless supervised some delicate digging and disentangling of items by hand. Lifting the armoured seat back revealed mangled instrumentation and cockpit controls, including the broken spectacle grip. Crushed amidst the debris were the pilot's seat and harness, the remains of his dinghy and

equipment, then, making a more profound impression, a parachute pack still clearly blood-stained. Recovering his body had evidently been a grisly task understandably undertaken without interest in the aircraft. Only history enables items from the wreckage to make a statement, to help relate the downfall of a young airman whose story might otherwise disappear.

Gently setting aside the parachute, we speculated why it had not been used. Perhaps the hapless pilot had been pinned by centrifugal reaction as his P-38 spun viciously earthwards, his last moments a grey screen of terror, the horror of hurtling from cloud too low to pull out. Such thoughts made our work sombre but determined as we continued to clear the cockpit. Enmeshed in debris and earth, there now appeared pieces of uniform, the largest being shreds from a pair of olive drab trousers. Pencilled on one of the pockets was a name, 'C. A. Smith', which confirmed the crash site

Above left   A brass 20mm cannon shell was still in the breech of the 20mm cannon.

Left   French Francs from the escape kit were found to be in excellent condition.

and added further poignance to the day's events. Folded inside the pocket were several English pounds, a handkerchief and a black, plastic comb, ironically manufactured by the 'Victory' company. The victory then still to be won was never seen by Curtis A. Smith, but his sacrifice was one of the many making it possible.

Such thoughts prevailed as we quietly continued to remove the remnants of the pod that had once entombed its pilot. Machine-guns and the great 20mm cannon emerged, the sinister glint of shining brass warning of a 20mm shell still in the breech. By now the quantity of finds was proving almost overwhelming: Smith's escape kit; flare pistol; radio equipment; jumbles of hydraulic and fuel pipes with associated pumps and valves. Little of Lightning 42-67895 had been taken during the war other than surface debris and the remains of its unfortunate pilot. Apparently the recovery team had dug through the top rear of the canopy to retrieve him, then simply back-filled.

Our finds had catalogued the cockpit contents and we now moved to the port engine. Cutting through a layer of sand into clay, we were soon some 12 feet down and picking out pieces of a badly smashed Allison engine. Clearing the crater we then recovered its companion in a similar state, but the range of other artifacts more than compensated for the condition of the engines. Most of our finds would eventually be displayed in the EAARG's museum on the former 93BG base at Hardwick, not far from the crash site.

Nothing we found offered any clues to the cause of the crash, and it is assumed that Smith suffered some difficulty maintaining formation, drifted away to become disorientated in deceptive conditions and lost control. He

Above right Mick Tipple (left) and David Wade remove loose components before the Allison engine is lifted. Note the propeller blade protruding from the soil top left.

Right Nigel Beckett (left) and David Wade clear a propeller blade from the crater.

apparently made no attempt to bale out, nor transmitted any distress calls. Few witnessed his last moments, but Derek Hammond, then 17 years old, was working in the coal yard office at Tivetshall railway station. The crescendo of engines caused him to rush outside expecting another exhilarating buzz job by a fighter on the nearby 445BG base at Tibenham. In an instant of transfixion, he saw Smith's last moments.

Disgorged from the cloud's embrace, the P-38 howled straight down, plunging into a field on Charlie Colchester's Farm, barely 500 yards distant. An enormous flash of erupting fuel tanks stunned the teenager as the echo of screaming engines was chased over the countryside by the climatic, terminating *boom* and then a shocking silence. Disfiguring the skyline was an ugly pall of smoke towards which came a rush of USAAF personnel. Clearly it was to no avail for the pilot, and Flying Control at Tibenham contacted Honington to advise the 364th of the crash.

Smith's was one of three 364FG Lightnings lost over England that day. Lieutenant Vann survived a crash-landing at Knettishall. Second Lieutenant Kenneth M. Shaffer of the 384FS had been leading his flight, climbing through the overcast, when he reported instrument failure and had no alternative but to bale out. His P-38 left a smoking crater at Troston near Thorpe Abbots, home of the 100BG. Nearly 50 years later, parts of this aircraft were also excavated and imaginatively displayed in the 100BG Memorial Air Museum now established on the old airfield.

The three Lightnings lost by the 364FG could be easily replaced, but a life could not. There would be all too many 'Smith's' before the war's end, but at least Curtis A. Smith has been moved from historical anonymity by the diligence and dedication of enthusiasts anxious to ensure continued appreciation of the debt owed to him.

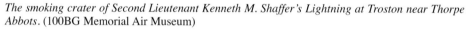

The smoking crater of Second Lieutenant Kenneth M. Shaffer's Lightning at Troston near Thorpe Abbots. (100BG Memorial Air Museum)

6: My father's son, at last

A PALL OF SMOKE over the Suffolk countryside on 18 May 1944 marked the creation of yet another war-widow. Several days later, that dreaded Western Union Telegram seemed unreal to Alice Underwood. Yet, remembering last night's dream, she had somehow expected it. In sleep, she had seen the sky open and there stood Kenny, smiling down. The vision had troubled her and, sitting on the porch swing with her sister Tess, she had felt a growing discomfort, one not caused by the baby's movements. When the two women had seen the telegram boy call at Bernie Miller's next door, Alice's fear suddenly focused. 'That telegram is for me, I *know* it is.' Now, heart-broken and seven months pregnant, its stark words stunned her emotions:

'THE SECRETARY OF WAR ASKS THAT I ASSURE YOU OF HIS DEEP SYMPATHY IN THE LOSS OF YOUR HUSBAND SECOND LIEUTENANT KENNETH H. UNDERWOOD. REPORT RECEIVED STATES HE WAS KILLED EIGHTEEN MAY IN BURY SAINT EDMONDS ENGLAND IN AN AIRCRAFT ACCIDENT. LETTER FOLLOWS = DUNLOP ACTING THE ADJUTANT GENERAL'

In disbelief Alice re-read Ken's last letters, still so alive, words still vibrant with love, laughing, teasing, seeking family gossip or, ominously, touching on the war and the task ahead.

'17th May, 1944… Gee, it seems I'm just rambling on but there isn't a darn thing to write about as nothing ever happens and the D-Day was not left up to me to set so we will just have to wait it out and hope its not too far distant. Everyone had the 15th picked out but my guess is the best … the next 5 years. It will be sometime between now and then so what's the hurry? If I came back all we'd have to do is eat steaks, ice-cream, bourbon, etc and that's not good for you. This combat is not getting me down, not getting me down, not getting me down. Or is it?… How is everyone making out on the home front?'

Alice Underwood, who became a war-widow when her husband died in a plane crash on 18 May 1944. (K. Underwood Jr)

His tender teasing, which now drew only tears, continued:

'Don't see why you aren't out working as you could work for another month yet and just think of the money you could be saving! I'd better be quiet as after all I've been spending in London I should bitch or should I?

Wish my new plane would come in so I could get it painted up and into action. The photo boy is a good friend mine … he had the bourbon last Thurs upon I proceeded to get skonko – and he promised me some pics if I get it fixed up. Sure hope so, so you can see how fat I really am getting… I still love you doll and always will even though it will be a long time before we get together again. Just take care of yourself and don't fall for any wooden nickels as I'll Be Around … sometime. Your ever loving husband … of this I am sure! and father of your unborn child…'

His last letter was also dated 17th May:

'The bomber boys are continually bombing hell out of the Krauts but yet they find the tenacity to hang on and I admire them while still fighting them. They are damn good soldiers and many lives will be lost before this fracas on this particular front is over. Here's hoping it lasts but little and that we can start the New Year out right but still the Jips must be next so on we go.

We are now being beaten up by a T'bolt and L'ning and with the noise and vibrations combined it makes a wonderful distraction from this typewriter … and I'm about done but still have an hour and a half before duty is ended and then into the jump sack to dream of you and how I will… Bye sweet little enceinte spouse as I sure do love you from the bottom of my heart clear up and down again. Here's one before I forget it:

As one Commando put it: "The Yanks are over fed, over paid, over sexed – and over here." How true indeed, how true indeed.'

Second Lieutenant Kenneth H. Underwood is still 'over here'. In a service conducted by Chaplain Bill Byrd of Ken's 55th Fighter Group, the 23-year-old flier was laid to rest on a gentle English hillside, in land donated by Cambridge University to be a cemetery for the gallant Americans who had already given their lives, and for many more who would perish before peace was earned.

Chaplain Bill's letter to Ken's mother contained the most comforting words received by the family from official sources, but they left unanswered many

'Your loving husband … and father of your unborn child.' A picture of Alice and Ken taken before he entered the USAAF. (K. Underwood Jr)

questions: 'Unfortunately there is little I can tell you. I'm sure you will understand that security reasons prevent exacting locations, etc.'

During the ensuing years Alice was never told what had really happened, and some stories filtering to the family fed a growing bitterness that Ken had wasted his life. Apparently he died 'hot-dogging' his P-38 over a bomber base, showing off to a friend based there or, alternatively, was killed 'rat racing' a British fighter, which crashed, and Ken hit a grove of trees by flying too low, checking the other pilot. Such tales tarnished Alice's husband's image, engendering an inner anger, difficult to assuage and alleviated only in part by the birth of her son, Kenneth H. Underwood Jr, on 3 July 1944. Writing in her new born son's 'Baby Book', Alice clearly cherished the love she had known.

'Everyone thought you were just darling … raved over your broad shoulders and chest. Most everyone thought you were the image of your Daddy, and you were. Everytime I held you it was like holding your Daddy. You yawned like him and stretched like him. Grandma Underwood said you looked like Ken when he was born.'

A few years later her grief was eased by the kindness of a new love shared with a gentle Kansas farmer, Ernest E. Carl, who became an adored stepfather to three-year-old Ken. Moving from Topeka to Onaga, a friendly farming community some 50 miles distant helped her build a new life, covering many scars as her son continued the reincarnation of his father. Duplicating not only looks and mannerisms, Ken Jr also developed an enthusiasm for aircraft and flying.

Sadly, the bitterness felt by his mother stifled her ability to easily discuss his father's death, and his corresponding care for her closed the door to many questions, leaving unsated the desire to know. A tribute to his father was the model P-38 curving in combat from the boy's bedroom ceiling. Touching the photograph on his dresser, young Ken would strive to draw from it some knowledge of what had happened to his Dad. Such emotional starvation, not deliberate or cruel, but nonetheless real, nurtured his determination to one day discover all he could about his father's final flight. Ken wanted to feel pride, not bitterness. Exactly where had he crashed? What had really happened? *Was* his Dad's death the result of pointless exhibitionism by a foolhardy flier?

Through his adolescence, college and early adulthood, the questions continued to haunt him, but all he could glean from his mother was the fact his father had sought several times to join the Air Corps and had bravely flown 23 missions only to die needlessly in an accident – for which she could never forgive him. Ken Jr's imagination saw the English countryside, the grove of trees, the fighter's final moments. What *had* his father been doing, and *why*?

In 1971 Ken became the first of his family to visit the grave. Just as Bill Byrd had written 27 years earlier, his father was at peace, but the austere and functional cemetery of 1944 had now been transformed into a beautiful 30½ acre setting, framed by wind-whispering trees honouring the heroes within and 5,125 of the missing listed on the wall. Ken was interred now with 3,811 other young Americans, notwithstanding that Public Law 368, 80th US Congress, entitled families to opt for a programme of final disposition of Second World War dead. Conducted by the American Graves Registration Service of the War Department's Quartermaster General, the programme allowed next of kin to have the bodies repatriated, and many had been taken home in the late 1940s.

Alice had chosen to leave Ken in the embrace of the countryside over which he had so often flown. To Ken Jr it felt natural to be with his father for a few moments, but he was not at peace. He knew now the landscape and sensed the gratitude of the British people, but this only intensified his feelings for discovering the truth. Time on that day was too short, but Ken also recognised that he could not live looking backwards, nor would his father ever have wished it, so, for some 15 years, he devoted himself to matters of the present: education, career, gaining his own pilot's licence. It was not until 1985 that his quest resumed.

His mother, conscious of her son's innermost feelings, heard of a 55th Fighter Group reunion in the fall of 1985 and arranged for the family to attend. The first day began with disappointments as Ken circulated, seeking those who might recognise his name. Then his despair dissipated when, from a cluster of veterans, someone responded.

'Yes, I knew him. I was his Chief Mechanic.'

It was former Technical Sergeant Donald W. Maloney from Maine. At that instant a key in Ken's life turned, unlocking tears as he talked to the man who remembered his father. In those emotional minutes, Ken absorbed Maloney's recollections of his father as a skilled flier, not fearless but with the courage to face combat, and certainly not a gung-ho, careless clown. He had been a man dedicated to his duty of defending the freedom that his son inherited. As the door opened into this sought-after aspect of his father's life, Ken felt more of the burden ease, but no one at the reunion remembered details of that last, fateful day. He and his mother still had no answer.

A few months later Alice died, and even on her death-bed she spoke virulently about her husband's irresponsibility. This intensified Ken's desire to discover more, initiating investigations that would climax several years later on the precise spot where his father perished.

Sometimes his search seemed imbued with spiritual overtones. Developments occurred that stretched the credibility of coincidence. It felt like forces unseen were weaving threads from other lives, disconnected now but destined to be drawn into the completed tapestry telling of the events of 18 May 1944. Inheriting more paperwork from his mother, Ken contacted Bert Shepherd, another 55th Fighter Group pilot, famous after the war for pitching with the Washington Senators despite a wooden leg acquired after being shot down. A meeting was arranged at the Chino Air Show, but some confusion created difficulties amidst the thousands present and Ken felt that finding Bert would be impossible. Remarking to a

'Yes, I knew him...' T/Sgt Don Maloney (left), Ken's Chief Mechanic, is pictured with Cpl Parrish. (D. Maloney)

neighbouring spectator on the superb performance by Lefty Gardner's P-38 'White Lightning', Ken was startled to discover himself talking to Bert Shepherd.

Ken learned from Bert of archives that might reveal more about his father's accident, and in 1988 received a copy of the 'Report of Aircraft Accident'. There, on faded microfilm, was information about that fatal flight. Signed by Captain John D. Landers, later a famous ace and Group Commander, was the Operations Order authorising Second Lieutenant Underwood to fly a training mission. There, too, were barely discernible Flight Reports showing engine numbers and hours accumulated – 98.55 for each Allison – and the fuel carried – 426 gallons with 52 quarts of oil per engine. The crew chief who pre-flighted the P-38 was T/Sgt F. H. Yarham, while La Clair, Farish and Bernards had checked armaments, radio and camera equipment. With military methodicalness, the flight data was denoted as take-off at 1345 'From' Station F159, but under 'To' was one grim word, 'crashed'. A summary attached stated simply:

'On 18th May 1944 2nd Lt Kenneth H. Underwood, SN 0-753761, took off from the airfield at Wormingford, Essex, England (AAF Station 159) to fly a local training mission in P-38J aircraft, SN 42-104334. The aircraft took off at 1345 local time, and sometime after departure, the aircraft crashed near Bury St Edmonds. The aircraft was destroyed, and the pilot received fatal injuries.'

His father's flying hours were given, 460:2 – 236 of them on the P-38 – but one critical question, 'Cause of Accident', had been censored. Ken was both elated and frustrated. Here were vital facts, even microfilmed photographs of the actual crash site showing the scarred bole of an enormous oak tree and wreckage of the shattered aircraft scattered across an English field. Captions for each picture provided another significant fact: '18.5.44 P-38 crash at Saxham'. The Kansas farm kid was closing the gulf in his past and hastened the pace of his research

A challenge was made to the Air Force General Council regarding the censored portion of text – not much more than one sentence deleted, but material to the knowledge he sought. Bert Shepherd also suggested contacting the 94th Bomb Group based at Rougham, near Bury St Edmunds, because the pictures had been taken by one of their photographers, Rougham being the nearest airbase. Several

Second Lieutenant Kenneth H. Underwood, and the identity bracelet returned to his family following his death. (K. Underwood Jr)

months elapsed with no news from the 94th, but a letter from Lethbridge in Canada arrived, which, as Ken recalls, 'would forever change my life'. Written by Dr Brian Tyson, it related boyhood memories of wartime around his home at Risby, the village next to Little Saxham.

'Dear Mr Underwood

I am a "Friend of the 94th Group", who read with excitement your request for information about your father's crash in a P-38 "near Rougham". My brother Pat and I lived in the village of Risby, about 4 miles from Rougham in those days. In 1944 Pat was 15 and I was 11. We both attended King Edward VI School in Bury St Edmunds, whose playing fields lay alongside Rougham airbase. I have spoken with my brother (who still lives in Suffolk) about that crash, and we are absolutely certain that it was the one that we rode out to on his bike on the May day in 1944 to collect "souvenirs" as usual.

It is hard for people today to imagine the religious awe with which we young vultures regarded parts of crashed aircraft in those days. We were children of the War: we had collected incendiary bomb tops and parts of enemy aircraft and pieces of shrapnel during the blitz, and most youngsters, if you asked, would take you into a barn, or to a cupboard and proudly drag out a huge cardboard box filled with the grim detritus of war: pieces of twisted metal, perspex, bakelite, bolts and spent bullet cases. We were unashamed hero worshippers of all flyers whichever side they happened to be on. Some of our pieces of wreckage were quite ambitious. For most of the war, for example, we had the exit door from the nose of a Heinkel III, grey in colour, with "Rauchen Verboten" stencilled on it in red. This our parents finally got rid of because it was too big and always in the way. My brother also bought from a school friend a flare gun from a B-17 and a pouch of red flares, one of which he shot off, almost incinerating our gardener, an old man who snoozed in blissful ignorance in a thatched cottage which our flare missed by about 3 feet.

In short, we were, quite simply, obsessed by airplanes, and spent most of our waking hours cycling to the hundreds of aerodromes which surrounded our tiny Suffolk village of Risby. We were experts at aircraft spotting. We knew the sight of every silhouette and the sound of every engine. Originally this had been useful, in 1940 when the sound of German Junkers Jumo engines sent us scurrying for shelter; but by 1944 the sounds were mostly friendly and we could tell an Allison from a Wright Cyclone, could identify not only the type but also guess the airbase from which they came. We longed to see airplanes, to hear them, and if possible, to touch them. Security mostly forbade the latter (though I remember Pat climbing through the hedge at Chedburgh, a Halifax base, and getting into a hut; and I remember the day we both climbed through the hedge at Tuddenham, and walked round a Lancaster bomber, watched all the time by a man with binoculars in the chequerboard van at the runway's end).

Mostly, however, we spied shyly through thick hedges of may blossom at the aircraft as they stood on flat tyres waiting to be bombed up (if they were bombers) and fantasised about where they were going, and what it must be like to fly one. We prayed continually for their safety. We listened in awe in bleak January mornings as their bombers lumbered off invisible runways. We wondered at their bravery as they formed up in dark dawns, dropping liquid fire of red and green flares in strange patterns, their engines throbbing as they strove for altitude. In golden afternoons, too, we saw them return in broken formations, stragglers with dead-stick propellers and buckled tailfins, and occasionally they would crash short of the runway, or in the

Suffolk fields, and we would cycle out to the crash site, and regard it with excitement mingled with awe and reverence. We saw fewer fighters – which were stationed nearer the coast for purposes of maximising their range over enemy territory; but occasionally a P-51 would bounce over at nought feet, his engine sounding like a giant tearing calico, or we would see P-47s, mere specks in the steel blue heavens. The pilots were gods to us.

Sometimes, however, the gods fell. On Boxing Day 1943, for instance, a Canadian Mustang, performing aerobatics with an American P-38, stalled and spun in, crashing just behind our biggest barn. This was one of the few crashes that we saw from beginning to end. It was terrifying. I remember the ammunition exploding in the wings as it burned, and the layer of foam sprayed on the smoking fuselage by the firefighters. On another occasion, one dark night, a Lancaster collided with another on take-off from Tuddenham, ran into a small copse of trees just outside our village, and blew up with a full bomb load, rattling our back door and making the oil lamp jump in its brass bowl. I can still hear the sound of the Merlin engines racing up to full pitch just before the final explosion. More often, though, we came upon the results of crashes; for example, when two B-17s collided over our school, we were on holiday, and we returned to find the end of a wing leaning against the headmaster's house, and an engine in the centre of our playing field.

Thus it was with your father's crash. I remember coming home from school on that day – a beautiful May day it was – and being told that a P-38 had "gone in". Mr Wakefield, the station master at Saxham & Risby railway station – a tiny "halt" on the brow of a windy hill, just off the old A45 (the Newmarket Road) – told me that the "Lightning" had been "buzzing" his station for quite a little time. It was the only P-38 crash we have ever visited (there were no P-38s stationed near us), and we set off on Pat's bike (myself seated on the crossbar! – I don't know why I didn't take my bike) and I remember that as we wobbled along the main road we saw a line of cars stopped or moving slowly, and it turned out that there was a young bullock on the loose. He kept hopping over hedges on long spindly legs and occasionally running into the main road, hence the traffic snarl-up. Although young, he was very large, and had I been in charge of the bicycle I should have turned around and headed home; but my brother continued and we passed the bullock safely, though I remember seeing him butt his head on the mudguard of a car, and noted the thin line of drool from his nostrils.

As we approached the crash site, we had to leave the road and wheel our bike through farm gates and along rut-filled tracks, until we reached two large wheatfields – the wheat small and green at that time of year – separated by a line of windblown trees. The first indication of the disaster was a twisted propeller lying in the first wheatfield, several hundred yards from the crash, which we now saw had occurred at the line of trees. We later speculated as to whether he had come in too low, and his propeller had struck the ground and torn off, thus depriving him of power and stability, because he had clearly flown into the line of trees at full speed. When we arrived at the trees you could see where the root of one of the P-38s wings had thudded into an ancient gnarled oak, about 10 feet from the ground, almost severing the trunk. But it had been the aircraft that had disintegrated; the twin booms and elliptical tail and the outer wings had been stripped off clean at that line of trees, the smaller of which had been chopped to the ground in the process; and the body of the aircraft and the engines had hit the ground just beyond the line of trees. Your father's death must have been instantaneous; by the time we arrived he had been taken away, and most of the nose section had gone too, except the nose cone itself, with the machine guns protruding from it; and the scene was peaceful and green again, apart from the shocking scar in the earth, and the cluster of aluminum debris, marking the point of the P-38's impact. There was also, I recall, burned film scattered around the site, and my brother and I thought perhaps the pilot was from a Photographic Reconnaissance Unit.

A young American soldier (or airman) was guarding the crash site with a rifle, and he seemed very nervous, I remember. He must have been extremely young, because usually to an 11-year-old anyone over 20 seems practically elderly, and yet I remember him as young! Perhaps it was his nervousness that gave the impression of youth. His nervousness was increased by the sight of the same young bullock my brother and I had seen earlier, which had managed somehow to get into the first of the wheatfields, and was galloping around at a distance. I remember the guard saying (with an oath) that he would shoot the son-of-a-bitch if it came too close. Of course, I got chatting to him, and my brother Pat surreptitiously collected one or two items as souvenirs.

The point of this is that I telephoned my brother in Suffolk when I read your letter and he tells me that he still has a rudder pedal from your father's P-38! Moreover, he could still lead you to the very place where the crash took place. He was older than me, remember, and may have a more accurate picture of the events that day. However, I too remember the place well, because we went back to that copse of trees and the wheatfields several times, trying to imagine how the accident had occurred, and we noted that no wheat grew there for some years (presumably because of the oil that had soaked into the ground at that spot).

'When we arrived at the trees you could see where the P-38's wings had thudded into an ancient, gnarled oak.' Note how the ground is scoured by tracks from the crashing aircraft heading towards the tree. (USAF Official)

The aircraft had disintegrated. (USAF Official)

Enlarged from microfilmed records, this photograph shows the tail of the aircraft lying in the foreground as local people look on from a distance. (USAF Official)

It may be that your enquiries have located an adult survivor from that time, perhaps from the 55th Fighter Group itself, or from the 94th Group, who knew about your father's visits to Rougham, and who may know more about the reasons for the crash. I truly hope so. I fully understand your need to come close to your father, and to find out as much as you can about the events of that day. The above impression is, alas, all I can tell you about your father's death. He remains a god to me. The men who flew those machines and who came from the USA to take the burden of the war from our brows were all heroes and deserving of the highest praise. They made it possible for boys like us to grow up in a peaceful world, and realise our dreams and ambitions. Of course, I am now elderly myself, and little of the young red-haired boy that I was in 1944 remains, except vivid memories of a May day, of green wheat in windy fields, torn trees, and the glint of silver in the sun.'

Contact with the elder Pat Tyson elicited more memories:

'When we were at the rise of the bridge something sparkling hit the road some way in front of us. There were several aircraft in the sky and amongst them some P-38s, B-17s and other aircraft. The P-38s were dodging up and down as fighters do, and a Yank lorry driver coming the other way shouted something about a cockpit cover of "plexiglass" on the road. We knew that the American word plexiglass was their equivalent of our perspex and began looking for something of that nature on the road ahead... As we rode towards Risby, we saw bits of perspex on the road which we took to be off the lorry that had just passed. The Army driver who had shouted had now stopped his lorry and several behind it drew into the verge and, as we looked back at him, he pointed to a P-38 which had broken away from the other aircraft and was heading quite low towards the woods on the other side of Saxham Station. Although not as high as the driver standing on his running board, we saw a cloud of dust go up as the aircraft obviously hit the deck and there was a dull, familiar boom as it went into the wood amidst a cloud of dust and smoke.'

Keeping their bicycles clear, the boys watched as several trucks turned and tore away towards the column of smoke, now ugly on the spring skyline. They followed but soon encountered a crowd of spectators and further progress was impeded as they heard the bells of a fire engine clamouring closer. 'We knew by many experiences that it was far better to wait until the rescue services had done their job if we wanted to have any chance of picking up souvenirs.'

Returning to the scene about 4.00pm, Pat recalls, 'I remember part of a propeller sticking up and part of an engine nacelle in the field before the wood... It was as if the aircraft had hit the deck in that field before the wood, travelling towards the bridle path, and had shed some parts. One prop must have been the first to hit and it must have hit pretty hard to tear the nacelle and reduction gear out, as the rest of the P-38 bounced or rolled and cartwheeled as it went through the trees lining the bridle path, hitting the largest oak, which still stood smouldering, and tearing a path through the rest. You could see the swathe it had torn in its final passage... There was still a fairly large crowd, most of the village people and a lot of Americans clearing up ... taking photographs. Basically, it was all over and certainly they would try to get it all done and cleared up before dark because they would not want any lights on the scene ... it was wartime with a full blackout... The pilot, if any, had been removed... I was of the opinion he had baled out. As young lads it seemed that the pilots and crews of these crashes were completely impersonal. That is not to say that we did not understand that they were human beings, almost of our own generation, but we thought of them as military airmen first and their fate went with their role even if we did not exactly disregard their civilian backgrounds. But, not being aware of their home life and loved ones, we did not consider it. We all had relatives and friends who were getting the chop daily and nightly so what few emotions we felt or expressed about these things had to be reserved for those closest to us – when a parent or teacher called us in to tell us that this or that cousin or schoolmate was missing or presumed dead, etc. It was only in later years that we began to consider these airmen who had died as having families and loved ones back in the States or over here.'

As youths untroubled by any misgivings, the boys were soon gathering their trophies – sinister cannon shells, shiny belts of .5 machine-gun ammunition, electrical wiring and aircraft components, some smeared in oil or hydraulic fluid to which the soil had adhered, giving a gritty coating. American aircraft had a distinctive aroma when burnt, strongly metallic, unlike the odour of dope on British sites, and they associated the smell with things new and mass-produced but with supreme quality. Such were Pat's thoughts as he secreted away one of the plane's rudder pedals, a prize that would one day pass in pride to the pilot's son.

Later, heedless of the danger, Pat experimented with their collection of ordnance:

'The cannon shells were particularly dangerous as they had an explosive charge in the nose, but all my attempts to explode them by putting them pointing upwards on a piece of brick near the barn, then going into the pigeon cote and dropping another brick on the nose did not work… The .5s, again, had various colour-coded noses… I did start to saw off some of the noses and found that some had a high silver magnesium powder, which I put in a tin lid, laid a trail with paraffin-soaked string and paper and managed to get this stuff to explode, which it did with a white magnesium flash and a dull bang.'

Soon the shells had all gone, and the rudder pedal was packed when the Tyson family moved and the boys grew up, had their own adventures in the RAF and became successful in the careers they chose. Their response to the appeal by Ken Underwood now triggered the climax to his search.

Ken himself, meanwhile, had received heartening words from his father's former Flight Leader, Lt Colonel Arthur L. Thorsen:

'Everyone, I suppose, saw your Dad from a different angle and did a lot of second guessing as to what happened that day he crashed. There were no witnesses, just a lot of different scenarios offered by some of the other 38th pilots. I decided to try to remember things about your Dad from the days of flying school up to combat in the ETO. It might give you a better insight into the personality of your father.

Your Dad seemed to have drawn a wall around himself. He didn't have time for nonsense, not as a Cadet and not as a Commissioned Officer. Ken Sr never horsed around with the other men. He was a very serious person, not an easy man to get to know. I believe I was as close to him as any of the others, maybe more so … except for one other pilot. This pilot's name was Charles Harris Hodges, another classmate. He and your Dad spent much of their time together and I suppose one could call them buddies. Hodges crashed and was killed one week before your Dad went down. The crashes were very similar… You mentioned "hot-dogging" in your letter. Don't believe that. He had better sense then that. I believe the truth is, he was practising low-level flying.

It was at that time that we were ordered in on close ground work – a series of attacks at below tree-top level … we were to destroy everything we observed: locomotives, tanks, aerodromes, troops and truck convoys. This was very dangerous work and everyone had to have their wits about them if they were to survive. Ground gunners always used us for a turkey shoot. So I believe your Dad was merely developing his low-level skills that day and something went wrong and he crashed… Your Dad was a good pilot, one that I, personally, had no qualms about going into combat with. He was courageous, serious and determined to do his job as best he could and return home to his growing family. Unfortunately, fate saw otherwise, but you have every right to be proud of him. Your Dad would be proud of you too in your continuing search for your father you never saw.'

Inspired by events, Ken now resolved to visit England and visit the crash site with Pat Tyson. By 1992 Ken's bond with 55FG veterans was such that they bestowed on him the honour of laying their wreath at that year's Memorial Day Service at the Cambridge Military Cemetery. A chance meeting with my friends Clifford and Rosalind Robinson, wreath-layers for the 389BG, would eventually prompt my own contact with Ken and the privilege of using his story. More personal than the official services was Ken's visit to the crash site organised by Pat Tyson.

Exactly 48 years to the day, Pat's plush saloon was edging cautiously along the sun-speckled bridleway until the ruts dictated that they continue on foot. Subtle changes over 48 summers together with the fallibility of memory made Pat anxious about his responsibility in determining the exact location. Certain childhood

His father's son at last: Kenneth H. Underwood Jr at his father's grave in the Cambridge Military Cemetery on Memorial Day in 1992.

experiences had encouraged a belief that he was 'somewhat "fey" (as the Irish say), particularly when it came to aviation'. A reconnaissance in April had induced some eerie, spine-tingling shivers on reaching what he felt was the scene, but his practical self sought proof positive, not prods from the paranormal. Now, nearing the site again, he felt a sensation of being guided by forces beyond his control. None of this had been communicated to Ken, yet he and Pat's wife, Pam, were also aware of the power intervening in their actions. Their steps were somehow guided, 'being controlled by something other than our own desire to do things'. Simultaneously, he and Ken felt the same idea, to try the cottage nearby for help.

Two men acting imperatively may have deterred Mrs Julie Kilner when she answered the door, but Pam Tyson was reassuring and established quickly the existence of common acquaintances. Soon they were in the lounge, Pam playing with baby William while Mrs Kilner made tea and phoned Tom Mann, owner of the surrounding fields. Ken was enchanted with this kind invitation to tea in an English country cottage. Mrs Kilner knew nothing about his father's crash, but those unseen forces now continued their support. Idly perusing pictures on the mantelpiece, Pat suddenly realised he was looking at the same scene shown to him earlier in Ken's enlargements of the microfilm crash pictures. The same great oak, only this time it was the background to innocence in a picture of one of Mrs Kilner's children. Two photographers, decades apart, had positioned themselves in exactly the same spot, one to portray the scene of a young pilot's death, the other to picture a child, carefree thanks to the price he had paid.

Moments later Mrs Kilner returned to her now excited guests and quickly identified the tree as one visible from the cottage. Ken was awestruck by the significance of events. Years of wondering, a lifetime's entrapped emotions were like water flooding near the brim of a dam.

Farmer Tom Mann arrived and, brief but warm introductions made, Ken now took the steps that brought to fruition his very personal pilgrimage to honour the father he had never known but always loved. Solemnly the party moved along the bridleway, the branches above roofing the aisle; the oak was the altar, and a gentle choir of leaves created an idyll for the man below, deep in personal thoughts.

Stooping, Ken peeled away some dry bark from the base of the ivy-encrusted oak. Revealed were charcoaled fragments undisturbed since that catastrophe had torn away the life of a young father to be and killed the oak itself. Climbing through the hedgerow, the party eased amongst the deepening

The catastrophe had torn away the life of a young father and killed the oak itself. Pictured in 1992, the ancient tree still carries scars from a wartime tragedy. (K. Underwood)

young crops into the field where most of the wreckage had settled. In Pat's memory and Ken's imagination lay the torn-off tail section, the broken booms and twisted propellers. Settling gently on the scene were thoughts of a spirit now eased by a visit from his son. Conversing in hushed tones, Pat described the picture 48 years earlier, while Tom Mann, listening with interest, kicked casually into the soil and unearthed a long buried piece of the P-38 – a small, nondescript fragment, but revered by Ken as he retrieved it and, close to tears, brushed earth off the rivets and paintwork.

As Pat related, 'We were all a little overcome for this quiet American who had come such a long way to find the spot where his unseen father had been killed. For me, the memories of 1944 seemed more acute, as I had always thought the pilot of this crash had survived.'

Later that day they revisited the site and, with media in attendance, Pat presented the preserved rudder pedal to Ken.

The following year Ken faced a disappointing letter from Walter A. Willson of the Air Force General Counsel in the Pentagon, but tried to understand their reasoning:

'This is in response to your 8th March 1993 letter requesting additional information about the 1944 crash of your father's P-38 aircraft. Your letter has been properly reviewed under the Freedom of Information Act (FOIA).

The Office of the Secretary of the Air Force has considered your appeal, and I have determined it should be denied.

Some information responsive to your request has been made available to you. I have further determined that there is no reasonably segregable non-exempt material withheld.

I understand your desire to learn more about the unfortunate accident which involved your father. However, the information you did not receive was properly withheld. Accident safety mishap reports are prepared solely for flight safety purposes and are used only to prevent future aircraft mishaps. Investigators are told that theory speculations and opinions will be reviewed only by those persons within the Air Force whose duties are to promote aviation safety. Due to this policy, investigators feel more disposed to assess blame and to speculate as to causes of the mishap. Disclosing such opinions and deliberations to those not directly involved in accident prevention would discourage candour, to the detriment of the flight safety program. Thus a significant governmental purpose is served by withholding the findings and recommendations of the board members. This privilege is not eroded by

Pat Tyson presents the rudder pedal to a proud son. (K. Underwood)

the passage of time. Violating the promises of confidentiality made to past investigators and other involved parties will damage our credibility with future safely investigators to whom the same promises are made, thus destroying the process whereby safety information is gathered and evaluated. This material is therefore exempt from mandatory disclosure under the provisions of 5 USC 552 (b) and Air Force Regulation (AFR) 4-33 paragraph 15e.

The same rationale applies to the witness statements in the safety investigation. Statements of witnesses before the investigation board are similarly exempt under 5 USC 552 (b) (5) and AFR 4-33 paragraph 5e. Witnesses were promised that their testimony would be used solely for accident prevention purposes and would not be used in any military or civilian disciplinary, administrative, or other proceeding. The promise of confidentiality was used to induce each witness to tell the board everything he or she knew about the accident, even if some statements might have been against a personal interest. Failing to honour this promise, in addition to breaking faith with the person concerned, would set a precedent that would effectively eliminate essential sources of information and adversely affect the Air Force flight safety program. See Weber Aircraft Corp v United States, 465 US 792 (1984).

This constitutes the final Air Force action on your appeal. The Freedom of Information Act 5 USC 552 provides for judicial review of this determination.'

Despite this set-back, Ken now felt that his father could be vindicated and is convinced that his mother would have endorsed those feelings. It was possible that pilot error played a part, but, if so, it was a tragic misjudgment by a dedicated airman honing his skills, not the result of aerial showmanship. A note in my files supports this view. Equally plausible was an overwhelming catastrophe too low for him to escape. The emergency hatch jettisoned before the crash is possible evidence and was unlikely to have been known about by those preparing the Accident Report.

Ken Underwood Jr is now a father himself. One day, almost certainly, Ken will return so that his children can pay their respects to the grandfather they lost. Although more remote, they can share pride in the place of true honour their father regained for his father in the family history. As for Ken Jr, he no longer has to imagine the scene – he has been there.

'When I walk those fields, I feel close to my Dad... I am my father's son at last.'

In October 1997, Ken returned to England and re-visited the crash site with his family. A crew from Anglia Television attended as did the author and a bleak, drizzly day suited the occasion's sombre tone. Once again, soil turned for another season yielded further evidence of the fallen fighter but an even more poignant discovery was a section of leather flying boot. Eyes brimming with tears, Ken cherished this tangible link with the father he had lost. This time, however, his grief was imbued with pride that his son, Kenneth Harryson, and daughter, Naomi, would not just share the family's sadness but could carry forward the knowledge that their grandfather had not died in vain.

7: Other men's Mustangs

MOST FIGHTER PILOTS sought the status of an aircraft assigned predominantly to them. These ambitions were not mere vanity, but allowed features such as seat, trim, and gun-setting adjustments to be tailored for personal preferences and recognised individual idiosyncrasies of both man and machine.

New pilots sometimes 'borrowed' aircraft from old hands and, when resources allowed, older machines became relegated to training roles. Like pilots, aircraft had personalities and could become well known within a squadron or group. The 361FG had several such machines, two of which eventually embedded themselves in English soil, and one still eludes endeavours to establish where it fell.

The North American Aviation Company assembled P-51B-15NA 43-24808 in a batch of 150 identical models at its Inglewood plant in California, and it was allocated with others to replace P-47s of the 361FG based at Bottisham, Cambridgeshire. Arriving in early May 1944, '808 was adopted by Captain John D. Duncan, Operations Officer of the 376FS, and was soon adorned with the squadron code E9-D. Following the aircraft into the group was a replacement pilot, Second Lieutenant Dale F. Spencer, and the mission scheduled for 29 May 1944 saw Duncan's aircraft allocated to the inexperienced newcomer.

The role of the 361FG that day, their first mission to the Berlin region, meant providing close escort for First Air Division B-17s as the bombers again pounded Germany's oil and aircraft manufacturing facilities. Already airborne some 3 hours, the 361FG rendezvoused with 'Fortresses' homeward bound following a successful strike against the Focke-Wulf plant at Sorau. Barely had the fighters taken up station when Dale was ordered to cover Lieutenant Abe P. Rosenberger from the 375FS whose aircraft had developed engine trouble. Disappointingly, it seemed this essential shepherding would preclude any opportunity for combat. Even worse, when Dale broke formation he was unable to locate Rosenberger and circled west of the bomber's northbound track for 15 minutes searching for his charge. Adding to his despondency, excited voices on the R/T announced that his friends had found a fight and, eager to join in, Dale urged '808 anxiously back towards the bombers.

On board the 'Flying Fortress' dubbed 'Old Ironsides', Major Ralph J. White was pleased with the performance of his group. As leader of the 401BG, he had sensed his men's anxiety following the loss of seven aircraft the previous day, but today had gone well. So far. Twenty-one aircraft had taken off from Deenethorpe for the group's 78th mission and had bombed Sorau visually with good results. Leaving the target area and low on oxygen after a long, tiring flight, the 401BG was heading towards the Baltic Sea. Altitude had earlier been reduced to 15,000 feet to conserve oxygen, but the bomber crewmen's edginess had been eased by the comforting presence of escorting fighters. Until now.

The increasing intensity of fighter combat nearby had siphoned off sections of the escort until all were committed, and the 401BG was now vulnerably exposed to any new threat. Realising their predicament, worried gunners checked weapons and turrets, preparing to face any German fighters that broke through the cordon of their 'little friends'.

Nearing Weldenberg, Major White saw what he first assumed were four stray B-17s climbing towards his formation. The neat un-fighter-like formation, steadily gaining, proved deceptive, and his blood chilled when he realised that they were Messerschmitt 410 'Hornets', a powerful, formidably armed, twin-engined 'Kampfzerstorer', which could even carry rockets capable of being launched from beyond the range of the bombers' guns. Sidling alongside the B-17 formation, the 'Hornet' crews stood off some 1,500 yards, surveying the scene and undoubtedly surprised over their good fortune – no escorting fighters in view. Poised to defend themselves if the enemy came within range, the 401BG gunners made ready for the expected assault. After assessing that their advantage was genuine and not a trap, the Me 410s could now engage the unescorted heavy bombers.

Captain Scribner C. Daily, Deputy Group Leader, saw flames spurt from the wings of two of the Me 410s and told his crew that there were in-coming rockets – B-17s hit by these missiles could simply vanish in one terrifying fireball. But Daily was wrong. Major White had a clearer view. Just as the Me 410s were about to attack, he saw a solitary P-51 creeping up, slightly below and behind the Germans. Intent on the B-17s, the enemy seemed oblivious to it, unless they were deliberately ensnaring it within range of their rearward-firing MG131 machine-guns. Mounted in remotely controlled barbettes on each side of the fuselage, these guns swivelled like a lizard's eyes. Perhaps the P-51 had been seen and the apparent unwariness was a ploy?

Nearing the B-17s, Dale spotted the four 'Hornets' and quickly realised that he was the only fighter protection the bombers now had. Pushing '808 into a dive, he curved below the German aircraft hoping to avoid being seen by their rear gunners. Sliding in behind the nearest Me 410, he almost joined formation and clearly saw the Balkenkruez on the flight leader's rear fuselage. Lining his gunsight neatly over number four aircraft in the enemy echelon, Dale tweaked his trigger for a mere 2 seconds, then tabbed quickly across to number three. His first victim was already spewing flames while an alarmed number three tried diving steeply away to starboard. Dale followed and, from only 75 yards, jabbed in a

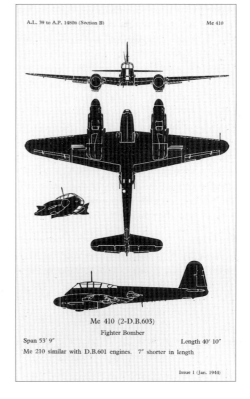

Me 410

A.L. 39 to A.P. 1480n (Section B)

Me 410 (2-D.B.603)
Fighter Bomber

Span 53' 9"   Length 40' 10"
Me 210 similar with D.B.601 engines. 7" shorter in length

Issue 1 (Jan. 1944)

A recognition chart for the Messerschmitt 410 'Hornet'.

2-second burst just as the cockpit canopy sprang off and two airmen emerged hastily. Twisting '808 further starboard, Dale dabbed another short burst from 100 yards and lanced bullets into the engines and wings of the third aircraft. All three attacked were now afire and falling earthwards. The fourth aircraft had vanished.

Viewing from 'Old Ironsides', Major White was astounded by the P-51s performance. In no more than 30–45 seconds the threat of four 'Hornets' had been eliminated, and all were now blazing pyres on the landscape below. He had seen a stunning display of courage and marksmanship. Barely had bullets finished entering one enemy aircraft before the nimble fighter had hit the second. Two parachutes only appeared from a possible four as the P-51 pursued the remaining 'Hornets' now nose-diving to escape. Another parachute from the third Me 410, then, it seemed, the P-51 hit the fourth, because Major White saw it explode on the edge of a lake. There were no parachutes.

Dale Spencer was credited with all four enemy aircraft using only 528 rounds of ammunition in under 45 seconds, a remarkable feat that undoubtedly saved the lives of many 401BG airmen. Having traced their hero, the Deenethorpe group invited him to a celebratory party on 4 June 1944.

On 3 June, Dale again used '808 for a 361FG sweep in the Rouen area. Skimming homewards towards Caen, Dale had tucked his plane into a valley when he sensed he was in trouble. Nestling in the cleft ahead was a small village fortified by several anti-aircraft guns. Creasing the hedgerows to the east, Dale wanted no dispute, but these gunners were very good. Two shells smashed into '808, one missing his starboard outer fuel tank by only 6 inches, the other ripping through his right stabiliser. The impact almost threw him out of control, but he recovered and dived over cliffs on the coast to get below their line of fire.

Ditching a P-51 was definitely not advised and striking the water at high speed would give him no chance, but, levelling off and slowing down out of range, Dale found that he could just control the yaw caused by his damaged stabiliser. Easing the lonely miles back to Bottisham, he set '808 down safely into the hands of her caring groundcrew. Next day, while the P-51 was under repair, he accepted the 401BG's hospitality.

On 20 June he again borrowed '808 to share in the destruction of a Gotha 242 while strafing the airfield at Putnitz. It was his only ground victory, but Dale Spencer was eventually credited with ten overall to become the 361FG's highest scorer.

Having established himself, Dale was assigned his own P-51, which he named 'Little Luke' in recognition of his training at Luke Field, Arizona. Mustang 43-24808 was also relinquished by John Duncan in favour of a new P-51D, but the now ageing aircraft continued to contribute to 361FG history. On 24 July she suffered damage in a minor accident, but was soon repaired and returned to work. At the end of September she and her sisters were flown to the new 361FG base, Station 165, at

One his way home on 3 June 1944 two shells smashed into Dale F. Spencer's P-51B 43-24808. Later that day at Bottisham he sits holding a piece from '808's damaged tailplane. (S. Gotts)

With blackout boards at the window, Dale Spencer relaxes with his 401BG hosts at Deenethorpe on 4 June 1944. Left to right are B/Gen Robert E. Williams, Dale Spencer, M/ Gen Lawrence S. Kuter, and Col Harold W. Bowman, Commander of the 401BG. (S. Gotts)

Dale Spencer with his ground crew and his personal P-51B 42-106538 E9-S, named 'Little Luke' in recognition of his training at Luke Field. (S. Gotts)

Damage sustained by 43-24808 in a landing accident on 24 July 1944. (S. Gotts)

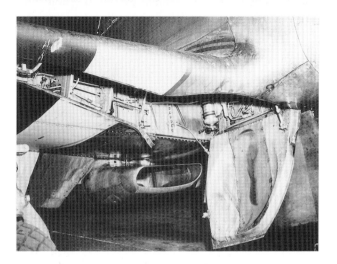

Little Walden, but the days of active combat for the elderly P-51B were closing. When the Group made its next big move overseas to Airdrome A-64 at St Dizier, the old aircraft remained as a trainer for new pilots.

The rookie who took '808 for its final flight on 2 January 1945 was Second Lieutenant Marion C. Kelly, a replacement pilot in the 376FS. Leaving Little Walden, Kelly flew north towards The Wash on a routine training flight. Climbing to 30,000 feet, he began to practise some manoeuvres useful for combat including one known as an Immelmann turn, after a technique introduced by the German First World War ace, Max Immelmann. This comprised half-rolling from the top of a loop, and Kelly dropped '808's nose, accumulated airspeed then smoothly pulled back the stick. Pressed into his seat by 'g' forces, he urged the Mustang up, watching the earth vanish until his vision was completely cerulean before entering a reversed world of earth above and sky below. Like Icarus before, Kelly was about to pay for the audacity of flight.

Rolling left, '808 slipped downwards and, before Kelly could recover, the P-51 was spinning over a giant-screen landscape seemingly rotating below. Straightening out in a fast, steep dive, Kelly's bronco bolted completely beyond control and, shuddering with ever-increasing violence, it shook his world into a crazy cacophony of screeching slipstream and tortured engine. His efforts to recover made no difference as the aircraft plummeted over 20,000 feet. Whether structural failure had triggered its demise is not clear, but the airframe was now totally overstressed. The port wing broke off and '808 spun like a demon, then, at 8,000 feet, the canopy snapped away hitting Kelly across the eyes as it went. Stunned, his vision impaired, he unclipped his harness and got thrown violently from the cockpit. Happily, his parachute opened immediately and the injured aviator was soon receiving attention. Mustang 43-24808 buried itself in frost-tinted farmland somewhere near Sutton Bridge, Lincolnshire, and has since evaded efforts by aviation archaeologists to locate it.

Turning back to 29 May 1944, when Dale Spencer had been unable to locate Abe Rosenberger and escort him home, Rosenberger had luckily returned safely, and his regular aircraft became a P-51D-5NA, serial 44-13926, but it, too, was being borrowed when it became famous as a photographer's model. During the Second World War the USAAF appreciated and actively endorsed good public relations, which often entailed sessions of aerial photography. One hot summer's day at the end of July 1944, Rosenberger's ship was borrowed by Major Urban L. Drew for some publicity pictures as part of a P-51 quartet. Coded E2-S (Easy Two-Sugar), the aircraft was then a

Second Lieutenant Marion C. Kelly took the P-51 for its final flight on 2 January 1945. (S. Gotts)

Mustang 43-24808 buried itself 'somewhere near Sutton Bridge'. Despite the dwellings and nearby road, the site has still not been pin-pointed by aviation archaeologists. (S. Gotts)

youngster and the only one with an empennage incorporating a dorsal fin to improve directional stability.

A few weeks later, on Wednesday 9 August, Second Lieutenant Donald D. Dellinger of the 375FS flew Easy Two-Sugar as part of a three-ship flight engaged in a high-altitude training exercise. Lieutenant Dean R. Morehouse was leading both Dellinger and Lieutenant Leonard H. Mottis when, at 19,000 feet, they were bounced by another flight of P-51s. Cavorting amid the cumulus like playful tiger cubs, pilots learned their own hunting skills and such training taught valuable tricks, but, like the jungle, the sky can be dangerous. In the ensuing chase Morehouse lost his companions, but, levelling off at 15,000 feet, he transmitted his position and altitude and told them to join him. Both acknowledged.

Four minutes later, at about 14.54 hours, Easy Two-Sugar dived almost vertically from cloud into the ground and exploded near the railway station at Stalham in Norfolk. Dellinger did not bale out. Perhaps his aircraft had malfunctioned, but, with only 6 hours 15 minutes of instruments experience since the preceding January, it is more likely that he suffered from vertigo in cloud and lost control. Weather reports show that there were three layers of cloud: three-tenths at 20,000 feet; seven-tenths at 10,000 feet and a low layer of seven-tenths at 3,000 feet. Eye witnesses heard the roar and surge of aero engines, then the distinctive wail of an aircraft hurtling earthwards.

Donald Dellinger's life terminated violently on Norfolk farmland, and, some 50 years later, fragments of his famous photo-call fighter were found and displayed in the Norfolk & Suffolk Aviation Museum. Dellinger himself now rests with many

A classic quartet: four 361FG Mustangs pose for publicity pictures during July 1944. Shown with 'Easy Two-Sugar' are E2-A, 44-13568, 'Sky Bouncer'; E2-C, 44-13410, 'Lou IV'; and E2-H, 42-106811, 'Suzy Q'. (USAF Official/S. Gotts)

comrades at Madingley, close to his former base of Bottisham. Shards of aluminium are meaningless in themselves, but those from Easy Two-Sugar whisper reminders of gallant young men and the cause they championed. If 43-24808 ever relinquishes the secret of her location, it is hoped that finds made will serve the same honourable purpose.

Donald Dellinger, who died in Easy Two-Sugar. (S. Gotts)

8: Why have we not heard from him?

SOMETIMES A PILOT'S OWN WORDS capture more effectively than any author the excitement and emotions of learning to fly. So it is with Arlen Richard Baldridge, 'Dick' to his family, 'Baldy' to his comrades in the 368FS, 359FG. Written during the trials and tribulations of training, Dick's letters to his mother, father and brother provide a fascinating insight into the processes of producing a pilot fit to fly fighters. His successes and failures are frankly revealed, as later, by the author, are facts that some will find shocking.

Joining the Air Corps in April 1942, Dick's flying career commenced two months later.

'Kelly Field, Texas, 23rd June 1942

Dearest Family,

Well, I am now an aviation cadet. I arrived Monday night at nine o'clock. Tell Billy Ray the first thing I did when I got here was to be checked out for any diseases I may have contracted along the way. I was then assigned to a tent. Things are very strict but not so much as I expected.

I never saw so many airplanes in my life. I haven't seen the field yet although it is about two hops and a skip from where I stay. Planes roar all hours of the night. I have to take my first physical tomorrow. I hope I pass. We were given gas attack drill today. I learned how to use a gas mask and was put in a tent filled with mustard gas.

The Baldridge family home at Cross Lanes, Virginia. Dick helped with its construction during 1940. (C. Baldridge)

My mask leaked around the eye piece and I got gas in my right eye but it will be alright in a little while. I also passed Randolph Field on the way down.

We certainly were given the best of everything. Instead of day coaches we had lounge cars. We were also reimbursed for tips we gave the porters. I will stay here for about a week after which I will be transferred to "the hill", if I pass my exams, as a pilot. The hill is the main part of Kelly Field and is where training begins. Pardon letter. In a hurry.

Love, Dick.'

'Kelly Field, Texas, 6th July 1942

Dear Bill,
…In the way of some friendly advice, I want you to think twice before you ever join the Air Corps. You really catch h—. I never was so disgusted in my life. It wouldn't be so bad if I were learning something. I haven't been classified yet and I don't know whether I will get in this class or not. I have been moved to a new area of tents which is about a mile from nowhere. It has been raining steadily for the last few days. Yesterday (Sunday) we worked in the rain nearly all morning to keep the tent from falling down. I finally got disgusted with it and managed to get out of a lot of work. This morning I built a table for the orderly room. I then tried to play possum and get out of some of the work details. Some son-of-a-gun finally caught up with me and put me to work. Tonight I have to walk guard all night and until five o'clock tomorrow. And it is raining to beat the band. So you see, William, why I think the Army is just so much shit. (Don't let mother see that.)

The motto of the Army is hurry up and wait; and everyone tries to get out of all the work details they can. After all, you derive no benefit or credit from them… I am going down to the orderly room to shoot the bull with the boys until I go on duty. It really is tough here but I don't suppose I would trade it for anything else because I am having a lot of fun too.

Your brother, Dick.'

'Grider Field, Pine Bluff, Arkansas, 17th September 1942

Dear Bill,
I am writing to let you know how flying is so that if you still want to get in you will know what to expect.

A person's flying depends upon the attitude he takes. When you go up you have to drive everything else from your mind and concentrate on flying, and flying alone. You can not take the attitude of a carefree sightseer. I have

'Well, I am now an aviation cadet.' This portrait of Dick hung proudly in his mother's home until her death in 1991, and has now been presented to the Mighty Eighth Heritage Museum in Savannah, Georgia. (C. Baldridge)

been doing pretty good until the day before yesterday. I went up and couldn't seem to do a thing right. The instructor bawled me out from the time I went up until I came down. When I had a chance I tried to think out each step I had done and what made me so poor that day. I finally arrived at the conclusion that I had been too confident. When my turn came yesterday I hated to go up because of the poor showing I had made the day before.

I made up my mind that I was going to do the best I could and, if that wasn't good enough, I just couldn't fly. Well, to tell the truth I did pretty good. So you see how important your attitude can be.

My biggest trouble is keeping the plane level. That sounds silly but it is really hard. I am gradually overcoming it tho. All Army flying is precision flying. If our precision work is OK we will get through, if not, we will wash out.

For example, say we are at 3,000 feet and you are told to pick a rectangular pattern. We spot a square field, cut the throttle, glide down to 500 feet, never gliding faster than 80 mph. When we get to about 600 feet, we open the throttle so the plane will settle down to 500 feet. We then must fly around the field with one part of the wing, almost a foot long, running along the edge of the field. We must fly around the field with this tab on the field at all times, at the same time we must account for the wind so it will not blow us off the course; we must keep the wings level, we must keep the rpm at 20–50, we must maintain a 500 foot altitude. Believe me there is plenty to do. We usually fly about 40 minutes a day and are we tired when we come down altho time really passes fast when you are in the air.

I am beginning to understand what nervous tension is. We are under a strain all the time but I suppose I will get used to it. Today, we will get stalls and spins. It is about time for classes now so I must hurry. Write soon.

Your brother and pal, Dick.'

'Grider Field, Pine Bluff, Arkansas, 24th September 1942

Dear Bill,

If you could see my face now you would realise how happy I am. The reason? Today I soloed, and is it a swell feeling. I'm really riding on air.

When I first went up this morning, the instructor said if I did OK, I would solo. Well, it seems as tho I didn't do a darn thing right and I got a bawling out from the time I went up until I came down. Was I disgusted.

After I landed I started to taxi into line and he told me to go on down to the end of the field, that I was going to solo. Boy, you could have knocked me over with a feather. After receiving instructions I took off (a perfect take-off). After I got to the proper altitude, I hollered and sang as loud as I could. Well my first landing was a little slack so I goosed into the field, fair landing. Next landing bounced some but I made a perfect recovery. The third time around I overshot slightly and gave it the gun to keep from landing. The next landing was only fair. After this landing the instructor called me to the end of the field and gave me some instructions. I took off and made two more perfect landings before I was thru flying for the day.

I still am not fully satisfied with myself tho. My instructor says I am the kind of guy who has to learn for himself. The fellows are washing out right and left. If I get thru here I will know I am one of the best.

Your brother and pal, Dick'.

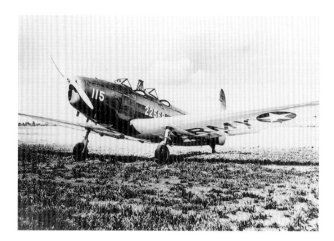

Dick Baldridge took his primary training from September to November 1942 at Grider Field, Pine Bluff, Arkansas, on the Fairchild PT19A. (Maxwell AFB/C. Baldridge)

'Grider Field, Pine Bluff, Arkansas, 22nd October 1942

Dear Billy Ray,

I know I have neglected writing to you for quite a while but I have been having very bad luck and was not sure whether or not I would stay here.

I was put up for elimination last week and was almost washed out. Sometimes I wish I had been, the way things are going.

Remember I told you I didn't like my instructor very well. At the first of the course he was a pretty good guy but along about 10 hours he started in bawling me out about every little mistake I made instead of trying to correct my errors. This is his idea of teaching. Well, I stood it just so long and then I went haywire, I couldn't do a thing and couldn't even think while in the air. After a while I didn't even try, knowing that no matter what I did I would get bawled out for it. As a result, I started worrying and I thought I was going to go nuts for a couple of days. This is when my flying hit rock bottom.

On my last ride with him he said that I did excellent flying but he put me up for elimination anyway. My first elimination ride was a civilian check ride given by the school, which I failed. I think I shall never worry, no matter what I go thru, as much as I did the night before this ride. My nerves were all on edge the day I took the ride but I still think he had made up his mind to fail me before he even saw me because I thought I flew very well. Anyway, after I failed this ride, I started making plans for something else, maybe bombardier or navigator or gunner. When it came time to take the ride I had the attitude that I didn't care whether I passed or not. (This elimination ride was given by an army pilot.) After we came down I was sure I had failed and was about halfway sarcastic with him. After I had answered the last of the many questions fired at me, he told me I had given him a satisfactory ride and he would get me a new instructor.

I don't know why but I almost cried when he passed me. I realised how very much I wanted to get through and that I had been kidding myself. I love to fly; in fact I would just about rather fly than eat. On my last "E" ride, when I was sure I had failed, I thought, "Well, Dick, it looks like this will be the end of your ambition, as a cadet, to become a pilot. I wonder what will become of you. Do you think you will ever make good at anything? Remember what Dad often said about your quitting everything you ever attempted. If I were you I would be ashamed to ever go back home a failure." These and about a million other things flashed through my mind on the way back to the field.

I met my instructor Monday and have been with him every day this week. I think he is swell and he doesn't eat me out like my former instructor. I am fighting an up-hill battle and don't know whether I will win or not but according to the way my instructor talked today I might have a chance. He said I am improving quite fast and if I keep it up I will get through. I still think I am as good as any other cadet here.

I have 38 hours at present and must have 60 before the fifth of next month. If I can hold out thru next week I will pass and I think I can pass if I don't worry, and take the "don't care" attitude.

I certainly would love to see all of you. When the going gets tough you can't realise how homesick I get. I think about all the little things I never thought of before, like the time I was learning the multiplication tables and was sitting in the high chair and mother was giving it out to me, and like the times I would come in late at night and knew just which of the stair steps that creaked and must be avoided to keep from waking Dad. These are all silly but they sure make you homesick.

I hope you can read this letter. I have a navigation test tomorrow and must hurry and start studying.

Love to all, Dick.'

'United States Army Air Force, Perrin Field, Sherman, Texas,
17th December 1942

Dear Folks,

...I am Officer of the Day today and things are getting pretty dull being as it is pretty close to bedtime. I am serving in the same capacity as a Commissioned Officer and a very busy job it is. I went on a cross country to Wichita Falls yesterday. About 220 miles. I also had my first night flying night before last. It really was a thrill to look out for miles around and see nothing but the moon and stars and a few lights. It is very beautiful. If we make three good landings at night our instructors solo us. I soloed after three landings. My instructor must think I am pretty good because I have less dual time and more solo time than anybody on the

Dick in the front seat of a Vultee BT-13A during basic training at Sherman, Texas. (C. Baldridge)

field. I haven't had my check ride yet but if I get it pretty soon and pass I will be pretty proud with so little dual.

We have been pretty lucky so far because none of our class has been killed altho I had as narrow a squeak as one could have and still get through. It was all due to carelessness tho and really taught me a lesson.

In the plane we have two wheels each about a foot in diameter and placed to the left of the seat. One wheel controls the ailerons and pulls the nose up or down according to which way you turn it. The other wheel controls the rudder and turns the nose to the right or left. Before we go up we check the wheels to see that they are in a neutral position. When I checked them the rudder trim was in neutral but the aileron trim was pulled as far back as possible, thus pulling the nose up. All the cadets have been merely noting the position instead of noting the degrees. It so happens there are about five of these "aileron trims" on the wheel and I didn't know this. When I took off I noticed something wrong but I didn't have enough runway left to try to stop my take-off. When I left the ground the nose went straight up in the air and I threw all of my weight against the stick to keep from stalling out. I managed to get a little altitude this way and kept the throttle cut back just above stalling thus lowering the tendency of the nose to rise. I tried to turn the trim (aileron) to neutral but it wouldn't budge. I started to jump out but decided not to because I realised I had made a foolish mistake. Believe you me, I was really sweating. By holding all my weight against the stick I managed to land again and got a mechanic to fix the trim wheel, which was stuck, and then took off. This goes to show that a slight oversight, no matter how small, may cost a pilot's life. Don't worry tho because I'll never make that mistake again…

It won't be long until Christmas now … write soon and let me know what you got for Christmas.

Love to all, Dick'

'Advanced Flying School, US Army Air Force, Foster Field, Texas,
22nd January 1943

Dear Folks

It probably surprises you almost as much as it does me to think that I have gotten this far. Believe me it really feels great. When I saw all the fellows dropping out along the way it sort of discouraged me at times. It isn't because I am good or anything but just because I worked like the very devil and really had my heart in flying. For most fellows Basic was much harder than Primary, but for me it was very much easier. I think I had as good a flying record as anybody when I left. I have only been up once in the AT (Advanced Trainer) so I don't know much about it. The instructors are so few that they can't get around to everybody. Maybe I will solo tomorrow, at least I am going to try hard enough…

We have open post every night and don't stand reveille in the mornings. It certainly is a life of luxury compared with what we have been used to. After all though, we are practically officers.

We ordered our uniforms last week. They certainly do run into money. I believe somebody is making too much money off them. Thirteen dollars for one shirt and 50 dollars for a blouse. I also bought a beauty of a class ring and some graduation announcements. I'll send you one when I finish up.

We only attend class for four weeks but it is extremely intensive. I could tell you a lot of things about our aces in this war compared with the enemy and a lot about gunnery, which is the best life insurance policy a pilot could take out, but all these things are secrets. But I can tell you that, beginning with the class that graduated before me, this field had developed an intricate method of aerial gunnery that can't be beaten anywhere in the world. Later on this very same method is going to be extended over all the US and England.

There is a fabulous pilot here who will probably go down in history after the war. He fought in the RAF and shot down some 20 enemy planes. His feats are become tradition here at the field. He is always on hand to give us lectures or help us out. We also have several AVG pilots lecture to us. Among them "Tex" Hill, the greatest ace of this war. So you see the time has come when all my skill and teaching and work is about to be put to the test. And I know I'll come through alright because we are getting the best training anybody can get. In just a few short months I should be fighting. I sincerely believe this is the best Advanced school the army has. Certainly they have more known figures. This former RAF pilot won the King's Trophy for aerial gunnery for three years in England, and cadets here have shown up his score several times since the field has developed our new method of attack. So you see we will be the ones to teach our pilots who are in combat now.

Incidentally, I am sending you a picture of the BT I flew at Basic. We called it the Vultee Vibrator…

Love, Dick.'

'Advanced Flying School, US Army Air Force, Foster Field, Texas,
25th January 1943

Dear Bill,

…Bill, do you still want to get into the Air Corps? Whether you do or whether you don't, I won't try to criticise you upon your decision. Anyway, it is rather dangerous (don't tell mother this). I think this is what I like about it most of all though. Nothing boring altho at times it gets a little tiresome. All in all though, I wouldn't trade places with the President.

I soloed Sunday after two hours which is fairly good. On my solo landing I had a

Dick's friend and fellow pilot Raymond L. Botsford with a Vultee 'Vibrator' flown for basic training. (C. Baldridge/Mrs M. Boussu)

The AT6-A Advanced Trainer as used for tuition at the 'University of the Clouds', Foster Field, Victoria, Texas. On his first solo, Dick landed with one tyre flat and was kept busy trying to maintain control. (C. Baldridge/Mrs M. Boussu)

flat tire but managed to keep the plane from being damaged. When you consider the fact that I touched the ground upon landing at about 80 miles an hour you can realise how busy I was in trying to maintain control of the plane. It seems that everything happens to me but I always pull through without a scratch...

Your brother, Dick.'

"University of the Clouds", Foster Field, Victoria, Texas, 12th February 1943
Dear Bill,
How are you getting along old boy? From what I gather from your letter you still want to get into the Air Corps. This is swell and I am sure you would make a success of it. Personally, I think it is the only way to make a living...

Before I joined up I would take a thorough physical exam if I were you and also brush up on my math and physics if only to pass the mental and psychological exams, which determine whether or not one becomes a pilot, navigator or bombardier. Even after these all-important steps are passed and you think your worries are over you find that flying is still a long way off. First there is the pre-flight one must go through. I believe it has been changed to nine weeks. A bit of it you will forget but the majority and most important you will retain.

Having successfully passed pre-flight, and with flying colours, that great and glorious day comes when the train leaves for Primary and those glorious days of flying. About three days after your arrival your instructor will take you up and let you handle the plane a little. At first I didn't get as big a kick out of it as I expected. In part, I was even a little bored on my first ride.

In about two weeks the fellows start soloing and you are wondering whether or not you will. Finally, you do and your worries really begin. If you have had a particularly successful day you will be sitting on top of the world; if you have not done so hot, you are sure you are ready to be washed out. And so it goes, day after day until you get the idea that you may get through after all because graduation day is only a couple of days off. And then another great day comes and you are off for Basic. In looking back over your career at Primary you come to the conclusion that nothing but hard work, a good attitude and the will to fly are what gets a fellow through, not the fact that he is a "hot" natural born flyer.

Upon arriving at Basic the BT-13 looks as big as a mountain and nobody but a superman could fly such a thing. It handles entirely different than the plane you flew at Primary. After a few days though you get the hang of it and solo with quite a few hours. And here, just as in Primary, the work and worry starts. Remember though, a great many fellows are washed out because they cannot fly well enough to solo. Basic flying includes the same manoeuvres you had at Primary with the addition of formation and night flying, also instrument flying. There will be a check ride anywhere between 18 and 60 hours, which scares a guy to death just to think about it. In all probability he will get his wings if he passes and will be washed out if he fails. Incidentally, these check rides determine for the school the progress the student is making and are extremely important. There are usually four in Primary, two in Basic and one or two in Advanced.

Having completed Basic a fellow should be able to fly most anything. I believe the BT is much harder to fly than the AT, certainly not as smooth. Everybody solos from 2 to 5 hours at Advanced and starts formation, gunnery and such right away. There is no long transition periods such as are encountered at Basic and Primary. Here the fun starts and the worries more or less cease. Even though the student seldom ever rides with his instructor he should, and is, able by this time to figure out his errors and correct them with no difficulty.

I tell you though, Bill, if it were humanly possible you should try to go to college. I wish I had finished although I know if I had it to do over I would take the same course. There is something about a well-educated man that everybody admires.

The first of our class was killed this week in a formation flight. I saw it happen and got first-hand information about how dangerous a plane can be if the pilot is not on the ball. A dangerous pilot is his comrades' worst hazard. If you are ever a pilot be a good one and think of your pals before yourself. I signed up for active duty today. I hope this letter gives you a general idea of the Air Corps. If you have any questions, don't fail to ask them.

Dick.'

'Foster Field, Victoria, Texas, Sunday 15th February 1943

Dear Folks,

This is a very unusual letter in that the most of it will be written above the clouds. I thought I would give you a first-hand account on what it feels like to be flying on oxygen about 5 miles up. I won't be doing much at the time anyway.

You see, we are going on a 300-mile cross country today and coming back by the way of the stratosphere. I'll have to hurry now because it is time to go out to the plane.

Here I am folks about 10,000 feet up and climbing 800 feet per minute at 115 mph. It is very awkward writing on my knee. It has begun to get cooler, about $-12°C$. The engine is getting rough so I'll have to lean the mixture out a little. Airspeed has dropped to 110 mph and the ship has slowed down considerably in vertical speed. I have it trimmed to fly by itself so I can write.

Am at 15,000 feet now and controls move very sluggishly. Can see a classmate far below trying to catch up. Temperature down to $-17°C$. Pretty chilly. I have turned on more oxygen. We start taking oxygen at 10,000 feet and keep it turned up to 3,000 feet above our actual altitude. Have checked all the instruments over and everything

'Here I am folks about 10,000 feet up and climbing 800 feet per minute at 115 mph. It is very awkward writing on my knee…' A flight of AT6s aloft over Texas. (C. Baldridge)

seems to be OK. Radio is dead. Can't hear a thing. Far below can see a few cloud, mostly clear tho. It is very smooth here altho very rough downstairs. Now at 20,000 feet. Have been climbing for 45 minutes. Getting pretty close to limit of plane. Have mixture control nearly all way back, full throttle and high rpm to get maximum power. Can't seem to get much higher. Climbing at 80 mph. Plane at 45° angle, vertical speed 200 feet per minute. Maximum limit 24,500 feet. Took 40 minutes to gain last 5,000 feet. Have lowered flaps to try and get higher; doesn't do any good. Can see for approximately 50 or 60 miles. Off in distance above the haze I can make out the curve of the earth. Ground looks like a toy miniature of the terrain, very beautiful. It is bitter cold –30°C. Controls are extremely sluggish. Fluid dropping out of instrument panel. Don't know what it is. Doing 80 mph with nose up high and not gaining a foot. Can see a town 40 minutes before I get to it. Trim controls frozen solid. My fingers stick to glass when I touch it. Breath turning to ice.

Way off in the distance can barely make out field. Be an hour before I get in to land. Beyond field can see the Gulf. Seems I am the only person in world way up here by myself. Very peaceful and restful. Gas down to 30 gallons. I'll have to go down to lower altitude and level off to save gas. See you when I land.

Landed successfully and through with flying for today. Certainly enjoyed today's mission. Have to fly tonight, another cross country. I flew 6 hours last night and I was plenty tired. We have finished ground school and am I glad. I guess I better hurry and eat so I can get back to the flight line. Time slips by so quickly it seems there is no time for anything. Hope you can read the letter and enjoy it as much as I did writing it.

Your son and brother, Dick.'

'Foster Field, Victoria, Texas, 19th February 1943

Dear Folks,

We arrived here on Matagorda Island yesterday evening. There doesn't appear to be much here except sand, water and mosquitos although the scenery with it is beautiful and vivid colours is some of the prettiest I have ever seen. From the setting and

13 March 1943: 'This will probably be the last letter I will be able to write you before I leave…' Later that month Dick sent home this photograph. (C. Baldridge)

background we have here we feel more like navy pilots than army. All of us wear life preserves, "Mae Wests", under our chutes.

I made two passes of 100 rounds each today. My gun was broken the first round and I didn't even come close to the target although the second time I think I did OK. Incidentally, we were firing on ground targets. We dive on the target at a 30° angle from 800 feet and are supposed to come no closer than 100 feet to the ground. I always dive down to within 20 feet and you should hear my instructor rave. I have more fun diving at the target then I do shooting at it.

While here we repair and take care of our own guns and are responsible for the planes assigned us. All in all it is made so nearly like actual tactical conditions as possible… We made a couple of night cross countries to San Antonio, Austin and Houston last week. The weather became so bad that we were forced to fly instruments most of the time. I guess we are a bunch of hot pilots. We have flown the beam the last 4 hours of instrument training and believe me it is quite a job.

Love, Dick.'

'13th March 1943

Dear Folks,

This will probably be the last letter I will be able to write you before I leave. We graduate in just six days and there is a lot to do in the meantime. I can hardly believe I have gotten this far. Remember when I used to talk about becoming a pilot. A lot of the thrill has gone since then and everything now is a matter of teamwork and precision flying.

We had our low-altitude mission today and simulated machine-gunning ground emplacements. In places we were no more than 4 or 5 feet above the ground. At times we flew just above a creek bed, down in between the banks out of sight. It certainly was a lot of fun…

Our graduation dance is to be Friday night and we leave Saturday morning for our new destinations. None of us know what we are going to get or where we are going although nearly everybody is praying for active combat…'

Many students had fallen, some literally, as the process of converting pupils into pilots gathered momentum, culminating in graduation and unit assignment. Dick Baldridge got his wish for an active combat unit and after 10 hours transition time with the 322FS, 326FG, he joined the recently established 359FG at Westover Field, Massachusetts. Promulgated in December 1942, the group existed only on paper for nearly a month until an order from HQ 1st Air Force appointed Lt Col Avelin P. Tacon as Commanding Officer. His command comprised an headquarters section and three fighter squadrons, the 368th, 369th and 370th, with support organisations. Dick was posted to the 368FS, but his training was not over yet.

Before being sent overseas, the 359FG had to cohere, to bond the men now funnelling from training units into a formidable fighter group. This process demanded wringing from men and machines the manoeuvres and techniques that they would take and hone in combat. Such activities had risks, as Dick would discover.

'Westover Field, Massachusetts, Sunday 28th March 1943

Dear Folks,

Arrived here without mishap and everything has been going fine although it is rather difficult to get used to all the privileges and courtesies attended an officer... We have been biding our time with the study of technical orders until we start flying, which will be tomorrow. We really have a lot of airplane (P-47) to handle now and the quicker we get into the swing of things the quicker we will get into combat, which incidentally won't be too long. You would be surprised at the great amount of studying one has to do before he is entrusted with this powerful piece of machinery. In fact I am rather proud to be flying the fastest and most powerful plane in the service of Uncle Sam. One of the fellows here passed out from lack of oxygen at 43,000 feet and when he come to he was 3,000 feet. He landed and due to the crumpled and battered wings the engineers estimated he had dived over 800 mph. From this you can readily see this is about the safest airplane in the sky today.

You can say all you want to about southern hospitality but I have never seen so courteous and friendly a people anywhere as I have seen here. The people certainly go after wings in particular... I have had several invitations to the homes of some pretty big businessmen. The girls at Smith Cottage threw a dance for us last night out at the college. We surely had a swell time. When we go into town we practically have to beat the women off. Boy, we love it though.

In all probability I will be leaving here around the 5th April for another tactical unit. It seems that this is more of an intermediate stepping stone in which we are supposed to get in 10 hours transition time...

Love, Dick.'

On 7 April 1943 the 359FG split up for more effective training and use of resources. The 368FS and 369FS moved to Grenier Field, New Hampshire, where the limited number of P-47s available were worked hard by enthusiastic pilots.

'Grenier Field, Manchester, New Hampshire, 17th April 1943

Dear Folks,

...This life of an officer certainly has its good points. I like the life better each day. We don't have the restrictions and discipline the enlisted men have, which makes our daily lives very nice. I suppose we worked for those bars hard enough though. Our training here is excellent and I cannot tell you of all the things I have learned. Things civilians don't even know exist. I don't think civilians know what we are up against. They seem to take the war too much for granted and don't work hard enough for our victory. Of course this is my personal opinion and doesn't mean that my training here points towards that end.

It won't be long before we leave altho I don't know the date and I can't tell you the month because of obvious reasons. Nobody knows where we are going and nobody cares... I made out a will to Mom and, Dad, you are my power of attorney. Also I am sending my entire pay check home for the duration. It will amount to something over $150 depending on the amount of war bonds I buy. I want you to put it in a joint bank account for us... I'll need something to get started on after the war... I'll give you 30 dollars a month and if it is essential that you have more you may draw it out. I am buying two or three bonds a month with mother as my co-owner... In case of my death you are entitled to $10,000 National Life Insurance ... six months gratuity pay and any arrears I may have been entitled [to]. You also may be getting a pension altho I am not sure. I'll write you a form letter later and explain everything you must do in order to collect.

My girl from Springfield came up over the weekend, and also my girl from Boston; the latter unexpectedly. Boy, did I have a time trying to keep them from scratching each others eyes out. I think I'll give up women as a lost cause. Incidentally, the girl from Boston is a millionaire and the one from Springfield I almost married a couple of weeks ago. I can't decide whether I should marry for love or money. Don't worry though because I have decided to stay single.

We are all getting to be hot pilots and as "HPs" we need our rest so I'd better turn in.

Your loving son, Dick.'

'Westover Field, Massachusetts, 5th May 1943

Dear Mom,

You must forgive me for not writing but you know how busy I have been. We have enough planes now so that each of us will probably be given our personal plane and it takes time to care for them. Maybe I will be able to fly home one of these days but don't count on it because gasoline is extremely scarce.

A lot has happened since I last wrote and as far as my own personal safety is concerned the closest call came today. My engine cut out at a low altitude and I was unable to keep it running. As a result I was forced to bale out just before the plane exploded. I got out OK except for a few minor cuts on my face. I consider myself lucky because a fellow baled out a few days ago and is not expected to live. I certainly am glad I have developed that don't-give-a-darn attitude or I would probably be scared to death. Anyway, I am now eligible for the Caterpillar Club made up of people who have jumped out of planes... Our training is getting down to

During his OTU days, Dick baled out of a P-47 similar to this and qualified for the Caterpillar Club. (C. Baldridge/ A. Chardella)

a fine point now and if the gasoline shortage keeps up it may be cut short. The shorter the better because I can't wait to get into combat...

Love, Dick.'

Some time later, Dick received a letter from the American Lady Corset Company enclosing his distinctively engraved Caterpillar Club pin and a membership card. They also wrote, 'That you were saved for America by a parachute of our manufacture shall be a source of never-ending gratification to us ... and it is our sincerest hope that your good fortune will see you safely through this war, and for many years to come.'

The faulty Thunderbolt that caused Dick's impromptu evaluation of their parachute had plummeted into woodland near Auburn, Massachusetts, and exploded. A few weeks later he narrowly avoided planting another P-47 in the centre of New York. Shielding his family from reality, his letter of 1 June 1943 opened laconically:

'Dear Folks,
Things have been going pretty smoothly and nothing exciting has happened to break the routine. I like our new field [Grenier] swell although our quarters are the worst one could find anywhere. Yesterday was my day off and my room mate and I went into New York to see the sights. It is plenty big but not nearly so big as expected. Since the gasoline ban the streets have become very bare and one often see horses and buggies on the streets.

We have acquired several Basic and Advanced trainers for use as instrument ships. It makes one feel like a cadet again to be flying them. When I look back and think of the tough times I had in school it makes me feel as though I must have been pretty dumb then. Those were the days...

I had quite an experience a few days ago. One that the engineers don't know much about. Our planes can dive faster than the speed of sound, from which dive it is impossible to pull out of except at very low altitude, and then the chances are nil. We had been flying at 35,000 feet and were playing around. I went into a dive at 25,000 feet right over the Empire State Building and couldn't pull out. Finally I loosened my safety belt and put my feet on the instrument panel and pulled with all I had and finally came out at 4,000 feet. This phenomena is known as a compressibility dive and is in the neighbourhood of 700 or 800 mph. Really pretty fast isn't it? And quite an experience to get into one of them... To tell the truth the only one good thing about this is that it makes you use your own judgement and teaches you to be self-sufficient. In school flying it is a lot of fun, but when you get into a tactical unit and learn to do everything in the books it ceases to be so much fun and gets to look like work. Well, enough for flying; I told myself I wasn't even going to mention it but you know me. Practically think flying all the time ... remember who loves you.

Dick.'

'US Army Air Corps, 27th July 1943
Dearest Mother,
...We are still plugging along trying to finish our training, but Lady Luck seems to be against us. It seems that everybody is all shot to h—-. We certainly have had our share of crack-ups and deaths, but everybody has become so hardened to seeing a man die no one thinks about it. We have fun though. In fact that is all we do when not flying. It has sort of become an essential... I certainly wish we could hurry into combat because I can't save any money in the US... I made an allotment to you

today of $120 per month… Please try to save it because I'll need a little money when I come back… I am sending a Will along so put it in a safe place and here's hoping you will never have to use it…'

On 15 August 1943 Dick's training officially ended and he became a Rated Combat Pilot. His aspirations had been achieved, and the 359FG was now preparing for overseas movement.

'Westover Field, Massachusetts, 14th September 1943

Dear Folks,

We are still here at Westover and I don't know when we will be leaving. I am getting very fed up with all the waiting… Since the surrender of Italy I think a lot of plans have been changed… Too many people think Germany will be a pushover now that Italy is out of the picture.

We had an air revue yesterday of 48 planes … tomorrow we are holding our dress parade. Wish you could be here to see it. The three squadrons had our group party the other night. It was a very impressive sight to see all the pilots in uniform at one gathering and made me very proud to be a member of such an organisation.

I want to compliment all of you on the way you said goodbye. Mother, you were swell and, Dad, I almost lost my voice when we shook hands. Don't worry though, I'll be back soon.

Love to all, Dick.'

On 8 October 1943 Dick embarked with the 368FS on the USAT *Argentina*, arriving in Liverpool 11 days later. Shuffling on quaint trains through bombed cities and close-hedged countryside, the 359FG eventually reached East Wretham, Norfolk. Station F-133 was situated on wind-scoured sandy breckland a few miles from the county town of Thetford, whence, 169 years earlier, Tom Paine had begun his journey into American history as a defender of oppressed and persecuted peoples. Dick Baldridge now did likewise as he and his comrades commenced the process of working up to their pinnacle of purpose, combat with the forces of an evil regime.

On 13 December their P-47s punched into Europe on a fighter sweep against a Luftwaffe that refused to take the bait. For a month this frustration continued, but 11 January saw first blood drawn, tragically all from the 359FG when four pilots were lost.

Censorship regulations restricted Dick's ability to relate details, but his early letters recounted impressions and experiences as well as continuing to reflect love for his family and Millie, a young lady who had won his heart shortly before he departed for service overseas. Dick's stable personality and dedication made him an ideal wingman, so most of his missions were in this vital role. Howard Fogg, his flight leader, remembers:

'I was the "old man", aged 26 and married. The average of "D" Flight was 22! I think they made me the leader because these guys could fly better than I could. Any one of them could have whipped my butt in a mock dog-fight. We were a damn good flight – and very close on and off the ground… Being a happy newlywed, I didn't see much of the young "wolves" during our summer 1943 training… However, on several happy occasions we would get together for an evening – supper, drinks, and a good "bull session". My wife, Margot, was our "house mother"… She thought Baldy was a great guy – he was her favourite, always a gentleman but full of soft-spoken humour and mischief… He was an excellent pilot – none better in our 368th

Squadron. He was deadly serious when flying, not a "hot-dog", always dependable and the total master of his aircraft at all times and under any conditions. There was no one in our squadron I would have preferred to have flying on my wing... I don't recall *any* pilot in the entire 368th Squadron who spent more time on the flight line checking his plane, talking and working with his groundcrew – making certain that everything was in top shape... In an overall sense, he may well have been the most intelligent member of our flight, possessed of a very enquiring mind about all things... I have never forgotten my impression that here was a guy who disliked war despite his skill as a pilot; had deeply religious feelings; had a "down to earth" attitude towards sex and marriage; wanted love; and had a strong love for home and family. A deep-thinking man.'

By March Dick had earned a seven-day leave, which he enjoyed in Scotland: 'The most pleasant week I have spent in a long time... The people are very friendly and are much less foreign to us than the English... I met a very nice girl the first day and she showed me the town. The women are just as beautiful as the American girls if not more so...'

    Dick could not reveal his other life, the fear and ferocity of combat as the 359FG's experience and casualties accumulated. Bomber protection was paramount and the group paid in lives fulfilling this and other tasks. Accumulating too were victories

P-47D CV-M 42-8617 'Lucky Pearl'. This aircraft, normally assigned to Andrew T. Lemmens, was flown twice by Dick during February 1944. (C. Baldridge/A. T. Lemmens)

Pictured on 14 February 1944, Dick discusses mission details with Lt Glenn E. Wiley, 368FS Intelligence Officer. (C. Baldridge)

over the Luftwaffe, but success in this sense eluded Dick because his purpose as a wingman was primarily that of guardian.

His mission hours mounted in travelling the European skies, ranging over the Low Countries, France, Denmark, Germany and into Poland. From his aerie amid the cliffs and canyons of cloud, his spirit still marvelled at the beauty of flying and the changing topography. Details of the human torment beneath were too minute, even remote, until flak spat viperous phlegm and shattered introspection into awareness that the land below was diseased by an occupying evil. Sometimes the American eagles swooped vengefully into 'some real old-fashioned dog-fights – just like in the movies'. Only there were no stunt men. Death played the leading role. Dick's youthful exuberance could deny such reality, preserving the necessary myth of it always being someone else. He hid the horror from his letters home, describing dog-fights as 'a lot of fun but 5 minutes seems like 5 hours'.

Early in April Dick's father was stirred into a poem expressing the pride and love felt for his son, little knowing what lay in store for them both.

TO MY BOY

I built myself a house by the side of the
    road,
Where the races of men go by.
You built yourself an aeroplane,
You fly through the sky.

I walk back through the fields,
I trod upon the sod.
You fly through the sky, my son,
You touch the face of god.

Upon my porch I sit at night,
At the end of the day.
While you fly among the stars,
Along the milky way.

But you will return again, my son,
Some grand and glorious day.
Back to our home by the side of the road,
Home again to stay.

Then we'll walk back through the fields
    together,
We will trod upon the sod.
I will walk again with my son,
Who has touched the face of god.

'To my Boy': proud father Arlen Baldridge enjoys playing with his baby son during the spring of 1922. Twenty-two years later he was inspired to pen a poem for his son, now a warrior. (C. Baldridge)

On 18 April Dick responded:

'Dad, the poem you wrote was excellent. I showed it to everyone in the squadron and the Squadron Commander had me put a copy on the bulletin board. You know, Dad, I am proud to be your son.

'...I want to marry Millicent when I get home.' Dick with Millie Bohr, the girl he left behind. (C. Baldridge)

Dad, as you know, I want to marry Millicent when I get home. You never liked most of the girls I used to run around with but I am sure you will like her. I think after meeting her you will be proud to have her as one of the family. She has a marvellous education and her friends are chosen through good choice. I know she loves me and I love her. Now here is what I would like you and mother to do for me, if you please. Take $250 out of the money I have at home and buy an engagement ring for me and send it to Millie. This may sound a little silly to you but, Dad, you know how you were when you were going with Mom. Besides, if anything should happen to me, I'd like her to have something to remember. You understand, don't you, Dad? I'd appreciate it greatly if you can do it right away.

It is a little late and I'd better get to bed. Write often, Dad, and I'll tell you how I'm winning the war.

Your loving son, Dick.'

The urgency demonstrates war's remorseless grip on Dick's desire for life while alluding to the spectre so frequently his companion.

On 4 April Dick flew a Mustang for the first time, and a month later, the 359FG officially relinquished its pug-nosed P-47s for the refined mane of this new mount. Two weeks later the Mustangs' extended range took them to Berlin where, shortly after rendezvousing with the B-17s, they became embroiled in a vicious combat with Me 109s, losing three pilots for claims of 10½ (one shared with the 352FG). The next day Dick wrote:

'Dear Mom,
...I am enjoying excellent health, having a swell time (?) and won't be home for quite a while.

I have been to Berlin and quite an experience it was. Got in a big scrap right over the city and finally hit the deck and came home alone (some 400 miles). Don't think I have ever been so lonesome for human companionship as I was then. Saw quite a bit of the country this way and was rather surprised that the people working in the fields were either very old or very young. One farmer saw me coming and jumped in a drainage ditch and the last I saw of him he was splashing water all over the place.

Dick's aircraft, CV-Y 42-4682, is nearest the camera as the P-47s take off for Germany on one of the group's last Thunderbolt missions in early May 1944. (C. Baldridge)

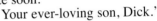

Guess everybody at home is all keyed up over the invasion. From the letters I receive and what I read in the newspapers it must be the main topic of conversation.

Billy Ray asked if I had any victories. No I don't. It seems everytime I get in a scrap I have to shake a couple Me 109s off my tail. I shot an enemy plane off one of our pilot's tail but he (the Me 109) didn't crash. Another time I got one in my sights and my guns wouldn't fire. Think I'll get a few before I go home though.

This about winds up my conversation for the evening – seems as if it was all about myself. All my love to the all the family and write soon.

Your ever-loving son, Dick.'

Fate now intervened, and there would be no further words from England.

An essential aspect of the impending invasion was the destruction of the enemy's railway network. This complex target of track, bridges, marshalling yards, freight wagons and locomotives was given high priority by both the RAF and USAAF. One plan, Operation 'Chattanooga', called for all available fighters and fighter-bombers to strike decisively against rail targets, and Field Order 344 of 21 May 1944 launched the first massive assault. Over 600 aircraft swept across Europe attacking some 225 trains and claiming nearly 100 locomotives destroyed. Other targets were airfields, road and river transport or anything else the pilot encountered as he skimmed the countryside. Low-level operations were perilous, and among some 50 aircraft failing to return was the Mustang CV-Y, serial 43-6962, flown by Lieutenant Arlen R. Baldridge.

Flown by Dick on 8 May 1944, this P-51B, CV-E 43-6491 'Wanna Honey', was normally assigned to Emer Cater. Dick finally hit the deck and came home alone: 'Don't think I have ever been so lonesome...' (C. Baldridge/ C. Doerson)

Throughout East Anglia that Sunday morning, church choirs were accompanied by the powerful chorus of piston engines as P-47s, P-38s and P-51s ripped over the roof-tops bound for Germany. Taking off at 10.25, Dick slipped easily into number three slot, Blue Flight, as the Mustangs ascended from East Anglia. Climbing over the North Sea, they found clouds covering the coast as they penetrated enemy airspace at 18,000 feet just north of Schouwen in Holland. Forty-five minutes had elapsed since take-off, but the 359FG was on track and on time for the area south of Lubeck to which it was assigned. At 12.34, near Ratzeburg, Lt Col Swanson ordered the lead section to give top cover at 10,000 feet while his remaining aircraft pulled off to scour for targets along the Hamburg–Lubeck railway.

Dick felt again the thrill of low-level flying as his 368FS rampaged through the region south of Wismar. Spotting a radar tower, Blue Flight snapped into action, hosing it with their machine-guns. Clipping the landscape, the flight became separated, losing sight of their leader. Dick now assumed command with Lieutenants Olin P. Drake and J. B. Hunter following him. With tree-tops blurring beneath their wings, the trio caught and quickly destroyed one locomotive, then damaged two more. Continuing their spree, they lacerated railway buildings, freight cars, power and telegraph lines before a more attractive but dangerous opportunity arose, an enemy airfield.

Hurtling over the surrounding hedgerows, the three Mustangs burst on to their target, raking an elderly Heinkel III and the distinctive outline of a Gotha 242 transport glider. A dance of bullets over airfield buildings and they were gone, pursued by the furious response of light flak. Low on ammunition, Dick pulled up, intending to turn homeward, but unwittingly their course crossed another, well-defended airbase.

A storm of anti-aircraft fire surrounded the Mustangs. Drake and Hunter remained unscathed, but Dick's aircraft was hit in the coolant system. Magnificent in aerial combat, the P-51 was more prone to ground fire than its sister P-47, and the wispy stream of white glycol trailing from Dick's aircraft was confirmed by climbing engine temperature. Rapidly assessing the situation, Dick realised that his experience and skills would be demanded in full. Too low to bale out and with the Merlin likely to seize at any second or, worse, ignite and consign him to a fiery oblivion, Dick searched for a suitable field. Ahead, a tiny community. Houses. A farm. In front, a small field. No power to go anywhere else. This had to be it.

Lining up, Dick judged his descent, slid the Mustang into the meadow and prayed as he gave the controls to God. Any dip or protuberance in the turf could have tumbled the aircraft to disintegration, but long grass helped as the P-51 slid across the field. For Dick it felt like hurtling on a tea-tray down several flights of stairs, but the Mustang lost momentum without mishap, pivoted, then stopped with its tail projecting over a small ditch.

Unsnapping his harness and parachute, Dick leapt clear. In the distance lay a forest promising cover. Jumping from the wing, he ran, but the tall grass that had helped his landing now entangled his feet, clasping like witches' fingers. Discarding his helmet, jacket and the weight of his .45 automatic, Dick fled across the meadow. The Danish border was close by – perhaps a boat to Sweden? Running. Running. Running. For now, all he craved was the forest and its green-black concealment.

Others recognised his intentions. Franz Bruhn, then a 13-year-old lad, welcomed the drama when the air-raid alarm sounded and several fighters skimmed overhead towards Rostock. Urged indoors by his parents, Franz and his elder sister dashed upstairs as the guns at Bargeshagen opened fire. Brimful of excitement, Franz felt that this was the most dramatic day ever for his tiny community of Bahrenhorst, and was enthralled to see one of the sleek machines slip below its companions and come down. Frightened that the aircraft might hit their home, both he and Ilse were relieved to see the fighter veer away and drop towards the field in front of their house. Racing downstairs again, they crowded for view in a front window as the aircraft made a good landing on its belly, then skidded to a halt some 200 metres away.

The drama developed as the pilot leapt clear and ran towards Heilengendam Forest. Realising the pilot's intentions, a soldier on leave in the village grabbed his gun, then commandeered a neighbour's motorbike together with its owner. Kicked into action, the motorcycle crackled down the road before swerving on to a track that intercepted the pilot's escape route. Adding to events came the howl of a diving fighter as Olin Drake's P-51 powered down towards Dick's abandoned aircraft. Unaware of the motorcycle, Drake had been cheered by Dick's hasty emergence and departure, but was determined that the fallen fighter should be of no value to the enemy. Two dummy runs confirmed Dick's evacuation, and Drake's machine-guns set the Mustang alight before he climbed for home, feeling comfortable that his friend had at least pulled off a successful crash-landing and may even have escaped captivity.

Meanwhile Dick continued breathlessly, barely aware of events behind him. Cursing the green tentacles trapping his ankles, he kicked off his flying boots as he ran, but exhaustion overcame his leaden limbs and the forest seemed no nearer. Then, despairingly, he saw the motorcycle. Further effort was futile – Dick had no choice but to surrender. For him, the war was about to begin.

Billy Ray Baldridge was alone when the telegram arrived on 2 June. He had heard of this moment for other families and feared it for his own. Seconds later he fled tearfully into nearby woods, finding solace amid the trees and begging for God to make Dick be alive. Unable to speak when his parents came home, Billy handed them the telegram.

'The Secretary of War desires me to express his deep regret that your Son, First Lieutenant Arlen R. Baldridge, has been reported missing in action since 21st May over Germany...'

Only a few weeks ago Mr and Mrs Baldridge had shared parental pride in the award of Dick's DFC – now they shared the anxiety. The irony of the letter that Arlen Sr had written on 19 May gripped their emotions:

'...Am glad you are on the "Ball" and have escaped injury and no doubt you have had some pretty tough scraps. I hope you will get to come home soon... Things are going along pretty well on the home front. Rationing of most foods has been discontinued and most stores are bulging out with merchandise. However, there is a shortage of some articles, such as automobiles, washing machines, household appliances, etc, but no one suffering for lack of necessities... You are to be congratulated for the fine record you have made so far and you bet we are proud of you. The citation you received is one to be proud of and proves your honor and loyalty to duty...'

The war had now crossed the family doorstep, and their son had entered the shadowlands. Their sufferings mirrored similar anguish throughout the land, but, like so many families, they could only wait. Their torment had barely begun.

Following the telegram came a letter from Brigadier General Robert H. Dunlop of the War Department:

'I know that added distress is caused by failure to receive more information or details. Therefore I wish to assure you that at any time additional information is received it will be transmitted to you without delay, and, if in the meantime no additional information is received, I will again communicate with you at the expiration of three months. Also, it is the policy of the Commanding General of the Army Air Forces upon receipt of the "Missing Air Crew Report" to convey to you any details that might be contained in that report.

The term "missing in action" is used only to indicate that the whereabouts or status of an individual is not immediately known. It is not intended to convey the impression that the case is closed. I wish to emphasise that every effort is exerted continuously to clear up the status of our personnel. Under war conditions this is a difficult task as you must readily realise. Experience has shown that many persons reporting missing in action are subsequently reported as prisoners of war, but as this information is furnished by countries with which we are at war, the War Department is helpless to expedite such reports. However, in order to relieve financial worry, Congress has enacted legislation which continues in force the pay, allowance and allotments to dependents of personnel being carried on a missing status...'

Helen Baldridge had never met Millie, but both women loved Dick, Helen as only a mother could and Millie as the fiancée whose future happiness with her handsome young flier was now held hostage by fate. Responding to the news, Millie wrote on 5 June:

'Your letter brought the saddest news I've ever heard – somehow or other I never imagined this would happen to Dick, although I did worry, it didn't seem quite possible, but the telegram stated he was "missing in action" – that leaves us so much hope. He might have baled out, or even made a crash-landing and was taken prisoner. I will not give up hope and I'll pray faithfully for his safety and his return after the war... War is such an unchristian thing – fighting, killing, and all the horrors. The young men of our country or any country fighting a war, when they should just be beginning their life, going to school and planning their future. The mothers of these boys are the ones that suffer most – you have brought Dick up, watched him grow from childhood into manhood, then watch him go to war.

It's hard to write my feelings to you, but I just can't give up hope – he just might be alright – he is such a good pilot and has such ambition to live. I do wish I could be with you and talk to you tonight... I do think we should know each other more.

Mrs Baldridge, I can't tell you how badly I feel about this – you have gone through so much, but we both love him so he must be alright...

Millicent.'

In later correspondence, still without news, Millie sought consolation:

'We can be thankful though if Dick is alright that he is fighting the Germans and not the barbaric Japs. I would feel then that there would be no hope...'

Her sentiments were encouraged during July when they received information advising that Dick had been seen to climb out of his aircraft and run. Several more weeks of strain elapsed before another telegram arrived from USAAF HQ in Washington:

'Report just received through the International Red Cross states that your son, First Lieutenant Arlen R. Baldridge, is a Prisoner of War of the German Government.'

A letter on 9 September confirmed the telegram, but, worryingly, it stated that the place of Dick's internment was not known and such knowledge might not be forthcoming for several weeks.

Buoyant that Dick was at least alive, Millie went Christmas shopping that November, confident that she would soon be able to send him some small gifts. She wrote happily to Helen:

'... maybe I could send him a couple of nice warm sweaters and some woollen sox – and a wonderful thing I saw last week ... it's a box containing cards, dice, chess mates, checkers and a board enabling them to play all these games. There are several others too...'

Back in that field on 21 May, waiting with the soldier, Dick wondered what would happen next, steeling himself to face interrogation and resolute that he would reveal only his name, rank and number in accordance with the Geneva Convention.

A woman living near the Bruhns had telephoned the police to report the downed fighter. Curious to see this 'terror flieger', young Franz joined a group of onlookers. The young pilot was clearly no demon and seemed not that much older than Franz himself. A few minutes later two sinister black limousines slid smoothly to a standstill nearby. Inside were policemen and, ominously, at least one member of the Sturmabeilungen – SA – ardent Nazis, infamously known as 'Brownshirts'.

Sturmfuhrer Peters lived with a local family, prominent in the building trade, and was well known for his fanatical fascist beliefs. Peters's companion was Police Sergeant Gosch, who had been posted to Bad Doberan earlier in the war. Franz saw the American pilot ushered into the automobile with Peters and Gosch, and the vehicle then set off towards Bad Doberan.

The following day, 22 May, would be Willi Selk's 46th birthday, but Willi was not inclined to celebrate births. His business was death. As cemetery caretaker for Bad Doberan, he was accustomed to dealing with death, but even he was shocked over the condition of the corpse delivered unceremoniously to the morgue by Sturmfuhrer Peters. A trail of blood indicated that death was very recent, and Willi could see that the young airman had been brutally beaten. Blackening blood congealing in the scalp resulted from savage strikes that had fractured Dick's skull from behind his right ear to his forehead. His mouth was pulped and bloody, and several teeth had been stove in, others twisted grotesquely, telling of the torture endured. Further pain had been inflicted by breaking his right arm before death, caused by a shot in the heart from close range, ended his torment. Afraid of challenging such brutality, Willi Selk could say nothing – yet.

Next morning, on his birthday, Willi had the grim task of burying the young pilot. Dick's barbaric treatment troubled the cemetery caretaker and he felt further revulsion on learning from Marta Müller how Sergeant Gosch had boasted about using his pistol to 'settle' the American.

November slid bleakly into a barren Christmas for the Baldridge family. Still without news of their eldest son's whereabouts, they also felt Billy Ray's departure early in January for service in the Marines. Helen wrote to him on the 23rd:

'We haven't heard a word from Dickie but I really believe he is still there somewhere. I am going to write to the International Red Cross and see if they can find him for me.'

Helen Baldridge. (C. Baldridge)

Tragedy had already struck the Baldridge family. This picture was taken in 1931–32; it shows Dick's parents and, in front of them, left to right, Dick, his sister Dorothy and brother Billy Ray. Dorothy died in 1941 after falling from her bicycle and suffering serious head injuries. (C. Baldridge)

Before Helen's anxiety could be expressed, another War Department telegram descended on the Baldridge family with devastating news:

'Report now received from the German Government through the International Red Cross states your son First Lieutenant Arlen R. Baldridge who was previously reported a prisoner of war was killed in action on 21st May over Germany. The Secretary of War extends his deep sympathy.'

Dick's father literally collapsed with grief and cried for hours. His mother could not comprehend it. The son they adored, were so proud of; the boisterous baby who had sparkled into their lives on 21 June 1921, and gave such love; the young warrior who never failed them, nor the cause of freedom, had gone. How? Why had they not been told before? Was he really dead or was this callousness of the cruellest kind? Helen struggled to find the words when she wrote to Billy, but the suffering she was to endure for the rest of her life was already evident.

'If we only knew how he was killed and if he was killed instantly. I imagine he was shot when he ran or maybe his own squadron killed him when they blew up his plane or maybe he was mobbed by the Germans. Oh, I can think of so many things... I will never get over Dickie's death... Several people say as there has been such a mix up about him he is probably still alive and in prison but why have we not heard from him ...? I am going to hope and not give him up entirely until the war is over and all the boys back again...'

Helen continued to cherish that hope, but with the passing of each painful week she felt more certain that her son had been shot by the Germans 'because he would not talk'. Her husband, racked with despair, lost interest in all that had once mattered, his life lying beneath the shadow of an overwhelming grief. Only slowly would that darkness lift, but he was robbed forever of the 'grand and glorious' day he once imagined for his son's homecoming. Later that year he wrote to Billy Ray:

'We have been torn to shreds with your going away and the news about Dick. I, myself, have very little interest in anything but realise I will have to get over that...'

Slowly the family reconstructed their lives, but Helen still felt compelled by the need to know what had happened, and in February 1945 she wrote to the War Department commencing a quest that was to continue for many years. Asking the War Department to investigate, she stressed her conviction that Dick had been shot after capture. Unfortunately, the war situation made it impossible to obtain further information.

Not until peace returned was Helen able to continue her pleas, and in November 1945 she persisted. Her anguish was still apparent:

'When peace was declared and the boys began coming home, we thought there was a possibility of our boy returning. We now are convinced he was killed; and we would like to know (if there is any way at all to find out thru the Red Cross) how he was killed, whether mobbed, shot as a hostage or really killed in action. Whether he was buried, and where, or what actually did become of him...'

Aware of its obligations to many families with loved ones still MIA, the US Army was translating numerous volumes of captured German records. These revealed that Dick had been buried at Bad Doberan, but gave no details of his death. In addition, many returning POWs were questioned and Lt Ben Hagan recalled hearing from his own, more civilised, interrogator, Bill Scharf, that Lt Baldridge had been 'shot while trying to escape'. While such evidence was only hearsay, suspicions were aroused and more material sought. By September 1945 it was known that several USAAF airmen had been murdered in the vicinity of Bad Doberan, and other evidence would accumulate.

Willi Selk had also not forgotten how the young pilot had been treated, and knew that a family, somewhere, would be anxious to know his fate. In April 1946 the cemetery caretaker came forward voluntarily and made a statement to the police in Bad Doberan. Records he kept gave the airman's identification number, 0-675653-2-43. Selk stated that the brutal Police Sergeant Gosch had been transferred shortly after this incident and Selk did not know of his whereabouts. Sturmfuhrer Peters had also vanished. Following Selk's disclosure, First Lieutenant Rowan A. Wakefield, commanding the 1st Searching Team, Soviet Zone, included Dick's name on a list requiring investigation by the 1st Field HQ American Graves Registration Command (AGRC), and commented:

'This is the greatest concentration of atrocity cases that this team has ever encountered, and for this reason it is brought to your attention with special emphasis in the hope that justice can be secured for these innocent victims of Nazi brutality.'

Regrettably, both Wakefield and the men at 1st Field HQ found their endeavours handicapped by towns like Bad Doberan being now in Russian-occupied territory. Ice was rapidly forming on the relationships between the former Allies, and

American investigators were frequently obstructed by obdurate officials and bureaucracy. By August 1946 a file had been created on the case of First Lieutenant Arlen R. Baldridge, and the Deputy Theater Judge Advocate for War Crimes requested a pathologist's report stating the cause of death.

On 18 September 1946 the AGRC Disinterring Team No 1 exhumed the bodies of two Americans from the graveyard in Bad Doberan. Sergeant Alexander Altman's Narrative of Disinterment grimly stated, 'No coffins were used and the bodies were badly decomposed'. The second officer was eventually identified as Lt John R. Rudnicky of the 95BG. The infamous Police Sergeant Gosch reported Rudnicky as being found dead in his parachute from wounds received in combat, a statement contradicted by a fellow crew member who told Rudnicky's family that he landed safely but was beaten to death by civilians.

For Dick, they established a 'partial identification' from cemetery records and dutifully filled in a standard check-list covering anything that would prove the identity or provide evidence. It was a sombre task. Dick's clothing had mostly rotted – there were remnants of undergarments, green trousers, shoes and his shirt. Still pinned to his shirt pocket were the outswept silver wings of which he had been so proud.

Second Lieutenant R. G. Johnson, the Laboratory Officer, noted under Remarks:

'Body wrapped in burlap bag, all bones recovered except right radius and ulna, advance stage of decomposition, fracture complete zig-zag extending from right interior portion of frontal bone through right temporal through zygomatic process to mastoid process. Est weight of remains recovered 65lb.'

Following the autopsy, Robert B. Mapes, Attorney for the Prosecution Section, War Crimes Branch, wrote a report requesting that an investigation at the scene of death should be undertaken, 'when and if permission from the Russians to do so is obtained'. Six months later, a note on the case file observed that, 'The perpetrator and an eyewitness are both in the Russian Zone. This is a good case if they could be obtained', but a later review, recognising the injustice of reality, closed the file.

In 1948 the American Graves Registration Command, still struggling to complete its work, visited Rostock with a Soviet escort officer. Once again, East German and Soviet Communist officials procrastinated, preventing the disclosure of information or files necessary to bring to justice Peters, Gosch and the local National Socialist group leader, Walter Kitman, also implicated in the atrocities against American airmen including Dick Baldridge. Dental records and other documents had confirmed Dickie's identity and he was given a proper military funeral in the US Military Cemetery at St Avold in France.

The US authorities did not disclose to his family the extent nor outcome of their research into his death. In June 1947 the War Department advised that they had Government authority to comply with his parents' wishes regarding the final resting place for their son. The administration of their request took almost a year because Uncle Sam had so many servicemen making this last journey. On 21 July 1948 family and friends gathered for a simple service both welcoming and bidding farewell to Dick as he was lovingly laid to rest, sharing the family plot in Cunningham Memorial Park, St Albans, West Virginia.

Happily, Billy Ray returned from war physically unscathed, but always remembering the elder brother of whom he had been so proud. Even more boastful of Dick's prowess and achievements had been six-year-old John. In Dick he had a handsome, heroic, full-of-fun big brother you could *really* look up to. Helen often called the family together and read aloud Dick's letters, and young John became convinced that every fighter flashing overhead was flown by *his* big brother and waved frantically at the departing aircraft. Lost to John was the adored potential mentor whose years had been forfeited for other families and children to enjoy freedom.

John grew up with that gap in his life. When his mother died in 1991, John and his wife Charlotte found the cache of letters, treasured over decades, as all that Helen had left of her eldest boy. Travelling home, John and Char read every one and were captivated by the way Dick 'walked off the pages and came alive'. So touched was Char that she determined to complete Helen's quest. The loss was more personal for both John and Billy Ray, but Char proved the catalyst. Helen's efforts had faltered against the barricades of bureaucracy, but the world had moved on since then. America had a Freedom of Information Act and, even more significantly, the Iron Curtain had rusted and collapsed.

From US National Archives, Char obtained documents that had lain dormant for nearly 50 years. Records claiming that Dick had been 'shot while trying to escape' were disbelieved, the very phrase mocking truth and undoubtedly concocted to conceal the brutal reality. Continuing her research, Char discovered the Atrocity File, the existence of which had been kept from Helen. Spurred on, Char even wrote to Berno Grzech, the Mayor of Bad Doberan. Now, instead of resistance, came a charming response offering to help.

Events climaxed on 21 May 1993, 49 years exactly since Dick's tragic descent into Bad Doberan. Char, John and Billy Ray arrived, anxious to establish more details of his death. Contrasting with events in 1944, their reception was warm, open and understanding. Guided to the Mayor's office, Berno Grzech greeted his guests, gesturing sympathy and support. It was later revealed that his support included alerting the provincial press and prompting local historians to investigate. By coincidence, the archivist for Bad Doberan was Frau Inge Bruhn, the wife of Franz Bruhn who had witnessed Dick's skilful crash-landing and valiant escape attempt. Frau Bruhn had kindly compiled a dossier of her efforts, 'Nachforshunger uber der Todd des Arlen Richard Baldridge' ('Investigation into the Death of Arlen Richard Baldridge'), which she now presented to his family. It was evident that Frau Bruhn had done her best to answer the questions previously faxed over by Char, and her gesture of friendship moved the American family to tears.

Even more had been planned. Tomorrow they would meet Franz Bruhn and be taken to the spot where Dick's Mustang had slithered to a standstill. They would also visit the cemetery where Willi Selk had buried the airman he knew had been murdered. For the remainder of their first day, they were shown around Bad Doberan by a local reporter, Lutz Werner. They visited the courthouse to which Dick had first been taken and then, behind the courthouse, they were shown the prison. Now converted to apartments, this was probably the building where Dick had been beaten, then shot by Gosch and Peters. Char imagined those grotesque creatures, armed and arrogantly vicious, crazed with the false bravado of cruel cowards whose courage came only when their opponents were helpless. These awful thoughts occurred again later when exploring, unescorted, they happened upon the cemetery where Dick's battered corpse had been first buried. An evening mist laced eerily amongst the tombstones and they found their steps guided along a gravel path to a large gap in the seriated ranks. As the crunch of footfall on gravel faded, an overwhelming 'presence' was experienced and they each stood in the caring silence, lost in their thoughts of the brother they might have shared.

Next morning they visited the crash site at Bahrenhorst with several local people including Franz Bruhn, who pointed to the precise spot where the Mustang stopped, then to the forest with its tantalising chance of escape. Franz recalled Dick's capture, then related how the burnt-out fighter had first been zealously guarded but later abandoned to a horde of excited children, innocent and oblivious of the pilot's fate. Eventually, a salvage team had winched the wings and broken fuselage over the tall trees lining the roadside and transported them to the smelters.

Questioning Franz about Sturmfuhrer Peters, Char felt the only sense of discomfort so far encountered. Clearly their hosts wished to disassociate themselves from such a person, but were apparently embarrassed because it had to be admitted that he was a local man who embraced the evil that once permeated their country.

Dick died challenging that evil. He had fallen into its grasp and suffered indescribable horrors before the life he deserved was stolen by murderous thugs who had, or have, evaded justice. It is most likely that they are now dead, but the creed they represented is still capable of infecting mankind. Unless we remember and respect the sacrifice of decent young men like Dick Baldridge, we risk again the rise of such despotism.

The Baldridge family took from Bad Doberan a sense of atonement, memories of friendship and gestures of goodwill. The people of that community cannot expunge the past. Good or bad, history is still history and revisionists cannot reconstruct facts. Char Baldridge still hopes that, one day, some undisclosed or misplaced file might emerge to reveal the exact identity of Dick's murderer. She feels that the family still need that final piece of evidence. Even now, legal action may be possible, but at the very least they want to identify all the men involved and verify that they are dead.

Fortunately, Dick's story does not represent the normal treatment meted out to German prisoners of war. His story *does* represent that of a young man, a patriot of a free nation doing his duty. It also represents the excitement felt by a young man who lived to fly fighters and who shared the traumas and thrills with his family. They continue to be proud of him, and so can his country.

Char eventually traced Millie. She had never forgotten her handsome young pilot, but, as Dick almost certainly would have wished, she eventually married and had children and grandchildren – a future denied to Dick.

May 1993: the Baldridge family visit Bad Doberan to discover more about their brother's fate. Left to right: reporter Lutz Werner; Mayor Berno Grzech; Franz Bruhn; interpreter Achim Stracke; John Baldridge; and Char Baldridge with her back to the camera. (C. Baldridge)

9: Engineering Officer

ASSURED AND SELF-CONFIDENT, fighter pilots may have seen themselves as paladins, but attending on each of them was a loyal band of servants on whom each pilot's life depended. His shining steed, an expensive amalgam of airframe, engine, armaments and fuel, required attention from skilled specialists and a support structure ensuring its needs were effectively met. A key figure in this organisation was the Engineering Officer, and George Hampson, then a Captain, was responsible for maintenance and repair of aircraft in the 486FS, 352FG, at Bodney.

George recalls that 'some fighter pilots regarded themselves as glamour boys, eager to show off ... an exclusive club whose members looked down their noses at ground officers. We were called 'paddle-feet', 'waffle-asses', 'gravel-scratchers' and 'dodo birds', but fortunately most pilots were intelligent people who disdained nurturing this asinine stigma. They realised the importance of ground operations and respected us for our efforts, and eventually the glamour boys learned that combat flying was far from glamorous.'

A typical group, the 352FG comprised three squadrons, the 328FS, 486FS and 487FS, initially with 16 aircraft each. For the 486FS, George's role was 'maintaining as many aircraft as possible in flying condition at all times'. Under his command would be an assistant, communications and armament officers, clerks, a line chief, and one crew chief and his enlisted men for each aircraft. Also required were radio technicians, fuel and oxygen truck drivers, a carpenter and a sheet metal worker.

Most Engineering Officers had an engineering degree and understood a range of technical aspects, but their philosophy was predominantly to remove and replace anything that malfunctioned rather than risk repair, although component shortages frequently forced a high level of ingenuity. Together, the men, 'worked as a team – there was no petty bickering or jealousy'.

Built on Norfolk breckland, Bodney first served as a satellite for nearby Watton and was a grass aerodrome later

Captain George Hampson, Engineering Officer for the 486FS, 352FG, pictured outside his quarters at Bodney. (G. Hampson)

laid with PSP (Pierced Steel Planking) to take the burly P-47. The status of every 486FS aircraft was chalked up on a large blackboard in George's office and he held a well-stocked rack of technical manuals.

'Pilots, including the CO, would come in and ask questions or check on their airplanes. Ground crews could come in at any time – it was very democratic. Sometimes they just came in to get out of the rain or get warm. That was OK, they deserved it. I wasn't always in the office; I spent more time walking or riding around the line in my jeep, checking on things.

'The word "line" was used loosely to designate the general area where the planes were; they were actually dispersed in random patterns to reduce vulnerability to air attack. Enlisted men are the ones who deserve recognition because they were out there in all kinds of nasty weather changing spark plugs, changing oil, cleaning the airplanes, even waxing them because pilots claimed it gave more miles per hour. Line chiefs and their assistants were the most experienced mechanics, and crew chiefs babied their airplanes like mother hens. These guys were not saints, none of us were. Our Air Force was famous for its lack of military formality compared to other branches of the service or the services of other countries, but there were problems that required discipline, and officers provided that. We also evaluated performance and recommended promotions when deserved or changes when needed. Sometimes we weren't popular. In general, on the field, relations between officers and enlisted men were more like those of civilians... Most of us were civilians at heart and we didn't go for military protocol.

'Life on an airfield spawned loose living. Since there was an effective treatment for gonorrhoea, some men were hardly more concerned about getting it than they would be about a common cold. Pilots didn't know if they'd be alive next day, while ground personnel endured dull routines and boredom, day after day, week after week. There may have been virtue in trying to clobber Hitler, but what we wanted most was to get it over with so we could go home...

'In bad weather, the airplanes could be grounded for prolonged periods and that was likely to cause all kinds of behaviour, drunkenness, fights, etc. Even the mildest and most docile amongst us might crack and go off on a tear. I don't mean to imply that all we did was drink. At times, though, it was a way of getting temporary escape from the rigours and dreariness, but hard stuff wasn't all that available. Pubs had mild and bitter, or you might get a shot or two of gin if you were lucky. Although the bar at Bodney had a supply of liquor, it wasn't unlimited.

'The English people had been suffering from the deprivation and misery of war and women took the brunt of it. Many of them had either lost their men or didn't know whether or not they'd ever see them again. They were sad and lonely. So here come the Yanks with their money, cigarettes, candy bars and tinned goods. For many of these women, the feeling was, "Well, they're not enemies, they're on our side and they're trying to accomplish the same thing we are. So why not be friendly with them?"

'The Yanks missed their women and were lonely too. We were appalled by the lack of everything to which we were accustomed. Hamburgers, steaks, eggs, whisky, beer, you name it. It took time to accept mild and bitter, but it was that or nothing... Anyway, we liked the English women, we had parties on the bases and we intermingled with them in the little towns and in London. With all this going on, many of us sympathised with the ordinary British serviceman who was on much more limited pay, rations and everything else. In contrast, for a £1 note we could join a "club" in London and get all the scotch we wanted, and restaurants there had steaks available from the black market, if you could afford them.

'To me, the dominant aspect of relations between Yanks and Brits at the time was a mutual feeling of trust, respect and common objective. Yanks had heard all about Dunkirk and the Battle of Britain... We saw the rubble from the bombings, we experienced a taste of the deprivation and we admired the people for what they had endured. The Brits knew we weren't over there for a joy-ride and that we were sacrificing lives, too. Most of them appreciated our participation and were grateful...

'So, when irritations or conflicts arose and tempers got hot, the atmosphere was apt to be, "Alright, let's get on with it". Warm friendships were established and there were acts of kindness on both sides. One night my train from London came into a different station to the one normally used so the truck from Bodney wasn't there. As I was walking along in the darkness, an English lorry came along and picked me up. The driver spoke right out and said, "I don't know what we would have done without you Yanks".'

Working on P-47s and, later, P-51s, George reflects on the maintenance merits of both machines.

'The P-47 Thunderbolt was a rugged, reliable workhorse which we called a nine-to-five airplane because it required so little "overtime" attention. After a mission, about all it usually needed was refuelling and routine servicing – it seemed that Pratt & Whitney radial engine would go on for ever. Even so, groundcrews had to spend many hours keeping them flying – changing spark plugs was no picnic and there was often an oil slick on the belly that had to be removed. The push rods that activated valves in the cylinders were covered by a metallic protective tube that had seals that prevented oil from gushing out. It seemed like these were forever leaking and had to be replaced. Oil on the windscreen could be disastrous, but I believe this defect was corrected on later models...

'The main problem with P-51s was rough-running engines caused by spark plugs loading up with lead and misfiring. If severe enough it could prevent take-off or the pilot might have to return and abandon the mission. Three squadrons would taxi out to the point of take-off, called the "funnel", and go off four at a time. The last ones in line had their engines running at low rpm for long periods of time before they commenced take-off.

Easter 1944: a P-47 provides the backdrop for a service, with fuel tanks as pews. George thought that the P-47 was 'a rugged, reliable workhorse'. (G. Hampson)

'Engineering Officers were sent to the Rolls-Royce plant in Derby where they were making the British-designed Merlin engine for the RAF. This was the basic engine in the P-51 made by the Packard Motor Co in the USA, but they beefed up various components so that it could be operated at a higher manifold pressure, hence more power. The instructor at Rolls-Royce was the best I've ever had. He explained that the engine was never designed for the manifold pressure we Yanks were subjecting it to. He suggested that, while pilots were awaiting take-off, they lean heavily on the brakes and maintain high rpm. This alleviated the problem, but it continued to occur occasionally.

'Another problem was coolant pump seals, which leaked frequently. When the pilot saw white smoke coming from the engine compartment, he knew there wasn't much time to get down on the ground before the engine froze up... I believe this was corrected on later models.

'During the conversion from Thunderbolts to Mustangs, some missions were flown with a mixture of both – it was quite colourful. After the last P-47 was removed from the field, we had a brand new Pratt & Whitney engine still in its crate. Since our efforts to dispose of it through channels were ignored, there it sat. After the last P-51 was removed and we received orders sending us home, we knew that an inspection team would visit to determine whether or not all the equipment had been properly disposed of. If not, our departure would be delayed until it was, and that would be like a death sentence. So what did we do with the engine? We hid it in the woods and it was there when we left. I've often wondered what happened to it.

'Engines, like people, can have idiosyncrasies with which mechanics become familiar, even if they're only nuances. For example, when it was dark enough, a good mechanic could tell by the colour of the flame from the exhaust ducts whether or not the fuel mixture was incorrect. Given a different engine, he had to start the learning process anew. Regulations required that, after a certain number of flying hours, the engine had to be replaced whether or not it was performing satisfactorily. This was sound maintenance policy, but tough on groundcrews – after having nursed the baby to near perfection, they had to throw it out with the bath-water... If the replacement engine was a new one, everyone was happy because it would only require fine tuning and not much else. Sometimes, however, the replacement was one that had been overhauled at a depot somewhere, so groundcrews were leery and started gnashing

A P-47 and P-51s parked outside the 486FS blister hangar during the transition period. (G. Hampson)

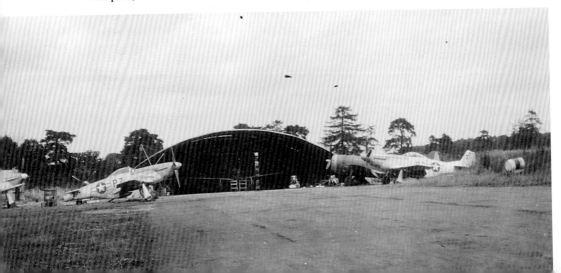

their teeth... Believe it or not, we installed some that weren't as good as the ones we took out, much to our dismay.

'There was a big mound of earth at Bodney that was used for test firing the guns and synchronising them with the gunsights. The 50-calibre machine-guns in each wing were usually adjusted for maximum firepower at 250 yards, but the pilot could request whatever pattern he preferred. Tracer bullets enabled sighting as the guns were fired into the bank, and the tail of the airplane was raised by jack or hoist until the airplane was in a horizontal, flying attitude. The trigger was on the control stick and a safety switch mounted in the cockpit to the left. When this was in the "off" position, the guns could not be fired. At some point during a mission the pilot would flip the switch to be ready for combat and, during his return and when well clear of enemy territory, he would flip if off to avoid accidental firing, particularly during landing.

'Upon returning from a mission, the pilot would taxi to his dispersal area and manoeuvre the airplane on to the steel-mesh parking mat. He would then cut the engine and the crew chief would usually climb up on the wing and talk with him. After the pilot left, the crew chief would climb in and run up the engine to clear it and check performance. In so doing, he'd pull back on the stick to keep the tail down and, simultaneously, his assistant would put chocks under the wheels to keep the airplane from moving.

'On one occasion, as the chief pulled back on the stick, his assistant had just started leaning down to position on a chock and three machine guns went off inches above his head. The pilot had forgotten to turn off the arming switch and the chief forgot to check it, so when he pulled back on the stick, his finger activated the trigger. Fortunately, the bullets didn't hit anything, but we swore that the assistant was as pale as a ghost for a week...'

But death did arrive. On D-Day George witnessed and would never forget its macabre brilliance. He and many others saw at first hand the sacrifice of a young pilot, Bob Frascotti, from Milford, Massachusetts. Only two months past his 21st birthday, Bob had a superb singing voice in the style of Vaughan Monroe, and his rendition of 'Racing with the Moon' had captivated and calmed his audience in the mess. It was, George recalls, a grim irony that clouds scudding across the moon may have robbed Frascotti of a few vital seconds' visibility.

During the afternoon of 5 June 1944, orders arrived sealing the base. Armed guards positioned themselves at key points while other ground staff suddenly found themselves in receipt of unfamiliar weaponry.

'The night before D-Day,' George remembers, 'our airplanes were dispersed in small groups with a guard on each group. They wore tin helmets and were armed with carbines, billy-clubs, etc. There had been mumblings about German paratroops, and ground personnel were edgy. Untrained in combat, we knew that if there were shooting, we'd all unintentionally kill each other and that a few trained paratroops could take the whole field...'

In addition, groundcrews were ordered to violate their pristine P-51s with hastily daubed black and white invasion stripes. The sense of expectancy grew as pilots tried to sleep surrounded by the swelling crescendo. 'Breakfast' occurred around 10.00 pm, with briefing set for midnight. A lid dropped on the fermentation of chatter as Colonel Mason strode in. D-Day for the pilots had begun. The task for the 'Blue Nosed Bastards from Bodney' was to help shield the invasion force from air attack, and the 486FS would be the first off at 02.30, still in darkness.

It was Bob Frascotti's 89th mission. In darkness, the familiar undulations were

Above *The evening before D-Day, groundcrew were ordered to violate their pristine P-51s with hastily daubed invasion stripes.* (G. Hampson)

Left *D-Day saw Bob Frascotti's 89th and last mission.* (352FG Association)

concealed as P-51s waggled like walking swans from the dispersal areas. Night operations were unfamiliar to most and a new experience for some. Bodney's lack of runways handicapped pilots with the absence of illuminated, clearly distinguishable, line-of-sight features, and the airfield turf soaked into the night sky like blending black velvet. A string of temporary lights was laid out, but one of the first fighters taxiing out snagged and snapped the connection. Pilots now faced the prospect of positioning themselves for take-off in drizzle and darkness.

To armourer Sergeant Jim Bleidner, 'the blue exhausts looked like tiger's teeth in the dark' as the snarl and rasp of impatient engines rose and was carried into the surrounding countryside. George saw the red and green wing lights jostle from the 486th dispersal area and the first flights were now positioning themselves near the tower, almost ready to take off. Unusually, Bodney had two control towers. One was in use on the western edge of the airfield and another, still under construction, lay almost directly opposite to the east, in the direction of take-off.

With a burst of power, Lt Martin Corcoran swivelled his P-51 into the wind then taxied forward a few feet, holding the stick back to lock his tail wheel. Unwittingly he was slightly right of the intended take-off line and flames crackled from exhausts as the rest of his flight gunned into position on their leader. In the cockpit of 'Umbriago', Bob Frascotti gave his instruments a final check, then, on command, all four fully laden fighters powered forwards into the darkness. Four Merlins chorused in the glory of release as pilots applied power and rudder to compensate for torque: 50 … 60 … 80mph as lift lightened the load. To climb away, an indicated airspeed of 150 mph was advisable, and all four Mustangs were heavy. Very heavy.

Lieutenant Bud Fuhrman, on Frascotti's right, held his Mustang, gathering speed until he sensed its hunger for flight. Trailing slightly, it seemed to Lieutenant Charles Griffiths that his P-51 was glued to the ground. 'Paddle-feet' and pilots prayed for a safe lift-off. The lights on Corcoran's aircraft confirmed that he was up. Fuhrman followed. Frascotti's wing lights were to his left, slightly lower. Then, at well over 100 mph, 'Umbriago' slammed into the darkened, unfinished control tower. Bob Frascotti's future vanished instantly. An enormous smear of fire, spewing like dragon's bile, burned over the tower balcony and flared malevolently onwards as the aircraft disintegrated.

His cockpit illuminated by that horror, Griffiths punched his engine into emergency boost. Racing from flames and cascading debris, the stick shuddering in his grasp, he sensed the sweep of death's scythe closing swiftly behind and, simultaneously, standing before him, because his own P-51 failed to lift. Then, unsticking, it bounced, settled back, then bounced off again. Barely airborne, it thumped a net post on the 328FS pilots' volley-ball court but miraculously kept going.

A gaping hole was ripped in the as yet unfinished new control tower at Bodney by Frascotti's plane. (352FG Association)

The engine torn from 'Umbriago' lying amid the rubble on the second floor of the control tower. (352FG Association)

In the nearby 328FS pilots' hut itself, pilots were at briefing when Frascotti hit the tower. A blinding flash then a blast hit the building, followed by bullets zinging past as ammunition overheated in the wreckage. Diving for cover, some pilots thought that German paratroops were attacking but, other than fright and a few bruises, no further casualties occurred.

No one present that night would ever forget the violence of Frascotti's fiery death. Flames, flickering and dancing, were grotesquely mirrored in polished aluminium as the remaining P-51s roared past. The 352FG still had its duty to fulfil, troops to protect. As dawn slid, silvery-grey, across the airfield, the charred remnants of 'Umbriago' released a stench of fuel, oil and burning rubber. A gaping hole ripped in the unfinished tower had swallowed the fighter's engine, still smouldering amid rubble on the second floor.

The war, stepping straight into Bodney, spurred pilots and ground crews as never before. Refuelling, re-arming, their teamwork shouldered an even greater sense of purpose. In supporting soldiers on the beaches, every man played his part, but Bob Frascotti had paid the highest price.

A few months later, the tentative toe-hold earned that day had expanded, and freedom for Europe seemed certain. Then, in December 1944, Hitler launched his last, desperate bid to force a repeat of Dunkirk, and broke through in the Ardennes. Part of close countermeasures, George Hampson found himself with the 352FG on European soil as the blue-snouted Mustangs strafed and bombed German troops. Operating firstly from Asche, the group then moved to the former Luftwaffe base at Chievres where George was impressed by the solidly built, carefully camouflaged hangars. One had earthen walls 4 feet thick and was constructed to simulate a farmhouse complete with dummy windows.

Finally, in April 1945, it was back to Bodney and the end of hostilities. Lingering until November the 352FG sailed home on the *Queen Mary* and disbanded, so ending George's career as Engineering Officer for the 486FS. He and many other 'paddle-feet' could be proud of the role they had played.

Wagons enhance the scene in front of an ex-Luftwaffe hangar, carefully camouflaged to look like a farmhouse on the airfield at Chievres. (G. Hampson)

10: Discovering Delbert

'DISCOVERING DELBERT' is a story not only about Second Lieutenant Delbert E. Schmid, but also of the dedication shown by French aviation historian Rémy Chuinard, whose research revealed the heroism of French families risking their lives to help a young aviator.

Drawn from the family farm near Jefferson, Missouri, Delbert's adventurous spirit was more attracted to the freedom of the skies than plodding the soil, and he volunteered for the USAAF. His parents were Swiss immigrants from Bern, and Delbert, the youngest of six children, found many benefits in having four older sisters to tease plus a brother to emulate. Although recently married, Delbert followed his brother into the Army where his 'happy-go-lucky' nature was tailored by training into the temperament of a fighter pilot – stable extraversion, confidence,

*Rémy Chuinard (**below left**), the dedicated French aviation historian whose research revealed the risks taken by French families to aid the fallen aviator Second Lieutenant Delbert Schmid (**below right**). (R. Chuinard)*

The 367FG went operational on 9 May 1944. (R. Chuinard)

individualism, but an ability to work in a team. The team into which destiny moved Delbert was the 392nd Fighter Squadron of the 367FG in England.

His enthusiasm was somewhat dampened by that dreary little war-weary country. On 31 March 1944 a Vee mail home read, 'Greetings from somewhere in England. It's quite a place, but a better place to be from.' The farmer in him found the verdant countryside attractive, but the blackened, bomb-soiled cities were depressing, while the populace overall were 'very friendly but have peculiar ways'. He respected the indomitable British spirit, but became increasingly homesick as the weeks of overseas training, preparing for combat, wore on.

On 24 April he wrote, 'I'm at last in my permanent fighter squadron and will be ready to swing into action very shortly. I'll like it fine because of getting my own airplane, a brand spanking new one.' Flying P-38s, his group went operational on 9 May, and Delbert wrote a few days later, '...I'm flying combat missions now and am still alive. Boy, you sure get a hell of a feeling in your stomach when you get over enemy territory and they start shooting ack-ack up at you.'

A paradox for the American pilot produced opportunities to tour, but disillusionment still dominated: 'I have just gotten back from London where I was on pass. Saw a lot of famous places, such as Westminster Abbey, Houses of Parliament, and Buckingham Palace where the King lives. Outside of these places I think London stinks as does the rest of England. To my conclusion they would be better off if they would cut the balloons loose and let this island sink. Unquote.'

Combat fatigue, eroding each man's quota of courage, affected Delbert. He feared what lay only minutes over the Channel from Stoney Cross as he clambered up his Lightning's access ladder: flak, frequently unavoidable, often unseen until it lanced the belly of a P-38, converting in seconds a sleek machine and its pilot into a defiling stain of fire on the countryside. Nervous fingers now welcomed his post-mission slug of whisky as his group made and paid for its contribution to D-Day. 'The morning of "D" Day,' Delbert wrote afterwards, 'my good old outfit was Johnny-on-the-spot over the beach protecting our Yanks on the ground and was darned proud to do it.'

Within weeks, many of these proud airmen would die as place-names from high school geography lessons now closed blood-stained books on pilots so recently pupils. The boyish jest by his squadron chums, nicknaming him 'Messer' Schmid, rang hollow as voices and faces became memories. Seven over Cherbourg on one day alone. On 22 June, a prelude to the Army assault witnessed over 1,000 fighter-bombers attacking the heavily defended port. Delbert was lucky to escape, crash-landing his flak-lacerated P-38 on a recently liberated airfield at Beuzeville au Plain. It was 3 July before he returned to operations, a shaken and apprehensive young pilot now needing every sinew of courage.

In the ten days since Cherbourg, the Allied armies had overcome tenacious resistance, battling to secure positions. Plans for penetrating further into France were behind schedule. Many D-Day objectives remained untaken, and General Omar N. Bradley still sought the opportunity for a southern thrust after bitter fighting on the Cotentin peninsula. Combat in the 'bocage', a landscape of roads recessed between tough hedgerows, favoured a determined defence. Field Marshall Gerd von Rundstedt effectively used the superiority of German tanks over most Allied armour, but, lacking air supremacy, his Panzers depended increasingly on flak for protection. Light AA units could swiftly deploy around his armour and make any low-altitude attack very dangerous.

The Cotentin peninsula was divided, with Americans in the north still thwarted by stubborn German resistance. From Mont-Castre to the east of la Haye-du-Puits, the 90th US Infantry Division found its advance blocked, while the 79th Infantry Division was similarly detained nearer the west coast of the peninsula. Allied air support maintained a constant shuttle from Southern England to pound German positions and the communications network on which they depended. During this phase of operations, the 367FG enhanced its reputation as 'The Dynamite Gang', and the targets on 3 July were typical. The 393 and 394FS attacked rail and road traffic, while Delbert's 392FS received a special briefing for their objective, a clutch of Panzers, possibly to Division strength, encamped near Mesnil Garnier, north-east of Villedieu. An officer from a US armoured division warned the squadron that their target would be well-protected by AA batteries, and they should avoid going below 5,000 feet to release the two 1,000lb bombs burdening each aircraft.

Airborne at 8.17 pm, Major R. C. Rogers led the 392FS seawards, but, as so often before, the weather failed to meet predictions. Encountering a dense overcast over the Channel, he found that the clouds continuing into Normandy covered landmarks necessary for precise navigation. North-west of St Lo, the three squadrons separated for their assigned targets and Rogers guided his 12 Lightnings south of known flak at Coutances, intending to manoeuvre into Mesnil Garnier from the direction least expected. His calculations put them near the target, but finding it now forced a cautious descent through the concealing cloudscape. Ordering one section of four to remain overhead, Major Rogers eased the other eight into the overcast.

P-38s of the 367FG. The unit earned its reputation as 'The Dynamite Gang'. (R. Chuinard)

Left   Clark 'Doc' Livingstone shared some of the hazardous missions flown by Delbert. (R. Chuinard)

Above   *Fellow pilot James Paschall with his P-38 'Viking 2' pictured later in the war.* (R. Chuinard)

In the countryside below, Captain Fritz Hofmeister of the Leichte Flakabteilung 752 (v) 2.Batterie had positioned his 12 3.7cm cannons for just such an occasion. Reacting swiftly to the alarm, Hofmeister's experienced gun crews took action stations, barrels swivelling towards the thrum of Allison aero-engines.

The P-38 pilots descended warily, hands poised to power on the controls like gunmen in a shoot-out. At 21.02, Hofmeister saw the familiar twin-boomed silhouettes slide from cloud at an altitude of some 1,200 feet or less. Visible to the pilots was the cathedral of Coutances, but the illusion of serenity now shattered as the first and second of Hofmeister's platoons barked into action, followed swiftly by numbers three and four. In seconds, the rapidly firing weapons hurled 108 shells into the American formation, lines of tracer lacerating the summer evening sky.

Ambushed, the P-38 formation scattered like startled starlings, engines shrilling urgency as they climbed, twisting away from danger. Except one. Piteously, a

A 3.7cm Flak 18 anti-aircraft gun similar to those that caused Delbert's downfall. (T. J. Gander)

Lightning now trailed a thickening streamer of oily black smoke from its port engine. Oberwachtmeister Bohme of 5./752 and Ogfr Feith of the LuftGauPost Amt (Air District Mail Office) witnessed the engagement. They felt not pity but elation at the accuracy of the early rounds pummelling one of the leading aircraft. Skilfully, the gunners tracked their stricken prey from one battery to the next. More strikes registered on their opponent; the pilot must be either dazed or dead, for he took no evasive action as his damaged aircraft, now smoking badly, listlessly drifted even lower.

Countering the will of his enemies, Delbert's comrades urged his damaged aircraft, 'Wee Willy', to climb. Vicious attention from the guns terrified Delbert and he froze with fear as more pieces were hacked from his P-38. When he tried to manoeuvre clear, the fighter failed to respond, trapping him amid the fury of further explosions. As his friends soared to safety, re-grouping out of range, they heard him screaming, 'I've been hit, I've been hit.'

Then, cutting across his distressed pilot, they heard Major Rogers calmly coercing Delbert to use his good engine, gain altitude and bale out. Suddenly Delbert's fear and sense of isolation diminished, and he even managed to encourage his fighter a few hundred vital feet higher. Steadying his nerves, he realised that it would not be many moments before 'Wee Willy' plunged uncontrollably earthwards, but every foot gave his parachute more time to deploy. Could he get out in time?

Ogfr Feith strained to steady his binoculars on the P-38 as it staggered away from the guns towards the village of Montaigu, its agony illustrated across the evening sky by a ragged black banner streaming from one spluttering engine. Then the trail stabbed abruptly to earth and the aircraft exploded on impact, leaving a dirty column of smoke in the distance. Was this also a funeral pyre for its pilot?

P-38J 42-104173 'Wee Willy' as flown by Second Lieutenant Delbert Schmid on 3 July 1944. (R. Chuinard)

Anxious to capture him or confirm the aviator's death, Oblt Kuhne set off on his motorcycle. Navigating the narrow lanes, he kept the plume of smoke in view until its density darkened the sky overhead. He was now in the village of Montaigu-le-Bois, only 300 yards from the church. Ahead, near the edge of a small meadow, lay the blazing remnants of their victim. One 1,000lb bomb had exploded harmlessly nearby, and the other had bounced wickedly away before embedding itself in the soil

The wreckage of 'Wee Willy' pictured at Montaigu-le-Bois. (R. Chuinard)

undetonated. The snap of cannon and machine-gun rounds exploding in the wreckage deterred Kuhne's curiosity about the pilot – other personnel had the responsibility for finding him.

Delbert had dragged a reluctant 'Wee Willy' up to 1,200 feet, but flames and faltering airspeed now forced a rapid exit. As the P-38 tipped into its final dive, Delbert unclipped his seat harness and tugged the emergency hatch release. Seconds later he was out, but seconds at low altitude can be as long as life itself. Pulling his 'D' ring, he was hardly aware his parachute had opened before terra firma surged up to meet him. An enormous blast announced the arrival of 'Wee Willy' moments before its pilot plummeted into the branches of a walnut tree about 200 yards away. Shielding his face, Delbert crashed in feet-first, creating a cascade of twigs and leaves before the canopy and cords ensnaring stouter branches arrested his descent with jaw-juddering suddenness. Deflating lazily, the remaining folds from his canopy gently screened his view before the stunned pilot grasped his surroundings.

His world became one of nylon-filtered light and green leaves, almost tranquil but for the discomfort, bruising and mounting fear of capture. This intensified when he realised he was entwined in a crazy cocoon of nylon lines and tangled harness. Helplessly trussed, he felt like a parcel ready for delivery to the first enemy soldier who appeared. It was then, through a gap in the nylon and foliage, that he saw a figure, knife in hand, heading towards him.

Farmer's son Alfred Bellais was fetching water from the garden well when the battle overhead disrupted the domesticity. Fascinated, he watched aircraft approaching, the rasp from their engines swelling in the evening air. One, flying lower, was on fire. Alfred knew it would crash when it tipped over and the engines screamed their final call. The blast when it hit shook the ground, but Alfred was even more startled when this white package came splintering through the nearby walnut tree. Only when Delbert came to an abrupt halt did Alfred grasp the situation.

Regaining his composure Alfred ran indoors, grabbed a kitchen knife and raced back to the entangled aviator. He knew the familiar, twin-boomed fighters were Allied and that this was a friend in distress, a brave pilot helping to liberate France. At this instant their roles reversed, with Alfred swiftly cutting the cords. No time for introductions – Delbert was breathless and both risked death if a German patrol appeared.

Demonstrating calmness beyond his 18 years, Alfred rapidly devised a plan. When Delbert dropped free, he ushered the airman into the farmhouse. Alfred knew no English but, thrusting an old jacket and trousers towards Delbert, he gestured for the pilot to hurry and get changed – quickly, quickly. Delbert, still shocked, glanced fearfully around before grabbing the clothes and removing his flying jacket and trousers. Taking the incriminating garments, Alfred quickly concealed them. Their actions had taken only minutes, but discovery now meant death for Alfred and, realising the risks that this unknown youth had taken, Delbert knew that he had to run from the farm and hide.

The burning debris lay close by, a clear marker for the enemy. Scared but desperately grateful, Delbert managed to smile and, gesturing his friendship, turned, raced down the garden and vanished into the undergrowth. Hurrying indoors, Alfred scooped up the flier's clothing and stuffed it into a box, which he hid beneath the stairs, intending to properly dispose of it later.

However, there was nothing to be done about the glistening white signal ensnared in the walnut tree. Hardly had the American disappeared when, simultaneously, Alfred's father Auguste and two German soldiers arrived. The Germans seemed perplexed by the parachute and the antics of the French teenager innocently attempting to disentangle this strange discovery in the garden. Inwardly, Alfred agonised about the box containing Delbert's clothes. There had been no time to destroy them, nor hide them more effectively. No doubt anticipating the appearance of an officer, the soldiers now postured threateningly with their rifles and marched Alfred and Auguste into the house. The search began.

It was too late to do any more about the box. Alfred knew the extent of German reprisals, but bravely quelled his fear, continuing the air of inculpability. His heartbeat quickened as one soldier stooped, peering beneath the stairs. There was no way he would miss the box. Even if Alfred now managed to dash free, they would shoot his family. The soldier stepped back, stood up and turned. The box … had gone!

How? Who? Alfred's bewildered expression went unnoticed and he quickly regained his composure, externally slightly obsequious for the German's benefit, internally puzzled but jubilant. The search found nothing, but the pilot's parachute plainly stated his arrival and the Germans' anger increased. Auguste Bellais, sensing that his family's lives were in jeopardy and that one wrong word meant violent retribution, now used every bit of guile he could muster. Pretending subservience, he explained at length how his son had found the parachute on returning home. No airman had been seen, it was a surprise to them. Neither soldier seemed to comprehend nor care as Auguste continued explaining how he and Alfred had seen the aircraft fall, now almost an hour since. They had gone uphill towards the crash site and seen how swiftly the soldiers arrived. Indeed, many were still there with an officer, and Auguste was soon bundled in front of them, the officer steely eyed and suspicious. Once more, Auguste related how amazed they had been to find the parachute, how they had no knowledge of any airman. He invited the soldiers to search the farm. The airman's whereabouts were a mystery; he wanted the parachute removed; he wanted no trouble.

Ordering his troops to bring Auguste and Alfred, the officer strode downhill to the farm and ordered a thorough search. Ominously, he unsnapped the flap of his holster and withdrew the pistol. Cocking the firing mechanism, he pointed it at Auguste and demanded, 'Where is the airman?' For some 90 minutes the German harangued and attempted to intimidate an implacable Auguste, who calmly and consistently denied any knowledge of the American airman. Thankfully, further searching found nothing in the farm and the Germans eventually departed. Showing supreme courage, the Bellais family had helped Delbert on the path to freedom. Today, a reminder of the risks they took still stands by the farmhouse wall. The second 1,000lb bomb from Delbert's aircraft was defused in 1946 and serves peacefully as a pot plant stand.

That the Bellais family survived can be credited to another fast-thinking Frenchman, their neighbour Monsieur Legallais. Seeing the flier descend he approached the Bellais home but, uncertain about events, concealed himself at the bottom of the garden. When the disguised Delbert emerged, Monsieur Legallais knew that Alfred had assisted the still-bewildered airman and felt that he, too, should help. Calling Delbert, Monsieur Legallais managed to make the American understand that he was a friend and quickly hid the pilot before darting into the farmhouse. It would have taken only seconds for a search party to discover evidence condemning the Bellais family. Monsieur Legallais easily found the box containing Delbert's clothes and fled with it from their house. In those few frantic seconds, no one witnessed his actions and he had not time to tell young Alfred, who was busy by the tree trying to unravel the parachute.

The Bellais family kept a souvenir of Delbert's visit: the casing of this 1,000lb bomb has served for over 50 years as a pot plant holder. Auguste Bellais is pictured with their trophy in 1946. (R. Chuinard)

Scurrying away, Monsieur Legallais rejoined Delbert. Supporting the shaken young pilot, he speedily guided him to a sunken pathway leading from the village. Further help now arrived. Etienne Marie and another young farmworker had seen the fleeing pair and ran to assist. Local knowledge and cunning kept all four men hidden as they stole from the village to an isolated former farm bakery still cluttered with old equipment and furniture. It was an ideal hiding place and avoided risking exposure until darkness gave time to plan Delbert's escape.

Etienne understood some English but the American seemed in shock or too scared to speak. At first he gave only his name, which the Frenchman accepted with some cynicism. It was two days before a dinghy with 'Schmid' stencilled on it was discovered near the wreckage to corroborate the pilot's claim. Whatever his name, the young aviator was highly agitated and very afraid.

Delbert was struggling to remain calm. Unjustly, he doubted these Frenchmen and was wrestling with this paranoia. More realistically, he knew that his presence endangered them and felt that they would be safer if they were less involved. After giving his name he was anxious to depart, because dawn would see a widening search and he was still too near the crash. Opening his escape kit caused his companions some astonishment over the amount in francs it contained, and this reaction exacerbated his irrational unease and desire to leave. Spreading his silk escape map, he pointed to the Villedieu area, then gestured north towards Allied lines. He figured that they were not that far away and were certainly advancing, but how to get through?

Etienne Marie sensed the pilot's fear and, in his best friendly English, sought to reassure the frightened American. Suddenly the pilot panicked, his manner became even more distrustful and he feverishly packed his escape kit, clutching the small bag as if for comfort. Kindly offering a blanket, Etienne indicated the need for sleep – he was with friends who would keep watch. Relaxing a little, the American accepted and lay back, trying to rest but increasingly tormented by doubt. No words from Etienne assuaged his fear of betrayal and capture, and, sitting sharply upright, Delbert grasped his bag and scrambled to his feet like a stag startled by the hunt. A fugitive as much from his emotions as from the enemy, he could contain himself no longer. His voice suppressing fear, he thanked his helpers then fled into the darkness, the Frenchmen powerless to prevent his departure.

Delbert's fear and claustrophobia diminished as he gulped in the pure night air.

True, he was alone, but the initiative was his and the friendly stars overhead eased his isolation. Moving with cautious speed, he distanced himself from Montaigu-le-Bois so that daybreak would see the search effort diluted over a bigger area. Bearing north, he avoided both paths and roadways, keeping to the countryside where high hedges and trees adopted his shadow in their own, concealing his movements. The landscape was a maze of hedgerows adding weary miles as he zig-zagged through gates and gaps. Crouching and listening by every roadside, he scuttled across to sigh with relief when no cry to halt echoed, no volley of shots burst the silence. He planned to go eastwards towards Vire before turning north, but daylight saw the distance travelled scarcely more than 3 miles.

Journeying without the protection of darkness was too risky, so he found a stout, deep hedge and crept underneath, camouflaging his position with more foliage. Exhaustion induced sleep. Later eking out his escape rations, Delbert hid most of the day before creeping out to continue his journey. For 48 hours he skulked across the French countryside, snatching rest or sleep where it felt safe.

Avoiding Vire, he turned north, intending to cross the lines near Bayeux. Despite the presence of numerous German troops, Delbert avoided detection and the early hours of 6 July saw him hiding close to the rumble of guns near Caumont-l'Evente, a town recently liberated by the British. His exact location he determined by a signpost for St Ouen des Besaces, but the community was too small to appear on his map. That it still lay in enemy hands was evident from the numbers of soldiers seen, and Delbert blessed the good fortune given to him so far. But how to cross the lines? Hide and wait for the armies to roll by? He could get killed by a barrage from either side. Take the initiative?

Reflecting regretfully that his doubts about the Frenchmen who saved him earlier were unfounded, he recognised that he again needed help. Evasion so far had given him self-assurance and he felt more confident in his ability to judge people and situations than he had after the trauma of being shot down. He had avoided further contact with the local populace, but he needed help whether he waited in some French cellar for the storm of guns to abate or deliberately sought local guidance to cross the lines. Moreover, his escape rations had almost gone, and he needed food and water to sustain him for the final hurdle. In a field near quarries on the outskirts of St Ouen, Delbert watched a young man working and eventually judged it safe to make contact and at least clarify his direction.

René Peretté realised immediately that the shabby individual approaching was not quite who he seemed; his demeanour looked too foreign for a farmworker. English? A German in disguise? Greeting the stranger warily, René was soon joined by his father who was milking cows in the same field. The foreigner looked haggard and gesticulated his need for drink. Monsieur Peretté's doubts diminished. Whoever he was, he lacked the air of a German. Monsieur Peretté's offer of some cider was politely declined, but proposing some fresh milk produced an enthusiastic sign of gratitude. At that instant the air was cut by some low-flying American fighters and, pointing aloft, the stranger said 'Comrades' and dispelled any doubts.

Thankful for the milk and USAAF timing, Delbert fingered through his Army phrase-book. Pronouncing phrases and pointing at words too difficult, he indicated his need for directions and was glad of the guidance their gestures gave. Smiling appreciatively, he waved his thanks and hastened on northwards. His progress slackened even more as he frequently hid to avoid ever-increasing enemy troop movements. Proceeding only a few hundred yards from his meeting with the Peretté's, he concluded that further travel was too dangerous. Selecting some bushes,

Claude Glémarec assisted the evading aviator during the final phase of his escape attempt. (R. Chuinard)

he crawled into the one most dense, covered his tracks and tried to sleep to a lullaby of guns and the tremble of bombs in his 'mattress'. But sleep he did until startled by fierce barking only inches from his face.

He could do nothing. The dog had clearly pin-pointed his position and he heard someone approaching. Peering fearfully through the foliage, he was relieved to see a young Frenchman, not the sharp end of a luger. Thankfully, the youth seemed immediately to grasp the situation, silenced his still enthusiastic hound and motioned for Delbert to stay hidden. Disturbing Delbert had embarrassed the young man because he was hunting illegally and this 'game' was more than he bargained for. Luckily, his dilemma was alleviated when he recognised someone working nearby he could trust. Claude Glémarec was now introduced into the final phase of Delbert's adventure.

Claude had moved with his family in 1940 to the nearby village of Les Loges. Their home in Le Havre had been destroyed and his brother-in-law killed during the evacuation, so the Glémarecs had no love for the Boche. Claude decided to help the fugitive flier, a fateful decision for them both. The farmer's son whose dog had found Delbert was too afraid of reprisals to help, but Claude had no hesitation. Convincing the worried airman of his good faith, Claude sent the other youth for food and drink, then signalled for Delbert to stay in his hide-out. An hour later the two Frenchmen returned with a makeshift meal and agreed with Delbert that moving in daylight was too

Odette Glémarec spoke English, so Delbert was able to unburden his recent experiences. (R. Chuinard)

hazardous. Claude made Delbert understand that he would return at nightfall to aid the beleaguered pilot.

That evening, brimming with apprehension, Claude revealed the day's events to his family, half afraid of their reactions. Unanimously they gave their support and, even though the village was awash with the Wehrmacht and the risks enormous, his father singularly embraced his son's decision, proudly proclaiming, 'You did a good job, my lad.' After dark, he and Claude moved stealthily to collect Delbert, safely smuggling the American home. Claude's younger sister, Odette, spoke English well, and Delbert, overjoyed with the warmth and courageous hospitality, was delighted to talk, unburdening his recent experiences and relating aspects of his family life. Here, in Les Loges, amongst friends with whom he could communicate, he slept soundly.

Claude's father had influential and trusted contacts who would be sympathetic: the Mayor and members of the local police at Mesnil Ozouf. More importantly, they could help provide false papers. Delbert's photograph was taken the following morning and a fake identity card for 'Albert' soon appeared.

Early on 8 July the Germans marched into Les Loges, ordering all civilians to evacuate immediately. Chaos ensued. Ordered to abandon their cattle and most of their belongings, the population were bullied from their homes. Snatching only a few possessions, they loaded hand- and horse-drawn carts before covering them with white sheets to make their civilian status more apparent from the air. The Glémarecs told other villagers that Delbert was a refugee made mute and traumatised after being caught in an intense bombardment. Acting the role, Delbert had no alternative but to join the wretched throng slowly wending south, away from the Allied advance and freedom.

Trundling from their homes, the citizens of Les Loges joined countless souls embroiled remorselessly in war's anguish. Worse was to come. Walking with the Glémarecs, Delbert's dismay deepened with every step. It was past noon when the convoy reached the crossroads at La Ferroniere and halted to rest. Out of earshot, Delbert stressed to Monsieur Glémarec how anxious he felt to break away from the refugee column and reverse his direction. Monsieur Glémarec promised to help, but persuaded patiently that it was impossible in daylight. German soldiers, pushing through the mass of civilians, would challenge anyone disobeying orders, and Delbert's disguise would not withstand scrutiny. Fortunately, the pace was slow and the two men decided to continue to Montchamp where they might get more provisions before sneaking out at nightfall.

Trundling from their homes, the citizens of Les Loges joined countless other refugees with their sheeted carts. (Author's collection)

Reluctantly shuffling south, they moved towards Vassy on congested roads now like a river of misery on which floated the unhappy flotsam from dozens of villages. Stretching several miles, the crunch of wheel strakes on stones and the slow clop of tired horses drew into a long afternoon for Delbert. The elderly rode where possible and frightened children clutched their mothers' hands, while the more boisterous enjoyed the adventure, weaving and skipping amongst the white-sheeted carts.

Hearing all day the background noise of aircraft, only a few heads turned towards a familiar drone, but this time coming closer. Then, as the noise increased, more people looked anxiously skywards to see a group of fighter-bombers approaching from Le Ferroniere. Black silhouettes against a screen of high stratus, they were following the course of the road. Some thought an air battle was in progress because one machine was wounded, trailing smoke, and seemed to be under attack from a fighter close behind. More engine noise, and the whine of diving engines came nearer and nearer. Suddenly, monstrously, bombs screeched from these swooping predators.

Claude Glémarec threw himself flat, his younger brother huddled alongside in terror. Both clasped their ears as the world around erupted in the earth-shuddering violence of bombs exploding nearby. More shocks, savage explosions. The deadly hot breath of blast scorched their backs, and shrapnel sang viciously overhead. Screams accompanied the cruel chatter of machine-guns and the whinnying of terrified horses. More screams, some silenced as bullets brutally invaded flesh. Then silence…

Lifting his head, Claude's ears still rang, and sounds seemed at first distant but becoming clearer through the darkness. Darkness? The summer evening had suffocated beneath a curtain of acrid, black smoke now slowly lifting on a stage set in hell. Claude's senses co-ordinated. He was unhurt. Strewn around were clods of earth, broken stones and branches, blackened leaves now settling like grotesque snow. Pieces of charred body littered the road, some horseflesh, some not. Blood. Lots of blood, already blackening into ugly stains spattered on victims and survivors. Some horses had hooves blown off, others fell gutted by shrapnel. Pinned beneath some still twitching animals were children. A few, crying with pain or fright, tried to wriggle free. Others lay ominously still. Claude noticed one cart driver sitting bolt upright, dead. An old lady perched in an armchair mounted on a cart had not stirred. The bullets that seared right through her body had merely caused her to stoop slightly forward, almost peacefully.

Then Claude saw his father, stunned and staring down in shock. Moving to him, Claude would never, never be able to erase from his mind the scene at his father's feet. Odette, his beloved, bright and smiling sister, lay on her back. Her face was burnt, and one leg had been torn from her body. Laying partly across her, as if he had thrown himself over to protect her, was the body of Delbert Schmid, his face also scorched, a large ugly hole gouged in his back. Delbert's desperate bid for freedom was over, but the final, bitter irony had yet to be discovered.

Still unaccounted for was Claude's mother, so he and his father began helping where they could, searching also in the confusion. Some of the injured were taken to a little house alongside the road. A German medical team arrived, nurses and doctors, moving amongst the victims establishing priorities for treatment and the waiting ambulances. It was near an ambulance that Claude found his mother, badly wounded; one of her feet had been severed, but she was at least alive.

Establishing order, German soldiers began shooting the dying and injured horses. The German presence still threatened the surviving Glémarec family, and Monsieur

Glémarec, alert to the danger, performed an essential but sad duty. Furtively searching Delbert's body, he collected any evidence of the pilot's true identify – dog-tags, escape map, his .45 pistol. The young pilot's belongings were slipped quietly to the priest at St Charles de Percy to be handed on in safer times to the US authorities.

As well as spiritual support, other French citizens provided what help they could, and Doctor Mauger with his nurse had rushed on foot from Bémy Bocage. They were too late. The wounded had been attended to by the Germans and a sad procession of carts conveyed the dead for burial, their bodies shrouded in the white sheets that had symbolised protection. Claude and his father helped identify the dead; 30 innocent civilians and the unfortunate 'refugee' would share the same temporary grave until circumstances made it safe to declare the death of Second Lieutenant Delbert Schmid, USAAF. Now, amidst the carnage, Doctor Mauger made a shocking find. Bending over, he picked up a bullet, gasping in disbelief as he stood up. It was American!

In one of those tragedies that war bestows, a group of USAAF Thunderbolts had bombed and strafed the civilian column. The 'air battle' had actually been a P-47 crippled earlier by flak, limping a few miles further on before its pilot baled out. Research by Rémy Chuinard also identified this pilot, who is believed to have been captured and executed, as well as the group that attacked the column. Their records were checked and, uncharacteristically, found to refer to targets 'thought to be civilians'. Rémy recognises that no air force had an unblemished record and no side had a monopoly on courage. However, one protagonist actively represented the reprehensible in mankind; the other made mistakes. Bombing French civilians under these circumstances was an error of judgement, but having himself survived Allied bombing intended for legitimate targets, Rémy feels that revealing the group involved would tarnish the record of brave men fighting on France's behalf.

Many innocent civilians perished under the weight of Allied airpower. Survivors saw in broken bodies and shattered homes the high cost of liberation. They also saw the heroism of young airmen and remember it today in the many monuments and carefully tended cemeteries. Resting at peace near Omaha Beach is Delbert Schmid. The date on his headstone, 3 July 1944, is wrong. 'Discovering Delbert' gives him those few courageous extra days, revealing also how ordinary French people rallied to help only for all to be so tragically lost in a cruel contortion of war.

Peaceful now: the road near St Charles de Percy. From left to right, Claude Glémarec, Alfred Bellais and the Mayor of St Charles de Percy at the spot where machine-guns caused mayhem and death. (R. Chuinard)

11: Lack of opportunity

FOR A FEW, FLEETING SECONDS the two fighter pilots stared at each other. One of them was about to die.

Leutnant Hubert Buschmann was a veteran of 1 Staffell, Jagdgeschwader 'Udet', with some 30 kills to his credit. Most were gained during service on the Russian Front, but, since entering combat against the Americans, the 26-year-old pilot had added several US aircraft to his score. Today, 16 August 1944, he intended to increase that tally and had tricked the American. The shiny, silver fighter, with its impertinent red and white spinner and red checkerboard nose, had misjudged and was now alongside his Me 109. Like a driver on ice, the Mustang pilot had recognised his error, but now Buschmann sought to take the initiative. Holding his Me 109, 'White 1', in its turn to port, Buschmann's ruse had caught the American off-guard and, looking over his starboard wing at his adversary, he guessed how the American felt. As an Iron Cross holder, Buschmann had already seen many men die, and had no compunction because the pursuing P-51s had just shot down his wingman.

Second Lieutenant Richard C. Penrose had recently arrived as a replacement pilot for the 504FS, 339FG, and 16 August had seen his first, and perhaps last, opportunity to fire his guns in anger. At briefing that morning, the 339FG had been ordered to escort Third Air Division B-17s attacking oil installations at Zeitz and Rositz, south of Leipzig. Take-off from Fowlmere had been at 08.25 hours, and they had crossed the Dutch coast an hour later.

Being a freshman, Dick Penrose had no aircraft of his own and was flying Captain James McLure's ship, 'Miss Priss', as 'Cockshy Red Four', wingman to First Lieutenant Hervey S. Stockman, Red Three. They were a small segment of the forces employed. Over 1,000 US bombers and nearly 700 fighters prompted retaliation by several hundred German interceptors in a day typical of

Second Lieutenant Richard C. Penrose, who had recently arrived as a replacement pilot for the 504FS, 339FG. (R. Penrose)

the times. Nearly 3,000 machines from two nations would be airborne in a war that was about machines and the resources required to produce and fuel them. Nations also produced politics, and war is about politics. Some political ideologies deserve to die, with war sometimes being the only option left to ensure their destruction. In the sparkle of gunfire and sun-flashed wings of high combat were the young men from these nations and, innocent or not of politics, many died. They simply represented the nation whose symbol endorsed the machine they flew.

It was at about 10.10 hours that the 339FG took up station protecting the B-17s, and within 5 minutes Major Bill C. Routt, commander of the 504FS, called in bandits approaching at 10 o'clock low. Luftwaffe tactics that day saw the formation of a 'Gefechtsverbande' comprising a 'stormgroup' of heavily armoured Fw 190A-8s escorted by Me 109s. The Fw 190s were to attack in 'Keilformation', a powerful wedge intended to split the bomber formation for easier assault by the Me 109s. German fighters were ordered, whenever possible, to avoid the American escort and concentrate on the bombers. Their controllers vectored them into the US formations over mountainous terrain bordering the River Weser. Ferocious combat saw casualties on both sides and the German formation had broken against the buttress of bombers and escorting fighters by the time the 339FG arrived.

Hubert Buschmann's unit had been scattered by combat. He and his wingman, Feldwebel Richard Karcher, were with a gaggle of Me 109s eager to renew their attacks on the B-17s when they crossed the path of Major Routt's 504FS. Dick Penrose heard Major Routt call in the enemy, but did not immediately spot them speeding in a shallow dive some 3,000 feet below and crossing behind the Mustangs. Drop tanks cascaded clear before the P-51s rolled over and swung about in enthusiastic pursuit.

Dick did not see the first Me 109 destroyed by Major Routt, but in the initial seconds of combat confusion he suddenly found himself off the squadron leader's wingman's wing as the Me 109 formation burst apart. Dick's role was to cover Stockman, not oust Major Routt's wingman, Major Propst. The two senior officers pulled up to resume escort but Stockman was overhauling an Me 109 as it twisted away in a steep, diving turn. Throttle to the wall and at full propeller pitch, 'Miss Priss' raced to catch up.

On 16 August 1944 Dick flew Captain James M. McClure's ship, 5Q-P 43-24804 'Miss Priss', seen here under tow from a cletrac at Fowlmere. (A. A. C. Jordan)

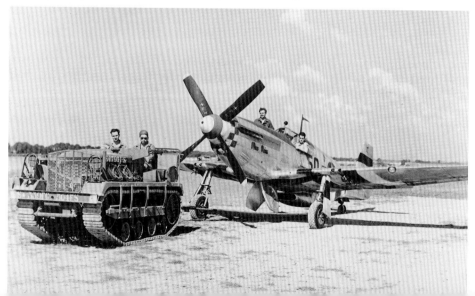

First Lieutenant Hervey S. Stockman, 'C' Flight pilot and Element Leader in 'Cockshy Red Three'. (R. Penrose)

Stockman's P-51, 5Q-X 'Fuxum'. (R. Penrose)

Stockman's bullets punched into Karcher's 'White 3', slightly wounding its pilot and setting the Messerschmitt on fire. Karcher had no alternative but to bale out, leaving the two Mustangs gaining on Buschmann. Intensely excited, Dick hurtled past Karcher's open parachute – he had not even seen the second Me 109 until now.

Diving steeply, Buschmann emergency-boosted more power from his protesting Daimler Benz engine. Now at 15,000 feet, the two Mustangs were closing in and a short burst from the leading American missed, but forced him into an evasive turn, prompting a difficult deflection shot from the second P-51. Tracers slicing the firmament caused Buschmann to steepen his bank, anxiously pressing to out-manoeuvre the leading American. Then, working hard at the controls, he flipped over and dived earthwards, simultaneously making a difficult target by rolling, half rolling, and performing fast, tight chandelles.

Soon Stockman had exhausted his ammunition, and Dick Penrose was also having problems with his guns. It was common for early Mustangs to suffer stoppages and, after barely 2 seconds firing, three of his four weapons ceased. Now armed with only one machine-gun, Dick still challenged the Me 109, conscious that even one hit from its cannon could prove fatal. While comparatively inexperienced in combat, he had acquired over 300 operational hours in America with the 408FG flying A-36s, an Allison-engined Mustang variant. He needed every vestige of this experience as he chased the gyrating Me 109 to 8,000 feet.

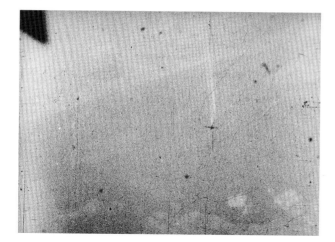

A gun-camera still from 'Fuxum' showing Karcher's 'White 3' Werksnr 165703 going down on fire. (R. Penrose)

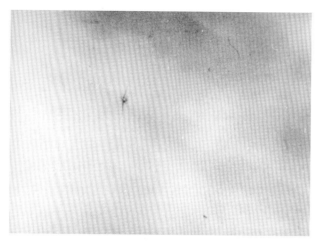

Banking steeply, Buschmann's Me 109 'White 1' closes head-on towards 'Miss Priss'. During this pass their combined closing speed was over 800mph, and Dick's single gun, with a 1.7-second burst, was no match for the Me 109's cannon. (R. Penrose)

At one point he and Buschmann were head-on. Scared but unflinching, his single gun rattled defiantly as he faced the on-coming Me 109. The whirling black and white stripes on its spinner surged in size as the two aircraft converged, their combined speed now over 800mph. Flashing past, Buschmann broke away and downwards once again as Dick pulled his P-51 round in a fast, diving turn. It was then that Buschmann deceived his opponent.

The Me 109 swung left, with the P-51 also banking steeply in pursuit, but the German suddenly cut throttle and dropped flap to decelerate so abruptly that the American risked overshooting as the Me 109 rolled out of its turn to fly straight and level. Chopping power and lowering his own flaps, Dick copied its manoeuvre, but was too close to fire and swung frantically to starboard to avoid colliding with his erstwhile quarry. Flying abreast for a few, fleeting seconds, the two adversaries stared at each other as men, not machines, now locked in mortal combat.

Then, pulling back on the stick, Dick sought to stall out before the German gained an advantage. Coasting past the Me 109 would invite a burst of cannon shells tearing into his aircraft from the jowls of the German fighter now so close. Dick's Mustang reared, nose up, his port wing obscuring his view of the Me 109. Instinct

Another 0.5-second burst chases the Me 109 as it banks and turns. (R. Penrose)

Seemingly impervious to a 1.9-second burst, Buschmann throttles back to trick the P-51 into overshooting. (R. Penrose)

and training combined as, in a last, desperate measure, he thrust 'Miss Priss' into evasive action and, for 4 life-long seconds, contorted his aircraft out of the predicament, knowing that the German, hidden below his left wing, might twist to get behind his P-51. Suddenly he became aware of Stockman calling, 'You are OK now', and realised, with relief and disbelief, that he had somehow avoided his opponent. Without that reassurance, Dick would have stalled out before searching for his enemy, which might have given the German time to better position himself. Perhaps the German had tried to attack and failed, or had simply broken away while hidden from view.

Banking steeply to port, he saw the Me 109 again speeding away below. Continuing the bank to become inverted, he felt his aircraft shudder on the edge of a high-speed stall before thrusting forwards after the fleeing Messerschmitt.

Closing in, Dick saw that the German's proximity to the hilly, treescaped terrain had forced him to level out. Wearing a Berger 'G' suit gave Dick an advantage, and he levelled off at speed without suffering either black- or grey-out. Gaining on the Me 109, he was alert to its previous tactic and opened fire with his solitary weapon in a series of bursts, peppering away from .2 of a second to a full 2–3 seconds. His

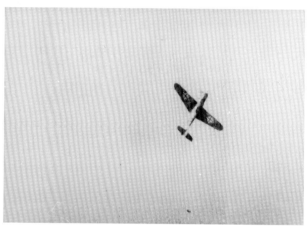

Dick's gun-camera catches Me 109 Werksnr 412806 performing as the elusive enemy banks, jinks and anxiously twists to shake him off. (R. Penrose)

gun-camera caught the elusive enemy banking, jinking and anxiously twisting to shake him off.

The German was good. Many of Dick's bullets found only air, and he had little ammunition remaining. A final .7-second burst, then silence. The few bullets that had hit the Messerschmitt had seemingly made no impression despite several spattering on its fuselage aft of the cockpit. Calling Stockman, Dick was both excited and frustrated as he reported his ammunition status. He was now only 60 feet behind the Me 109, close enough to admire its blue-grey paintwork.

His predicament now was how to stop feinting the hunter and avoid becoming the hunted, because the Me 109 could quickly turn on him the instant he broke away. Perhaps he and the German had fought each other to an ammo-less stand-off? During these few moments fate intervened – the Me 109's cockpit canopy whipped off and whirled past 'Miss Priss'. Dick elatedly yelled the news to Stockman: 'He's baling out!'

Moments later the Me 109 rolled on its back, then suddenly started spinning. Fascinated, Dick glimpsed its pilot somehow caught up at the back of his cockpit before tumbling free at about 1,500 feet, still in time for his parachute to deploy. Only seconds ago it was kill or be killed. Dick's emotions had catapulted from thrills to desperation, but now, as the figure fell earthwards, Dick could not avoid compassion when he realised that the German's parachute had malfunctioned. Instead of burgeoning folds, a miserable patch of material trailing from the pack mocked Buschmann's last terrified moments. Dick saw him slam into the merciless prongs of up-stretching woodland branches while the Me 109 exploded on a nearby field. Swooping over the scene, Dick sought photographic evidence of the burning wreckage, unaware that his gun-camera film had expired. He and Stockmen then headed home.

First back at Fowlmere, the two Mustangs announced their arrival in triumphant victory rolls, then landed to be greeted by jubilant groundcrews. When the 339FG assessed the day, four enemy fighters were claimed for the loss of First Lieutenant Charles Hunter, who had apparently made the mistake of loitering to photograph the parachute of the pilot he had just shot down and was himself bounced.

Hubert Buschmann would be the only aerial victory achieved by Dick Penrose. Short of competition in the air, USAAF fighter pilots foraged elsewhere for targets, and many lives were lost during increased strafing activities. Dick, like many of his high-spirited young counterparts, enjoyed the thrill of low flying and relied, like them, on the 'youth invincibility syndrome'.

On 18 August 1944 Dick flew his 13th mission, a dive-bombing and strafing attack on railway targets near Cambrai. He was assigned as Green Two, wingman for First Lieutenant Duane Larson, and after depositing their bombs on a small railway depot, they machine-gunned a junction and some rolling-stock. Larson then spotted a freight train, and eagerly dived to attack, dousing the locomotive in gunfire before soaring up and around for another pass. Dick then spotted two more trains further along the track, and they had selected one each when Dick saw his companion's

After depositing their bombs on a small railway depot, Larson and Penrose machine-gunned a junction and some rolling-stock. (R. Penrose)

This page and right Duane Larson strafes a locomotive, causing some damage as Dick closes in. In the final frame Dick has stopped firing, as shown by the pointer top left, and the camera is in 'over run' to catch the last rounds fired as steam and smoke boil from the target. (R. Penrose)

aircraft receiving fire from a flat-car-mounted anti-aircraft gun. Ignoring his own objective, Dick swung round and diverted the fire in his direction by opening up at long range.

He now commenced a deadly shoot-out with some equally determined gunners. Streams of bullets strode unswervingly over a recently harvested field, their dust trails stitching an excellent target reference. It was not all one-sided, however, as tracer streaks flashed past his P-51. Unseen by Dick, one shell went through his propeller arc; missing its vital blades by milli-seconds, the projectile skimmed over his starboard inner wing and smashed into the leading edge of his horizontal stabiliser. Tearing right through, it emerged fractions in front of his elevator hinge.

Pulled off target by the punch, Dick swiftly corrected and held the trigger firmly as his bullets again stormed across their objective. Even so, from within that maelstrom, return fire continued and Dick faced serious problems as he headed home. His rudder trim had been shot out and an excessive amount of right rudder proved essential to maintain control. A glance over his right shoulder revealed a gaping hole in the stabiliser. He could not maintain course at the normal 240mph cruising speed because the P-51 skidded dangerously, but Larson provided protection as he slowed to 200mph. Continuing home to Fowlmere he landed the damaged P-51 very delicately. The smashed stabiliser prevented him taxiing in because he could not push the control column fully forwards to unlock the tail wheel, but, on reflection, it could have been worse.

Another brush with flak while strafing an airfield on 20 November 1944 saw him again limping home. As he crossed the end of runway 29, propwash from a preceding P-51 threw his aircraft nose down to starboard and he narrowly avoided cartwheeling 'Beaver Chant' and terminating his career.

After flying a full tour, voluntarily extended by 50 hours, Dick Penrose finished combat flying on 28 March 1945 with 71 missions totalling 320 hours. Separating from the USAAF the following December, he returned to college to graduate as a

This page and above right Dick commences a deadly shoot-out with some equally determined gunners. The third frame catches, centre right, the flash of a returning tracer. Dick corrected his aim after his P-51 was hit. (R. Penrose)

Below 5Q-E 'Beaver Chant' assigned to Dick on 7 November 1944, who is pictured with his groundcrew, Crew Chief Sgt Sol Greenberg and Assistant Crew Chief Cpl Charles Mills. (R. Penrose)

Bachelor of Science in Forest Management. Life among the trees lacked excitement and, hoping to fly jets, he re-enlisted in 1948. His ambition was not initially realised and he flew Mustangs until 1950, when he at last converted to the F-80 Shooting Star. During the Korean conflict he amassed a further 100 ground support sorties before continuing his service flying a variety of early jet fighters. In 1956, his aviation appetite assuaged, he returned to the US Forest Service. Retiring in 1984, Dick became actively involved with the 339FG Association, researching its history and achievements.

His group had not been one of the top-scorers, but arrived in combat during April 1944, later than many contemporaries. Analysing their performance, Dick calculated that they had achieved the best average daily destruction rate for the 8th and 15th Air Forces on days when missions were flown. His single aerial victory was one of them, and he undoubtedly possessed the quintessential spirit of a successful fighter pilot. However, like the 339FG itself, he simply lacked the opportunity for further success.

Respected by pilots for their skills, 339FG ground crew refuel a P-51.

12: Silver wings

CRASH SITES lacking masses of wreckage can still yield small but powerfully poignant reminders of past events, as I discovered at Middleton, Suffolk, in September 1988. The freshly ploughed field was being prepared for re-planting as it had been for generations, and I imagined the scene in that same wheatfield during the harvest of 1944. Owned then by Water Hatcher, the harvesting had finished and shocks of wheat, symbolising the fulfilled energy and growth of another year, dotted the sunny landscape. Another wartime harvest – Britain needed every ounce of crop it could grow. Five harvests in war's shadow – how many more?

Untroubled by such introspection, 15-year-old Audree Georgina Longman of Hill Cottage hastened to get fresh milk from Valley Farm. It was a Thursday afternoon and already Audree was looking forward to the weekend, anticipating the excitement of another dance on the American fighter base at nearby Leiston. Girls from surrounding towns and villages boarded trucks and were taken to the dance, the younger ones strictly chaperoned. In Audree's case, the austere Mrs Marjoram had counted all the girls from Middleton both on and off the trucks, but the dance had been great fun.

A typical fighter airfield, set amid the Suffolk countryside, Station 373 Leiston was constructed in 1943 and known locally as Theberton/Saxmundham. Adding to the confusion, its 357FG had the name of 'The Yoxford Boys' after another nearby town. (M. Olmsted)

Audree's hosts on these occasions were men from the famous 357FG flying P-51 Mustangs – glamorous aircraft adorned with red and yellow spinners and the same dashing colours on each machine's nose in checkerboard pattern. Arriving at Leiston in January 1944, the 357FG had rapidly established their reputation as first-class exponents of fighter combat. Maintaining this reputation required dedication and training, inculcating the lore into new pilots. Acquiring skills meant hours of practice, and Second Lieutenant Charles O. Campbell, a newcomer to the group, enthusiastically embraced this doctrine. His plan for the afternoon of 17 August was to borrow an elderly 363FS machine and gain further local flying experience.

Recognising the familiar sound, Audree shaded her eyes to watch the Mustang, wondering if it was being flown by one of her recent dancing partners. Such wishful thoughts suddenly, terrifyingly, vanished. Before her eyes, in one unforgettable, frightening instant, the left wing of the fighter simply snapped off. Even before Audree's shocked gasp faded, the fighter whipped into a tight spin, spiralling earthwards out of control with no hope for its pilot. Momentum carried the crashing aircraft away from her, but, with growing fear, Audree realised her own peril from the shorn mainplane now corkscrewing rapidly downwards in her direction. Terrified she fled, but the crazily twirling aerofoil was so unpredictable that she did not know which way to run. Malevolently, it seemed to twist as if following her frightened movements. Seeking cover, she fled through a stack yard before diving headlong into one of the straw stacks just as the broken wing crunched heavily to earth only a few feet away.

Dances on the base were popular with local girls, and attractive Audree Georgina Longman had no difficulty in finding partners, albeit well chaperoned! (A. Buxton)

Second Lieutenant Charles O. Campbell faces the camera in civilian garb for his escape photograph. (M. Olmsted)

Having herself only narrowly escaped injury or death, Audree's next thought was for the poor pilot. Perhaps he had survived or been thrown clear and now lay injured. Scrambling to her feet, she raced across the intervening meadows to Title Road, then dashed along it towards the column of smoke. Reaching the entrance to a recently harvested field, Audree confronted dozens of blazing straw stacks preventing further progress and stared in disbelief at an horrific landscape of scattered, burning fragments, unrecognisable as the sleek fighter she had seen. The Mustang had fireballed, scorching a scar of flames across the stubble. Nothing could be done for the pilot. Stunned and upset, Audree remembered the embrace of fun-loving happy young fliers, the laughter and the excitement of big band rhythms. Now this, tears and hopelessness.

Dousing the wreckage in foam, fire personnel retrieved Campbell's charred corpse and later collected the smashed remains of his Mustang. Why his P-51 suffered such a catastrophic structural failure is conjecture, but similar calamities had occurred elsewhere. The aircraft, a P-51B, serial 43-6999, was old, and the 357FG were in the process of re-equipping with P-51Ds. During its service history 43-6999 had flown many missions and suffered some battle damage. Campbell could have exceeded stress limitations, or possibly a wing access panel might have come loose, the force of its opening into the slipstream, combined with other factors, wrenching away the wing.

Gathering every fragment from blackened soil or hidden amongst scorched stubble was impossible, and ploughing that year buried many small pieces that would turn with the plough's travels for decades to come.

Walking across the field, Nigel Beckett and I searched for evidence of the crash. Within minutes Nigel found a tiny, solidified globule of aluminium, evidence of the intense heat. Lack of signals from his Fisher deep-reading detector confirmed the absence of any large buried items from the lost aircraft, but my C-Scope's numerous

P-51B 43-6999 had many pilots and suffered some battle damage during its 357FG career. (M. Olmsted)

signals revealed a cluster of small but insignificant finds, mostly aluminium. Disappointed, I wryly remarked on our chances of a significant discovery such as the Mustang's manufacturer's plate or a pair of silver wings worn with such pride by pilots.

A warm autumn wind was carrying showers across the countryside, and threatening rain was discouraging. A few paces more to my next reference point, then I would give up. Then a crisp, clear 'bleep' suddenly triggered. I stopped, peering down at the jumble of soil and stubble. There, almost at my feet, resting face-down on the crest of a new furrow, lay Campbell's silver wings. All I had to do was stoop and pick them up – it was unbelievable!

Gently wiping the soil from my discovery, its significance and symbolism were not lost on any of those present. Sweeping outwards from a central shield, those wings spoke of the hopes and aspirations cherished by a brave young flier who had fallen and perished precisely where we stood. He had missed the dance that coming Saturday, but his loss, like so many, founded a freedom for future generations to enjoy their dancing, and we should not forget.

Audree Longman never forgot. Later, by coincidence, she married Ron Buxton, whose own wartime experiences, recalled in my first book *Final Flights*, caused him to become an avid aviation archaeologist. Audree had reason to understand his motivation.

Silver wings found at the crash site spoke of lost hopes and aspirations unfulfilled.

13: It's up to you, God

A PILOT'S FIRST MISSION was a nerve-racking affair, and Second Lieutenant Stephen C. Ananian of the 505FS, 339FG, would never forget his on 5 October 1944.

'We were awakened early. It was a cold and windy day. Briefing was the usual quick and efficient session. Mission for the day, Ramrod, escorting two boxes of B-17s … a short hop, four hours … target, Muenster, in the Ruhr Valley … lots of Flak expected … probably no fighter opposition … perhaps a few Me 262s … altitude, 27,000 feet … freezing level at 2,000 … violent up-drafts … gale warnings over the English Channel and North Sea … that means Air Sea Rescue won't be patrolling the flight path … "If you see any barracks in this area don't strafe them. It might be a POW camp, and we would not want to risk shooting our own men."

I was flying Chet Malarz's plane. It was a sleek P-51B, serial 42-106946. His mechanic told me that it was a good airplane and the engine was practically new. Only 10 hours flying time since it was installed. We were in White Flight. Tom Rich was flight leader and I was flying his wing. Take off was at 9.41…

We circled the field in formation while the Group formed up. Landfall out was at 10.26 and we headed out over the North Sea. I could see white caps on the water below us. It looked cold and grey. Just before we hit the Dutch coast we spread out in battle formation. We rendezvoused with the bombers as we made landfall in.

The route was almost straight in across the Zuider Zee toward Hamburg, then a 90-degree turn toward the Ruhr Valley. We had nearly crossed the Zuider Zee, flying over some small islands. Denmark and Sweden were to the north and the Third Reich was straight ahead. All was serene. It was hard to believe

Second Lieutenant Stephen C. Ananian's first mission was almost his last. Note the first aid kit and escape knife attached to his parachute harness. (339FG Association)

P-51B 6N-I 42-106946 now rests at the bottom of the North Sea. (339FG Association)

that we were at war and that the enemy was below. Suddenly BAM! One puff of black smoke, with an angry-looking orange centre – flak! My engine quit cold. I lost power.

"Upper White Leader, this is Upper White Two here, my engine just cut out! I've been hit!"

Tom's calm voice replied, "Upper White Two, this is Upper White Leader, I'll go back with you. Do you know what's wrong?"

I knew I must have been hit but it didn't make sense. One burst of flak at this altitude could never hit anyone … no smoke … no holes that I could see. I realised that the engine was running but it just didn't have any power. I checked all the instruments … oil temperature OK, coolant temperature OK, fuel pressure normal, oil pressure seemed a little low … had plenty of gas in my wing tanks, but switched to fuselage tank just in case … no help there … supercharger highblower is engaged… Or is it?

That's it! Oil pressure is falling off and the supercharger has disengaged. Since the supercharger is engaged with oil pressure I must have been hit in an oil line, or in the supercharger itself. That was bad news. I can't go far without oil. Five minutes if I'm lucky.

I was now at 20,000 feet over the Zuider Zee, and descending. Bale out here Steve, and you're a dead duck! If I'm really lucky I'll be a prisoner of war. Then again, there was Sweden nearby. But I didn't come all this way to become a prisoner of war in Sweden. On the other hand, I might be able to make it to the North Sea and bale out over the water. Then I remembered briefing! Storm warnings over the North Sea. No Air Sea Rescue boats patrolling today! No sense in worrying about that now. First things first. I called Tom Rich over the radio.

"Let's go home!"

Tom's reassuring voice came back, "Good luck, Steve, I'm right with you!"

That was the way it started. Two silver Mustangs, like knights of old, returning from the crusades wounded, heading back to England. We slowly descended, me in a flat glide with no power, and Rich essing back and forth to keep from over-shooting me; protecting my rear from enemy aircraft.

Tom was on the radio alerting Air Sea Rescue about our predicament. My hands were full trying to get my plane back home to Fowlmere. I thought, "And this is Chet's aircraft that I was supposed to take care of…" My manifold pressure gauge was reading 10 inches of mercury, the lowest reading on the dial. I had the trim tabs rolled back and the stick in my stomach in an effort to stretch my glide to the sea. I kept looking at my air speed and rate of descent.

We hit the coast of Holland and I was over the North Sea! Altitude 7,000 feet. At this altitude, atmospheric pressure was enough to give me the power to keep me aloft! I had hoped this would happen. As we hit the coast we were met by two P-47s from Air Sea Rescue. They were escorting me back. My rate of descent was now reading zero. Things were looking better, but I had a few problems too. Oil pressure was now zero and oil temperature was 40°C. It was obvious that my problem was in the lubrication system. I looked back and saw Tom. What a comfort! Still with me.

Down below the water was churning. I had to cool that engine somehow. If I could only get the oil in the bottom of the crankcase up on those cylinder walls. The automatic propeller pitch is similar to an automatic transmission on a car. Instead of transmission fluid the Mustang used engine oil to control the pitch. There was not much you could do except adjust throttle and the prop pitch controls and rock the aircraft trying to get oil to the propeller housing. It worked! The oil temperature started to go down. Tom asked what I was doing. "Lubricating the engine!" I said.

I kept looking ahead for the English coastline. Finally Tom called, "White Two, I can see the coast. We're going to make it! Great news!"

Then it happened! A run-away prop! While I tried to keep it from changing pitch, all hell broke loose! The coolant boiled out and smoke and oil filled the cockpit. The engine sounded like someone was pounding on it with a sledge hammer. The heat in the cockpit was unbearable! I looked at the altimeter – 300 feet! Minimum altitude for bailing out was 250 feet. It would be close but I had no choice. As much as I disliked it, the time had come for me and this aircraft to part company!

"This is it, Tom. I'm baling out!"

I lowered my seat, pulled my goggles over my eyes, lowered my head and released the canopy. I tore off my oxygen mask and detached everything that tied me to the plane. Just before I disconnected my earphones, I heard Archie Tower's voice on the radio. He must have been monitoring the whole thing back at Gas Pump. Tom answered him, "He said he's baling out."

For the first time there was a note of concern in his voice. Archie didn't answer. Then complete silence.

I raised myself to jump and the slipstream knocked me back in the cockpit. I rolled the plane over and started to drop out. Just as I left my seat, I looked back and saw the radio antenna and stabiliser just behind me. I was afraid of hitting the tail section. I pulled back on the stick a little as I fell and cleared the stabiliser. I pulled the rip cord. My oxygen mask went floating past my face … falling … falling head-first, spinning toward the water… Pop! The chute opened. Whitey (he was our parachute man) once told me that every chute packed at Fowlmere had opened… I'm glad the record was still intact.

Then a strange thing happened. My dinghy floated in the air past me. This dinghy was stowed in a canvas pack that you sit on. It was secured to your Mae West by a line aptly called an umbilical cord. The procedure for a water landing is to loosen your chute harness and drop out of your chute 10 feet above the water. The canvas bag is carried away by the chute. The dinghy is pulled out of the pack by the umbilical cord. You hit the water … splash … inflate your Mae West … inflate your dinghy … climb in, and wait for rescue. Simple! Right?

Wrong! I hit the water almost as soon as the chute opened. Once the harness was wet it was impossible to unfasten the buckles. Fortunately for me, when the dinghy floated past my nose in mid-air I reached over and pulled the CO_2 inflation cartridges and inflated the dinghy! This whole thing took place in a matter of seconds.

I hit the water and bounced from the top of one wave to the next. I was skimming off the top of the waves like a flat rock bounces off the surface of a lake. My chute, aided by the heavy winds, was pulling me for a roller coaster ride! I was flat on my back, struggling to dump the chute, and swallowing the North Sea like a pint of half and half at The Checkers (the local pub back at Fowlmere). I was in real trouble and on the verge of drowning.

Then this P-51 starts to buzz me. It was Tom! What was he doing? He made another pass and then I understood! Having seen my predicament he was trying to spill the chute with his propwash! On his third or fourth pass he succeeded. I think he hit the chute – at any rate it worked. I don't remember too much after that. I couldn't climb into the raft because the chute went down and started to pull me under. I just hung on to the raft for my life.

According to Tom, the P-47s from Air Sea Rescue dropped their four life rafts as soon as I hit the water. This caused some confusion, because there were now five rafts and five dye markers spread over 20 square miles of the North Sea. One of them was me, but which one? Tom said that when they finally located me, I looked like a drowning mouse hanging on to a doughnut. I tried to wave once and let him know I was alive, but I nearly drowned. Things were getting worse! The water was cold. I prayed, and I spoke to God.

"It's up to you, God. I can't think of anything else I can do." God didn't answer. He probably agreed with me.

I knew Tom would be running out of fuel soon. Besides, what else could he do? He must have been reading my mind. His plane passed overhead and wagged its wings. He was wishing me well and heading for home. The P-47s, having more fuel,

were still there … but for how long? I looked up at the circling Thunderbolts. They could not have had too much fuel left, and would have to go home too. Then I would be alone. What could they do anyway? What were they waiting for?

I became aware of a change. It was a sound. An airplane engine. Different! Then there it was! A Walrus! It was an Air Sea Rescue Flying Boat. A twin-wing Flying Bathtub! Now he started to circle about. There was one thing I knew. He could never land in this wind nor on this water with 10-foot waves! If this was Air Sea Rescue's answer to my problems, I was in deep trouble! God, it's up to you…'

God was receiving some practical assistance from Warrant Officer H. J.

Skilled piloting by Captain George Thomas Rich saved his friend's life. (339FG Association)

Bedford and Leading Aircraftsman R. H. Westbrook in Walrus HD933 from the RAF's 278 Air Sea Rescue Squadron based at Martlesham Heath. Scrambled at 12.15 with two escorting Spitfires, the doughty old 'Shagbat' found the P-51 pilot some 40 miles out, still clinging to his dinghy but clearly in a poor way.

Bedford was in a quandary. A Force 4 gale whisked white mares'-tails from the crests of countless waves and he recognised that conditions were borderline for the safety of his own aircraft. Surface vessels were hastening to the scene but, circling the enfeebled flier, it was evident that he could not survive without immediate assistance. Bedford and Westbrook decided to risk it.

Lining up for an approach, Bedford held the amphibian just over her stalling speed, judged his moment, and slithered into the sea. Spray streamed over the flying boat but Supermarine's sturdy product shuddered through to emerge like a duck startled by its own ability. Blasts of power from the Pegasus helped his rudder control as Bedford approached the downed aviator and Westbrook prepared to pull him on board. Stephen Ananian continues his account:

'I think I passed out then. I was aware of the sound of a plane taxiing on the water toward me, and came to. As I rose and fell on the wave crests I caught sight of the Walrus. It had landed and was heading right at me! Standing up in the hatch was an RAF airman with a big smile on his face.

"Here, Yank, catch this."

He threw me a line. Don't know how I managed to grab the line but I did! He hauled me toward the plane and grabbed me with a boat-hook. A waterlogged pilot is a heavy load under normal conditions – with a parachute and heavy seas I was an impossible load.

"Don't worry," he said. "There are two ships on their way."'

The trawler HMS *George Adgell* was first on the scene. Swiftly lowering a boat, its skilled oarsmen soon plucked the soaked airman from the sea's icy grasp. Barely conscious, Ananian scarcely realised he was safe:

'Someone gave me rum to drink. It was warm. I realised then how cold I had been.

Men with another kind of courage: 278 ASR Squadron pictured in front of a Walrus Mk 2 at Coltishall in April 1942. (P. A. 'Ginger' Rounce)

A seaman put a blanket around me and held me in his arms, like a father holding a son. I felt warm. How was that Walrus going to manage to get off? I passed out.'

The Walrus faced serious problems. Attempting to take off, strong waves tore off its port float and, struggling for stability, poor Westbrook was obliged to clamber precariously out on the slippery starboard wing, gripping struts and bracing wires as best he could. Another vessel, *RML547*, had now arrived from Felixstowe, and, after rescuing its crew, tried towing the Walrus, but conditions were too severe and the biplane capsized, then sank. Stephen Ananian would forever be indebted to that aircraft and its crew.

'That night I woke up at an RAF hospital on the Thames Estuary. The next day I was back at Fowlmere. The day after, 7 October, I flew my second mission… Ramrod to Bremen. I had it made! I knew that I was going to live through the war. I also knew that we were going to win!

I don't think I ever thanked Tom for all he did. He had called Air Sea Rescue and vectored two P-47s, a Walrus, a Spitfire (which never found me) and two ships. When the Walrus arrived at the scene I had been in the water for an hour. The pilot realised that I could not survive much longer and asked permission to land. He knew he would be lucky to make the landing, let alone the impossibility of a take-off! I had been in the cold water too long and he felt he had to risk it. Of course Tom's quick thinking, and expert flying, kept me from drowning on splash-down. All those people trying to keep me alive. I am very grateful.

All in all I was in the drink for 1 hour 20 minutes. That Mustang flew, losing oil, for over 45 minutes. I still can't believe I was hit by one shot from an anti-aircraft gun. I'll always be indebted to Tom Rich for his great flying and quick thinking! Flying low over the water and deflating a parachute is some sort of stunt! Why was I able to survive in that cold water, with gale force winds, and 10-foot seas I'll never know. To top it all, those RAF flyers, in Air Sea Rescue. Attempting a landing under those conditions, and making it! Yes, someone up there loves me!'

Steven Ananian flew wing for Tom Rich on many occasions because he felt he owed a debt and repaid it by protecting his buddy. Tom Rich later recalled, 'Never, ever, did I look back for Steve without finding him there. When we were close enough for me to see his face, he was always smiling.'

On 9 February 1945 Steve's smile was one of satisfaction when he became the first 339FG pilot to down an Me 262. Together the two pilots completed their tours and came home safely at war's end to share an enduring friendship sown in battle and grown in peace.

14: Misfortune of war

NOVEMBER 1944. The Allies had recent liberated the Dutch city of Kerkrade on the German border and five-year-old Maria Meys was having fun with these new soldiers. They made her laugh, they made her parents and brothers happy, not like those other soldiers. Everyday she was learning new words of their language and, even more important, they were jolly when she saw them and sometimes gave her candy.

Supporting this liberating army, Thunderbolts of the 36FG had followed the advancing troops through France from Le Mans to Tours sur Mont then Juvincourt. Now they crossed the frontier to airfield A-89 near Le Culot, and Captain William Van Stuck of the 53FS Intelligence Office spoke for them all when he described Le Culot as 'Belgium's worst mud-hole'. Using gravel and railway metals to aid movement over the glutinous morass, the men of the 36FG kept their three squadrons, the 22FS, 23FS and 53FS, airborne.

Harassing the enemy whenever the weather permitted that miserable winter, the 36FG had developed a 'routine'. Former pilot Tom Glenn recalls their tactics: 'We had been attacking fortified towns in support of the infantry and armoured forces. It had been a successful battle plan. We would destroy the German heavy guns, tanks and machine-guns, then withdraw; the ground forces would then attack and take the town. When one flight had expended its bombs and about half of its machine-gun bullets, it would leave the target and assemble over the town to the rear that had just been taken, maybe the day before. It was working well; we had done it before.'

On 7 November the 53FS was again in action and, having bombed and strafed its objectives, a flight of its Thunderbolts withdrew westwards to assemble over Kerkrade at 14.10 hours. Circling once over the town at only 500 feet, early arrivals waited for their comrades and commenced a second turn.

Five-year-old Maria Meys (right) pictured with her friend Marie-Louise Hendrichs. (B. Meys)

In Haghenstraat, yet another armoured convoy of American trucks had just arrived and the GIs were very jittery. This nervousness resulted from an alleged attack by P-47s, and there were even rumours of Germans using captured Thunderbolts.

Banking low over the town, the 53FS Thunderbolts triggered a renewed fear among the soldiers and, before anyone could prevent it, the first, frightened burst panicked a rash of machine gun-fire. Two P-47s were hit, one only slightly, but that flown by Second Lieutenant Charles A. Dimmock received a ferocious burst. Dimmock, a 21-year-old replacement pilot, had been with the 53FS since September and was showing great potential.

The bullets cut through the sky. Cut through aluminium. Cut through flesh. Cut off a future. Perhaps Dimmock died in that instant, perhaps he was wounded. Dipping its nose in a shallow dive, the stricken P-47 showed no sign of pulling out. Closer and closer to the rooftops of Kerkrade, then, clipping through the top floors of two premises in Bockstraat, the P-47 plunged into houses numbered 29 and 31 on the opposite side of the street. No 31 was the home of the Meys family. If not dead already, Dimmock died as his P-47 exploded, destroying both dwellings.

Racing to the scene, Dutch police and firemen were helped by American soldiers, but water supplies were erratic in the war-torn town and proved insufficient to douse the conflagration. Rescuers retrieved Maria Meys's badly injured mother, but there was no sign of her pretty, fun-loving little daughter.

Later that day, when the blaze subsided, Dimmock's body was extricated from the debris and preparations were made to lift the heavy Pratt & Whitney R2800 Double

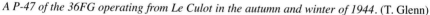

A P-47 of the 36FG operating from Le Culot in the autumn and winter of 1944. (T. Glenn)

The devastation in Bockstraat on 7 November 1944. (R. W. M. A. Putz)

Wasp radial engine still embedded in the rubble. Beneath the burnt engine they found the charred remains of a child.

Maria Anna Catharina Meys never grew up in the freedom she deserved. Charles F. Dimmock was among the first of 8,301 fallen to be interred in the US Cemetery at Margraten in the Netherlands where he rests today. Both were victims of a cruel misfortune in a war that one had not understood, the other had not wanted. Both names are testimony to its tragedy and wastefulness.

After clearing the street of debris, wreckage of the P-47 is extracted from dwellings destroyed in the crash.

15: A Mustang, blessed or blesséd

FIRST LIEUTENANT LUCIEN O. SONNIER named his Mustang 'T-Lou' after his girlfriend, and even had the aircraft formally blessed. At this precise moment, on 1 March 1945, it seemed certain that the next religious rites might be his last.

Climbing away from the 356FG base at Martlesham Heath for a bomber escort mission, Lucien was increasing power when the Packard Merlin backfired loudly, confirming yesterday's suspicions. Worried about the engine's behaviour, he had 'T-Lou' taken into the 359FS maintenance hangar for a compression check. The result was 11 cylinders at the normal 75psi, but one down to only 15psi, which Lucien felt was unsafe. However, a technical expert visiting from Rolls-Royce offered reassurances, but was not obliged to fly behind his judgement, as Lucien was.

First Lieutenant Lucien O. Sonnier had 44-15185 'T-Lou' blessed in a ceremony at Martlesham Heath. (D. Wade/L. O. Sonnier)

Seconds after backfiring, the engine belched a great burst of black smoke from the starboard side of the cowling. Rapidly turning white, the smoke signified sudden coolant loss, then the engine exploded and caught fire. Streaming flames, Lucien's P-51 dropped from formation in a steep dive to destruction.

On his milk round, Alfred Osborne was delivering to the Council Houses in the tiny Suffolk hamlet of Monewden. It had been a typical wartime morning in East Anglia. Earlier, the adagio of heavy bombers had accompanied the chink of milk bottles on doorsteps. Now, nearer the end of his round, a crisp allegro of Merlins crackled overhead as Mustangs arose and soared energetically eastwards. All but one. The roughness and spluttering drew his attention; he saw the climbing fighter choking out black smoke and his own knowledge of engines told him that the pilot had serious problems. Next moment, the smoke trailed white, then black again as flames spurted and the fighter curved quickly towards the ground.

Lucien had little altitude and little time. Releasing his seat harness and pulling the red emergency canopy release, he thrust upwards and the perspex dome vanished. Flipping the fighter over to port pinged him neatly from the cockpit but, at barely 500 feet, the earth was perilously close. A tug at his parachute 'D' ring produced a silken stream that burst open to snatch him from death barely 100 feet from the ground. His aircraft exploded close behind some houses and Lucien was now following it, descending directly into the flames.

Yanking hard on the rearmost shroud lines, he desperately spilled air to change direction. Skimming the roof of the last house in a small row, Lucien landed in a ploughed field some 200 yards from the blazing wreckage. Alarmingly, he now found himself on the receiving end of his own bullets as ammunition cooked off crazily in all directions. Snapping the parachute release, Lucien ran to put the security of the houses between himself and any indiscriminate round of .50 calibre. How ironic to shoot oneself, so to speak, after surviving such a low-level bale out!

Others nearby faced a similar danger. Working contentedly in his garden at 7 Council Houses, Fred Smith had thrown himself flat when the fighter roared over his rooftop before slamming into the pond near the bottom of his neighbour's garden. A tremendous blast cascaded flaming debris and sent burning fuel showering over a wide area. Several pieces of aircraft narrowly missed Fred's prone figure, and six of his best-laying hens died instantly.

Doused in fuel at No 8 next door, Alfred Kemp's garden sheds ignited, and so too did his rabbit hutches with the terrified creatures trapped inside. Rushing behind the houses, Alfred Osborne was relieved to find Fred Smith uninjured. Fuel on the pond's surface was burning fiercely and flames seared into surrounding trees before rapidly spreading across the grass into garden shrubbery. Fortunately a strong counterwind delayed progress towards the houses. The engine and cockpit of the crashed aircraft had vanished into the pond, leaving both shorn wings swept back on the banks.

Dodging patches of fire, Alfred hoisted wire mesh fencing to release trapped chickens and quickly undid the rabbit hutches; three of Alfred Kemp's rabbits were lost in the conflagration. His daughter Brenda, arriving home from school, feared for the safety of her family and neighbours, but luckily none suffered more than shock, although Hannah Kemp hurt her back diving under the bed! Mrs Kemp now stood anxiously outside worrying about bombs and savings left indoors.

Alfred Kemp had rescued his bicycle and was wheeling it out front when an out-of-breath Lucien arrived. Understandably Mrs Kemp kept retreating fearfully from her home until Lucien reassured the elderly couple that his aircraft carried no bombs.

To avoid risks from exploding ammunition, he told them to stay outside but use the protecting barricade offered by their home. Lucien was relieved that his aircraft had caused no human casualties and gratefully accepted transport from a British soldier who stopped his truck to help.

The authorities were soon dealing with the fire and, apologising for the manner of his arrival, Lucien left after suggesting that roast chicken might be appropriate for dinner. Little did he then realise that he would one day return to those dwellings at Monewden.

Some structural damage to the properties had occurred, but was repaired and events that day became part of local history. After researching Suffolk police archives, I joined a small team investigating the crash site in November 1976. Despite digging through the pond to a depth of 12 feet or more, results were disappointing. Our efforts and expense yielded only two machine-gun rounds and a few nondescript fragments. The name of the pilot and serial number of his aircraft were at that time unknown, not having been recorded by Police Constable Miller. We were also unaware that the size and shape of the pond had been altered, so our activities were off target.

Thirteen years later things were different, and US fighter research specialist David

Left OC-D 44-72148 'T-Lou II' proved luckier than her predecessor. (D. Wade/L. O. Sonnier)

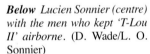

Below Lucien Sonnier (centre) with the men who kept 'T-Lou II' airborne. (D. Wade/L. O. Sonnier)

Wade had not only identified the Mustang as serial number 44-15185, but was also in touch with its pilot. The crash had occurred two days before his 20th birthday, an exciting episode during one of 47 missions flown between November 1944 and May 1945. Not only that, Lucien had gone on to fly F-86 Sabres during the Korean War and continued his Air Force career until retiring as a Lieutenant Colonel in 1971. His three sons also became pilots, but his wife Hilda disliked flying, leaving Lucien to solo for our excavations.

Bureaucracy increasingly intrudes upon aviation archaeology, and David, working with Jeff Carless and myself, now had to obtain a Ministry of Defence Licence, reach a legal agreement and further licence drawn up by the solicitor for Suffolk Coastal District Council, then purchase £1,000,000 of Public Liability (Special Events) Insurance Cover from the Prudential. Finally, on 18 March 1989, members of the East Anglian Aircraft Research Group gathered with friends and guests, including an enthusiastic Lucien Sonnier, to recover the remnants of 'T-Lou'.

Since the crash, much of the pond had been filled in, a fact that had thrown off-scent our efforts in 1976. Now, guided by better detectors and eye witnesses Brenda Smith, née Kemp, and Alfred Osborne, the group was successful in finding an assortment of trophies. These included armoured glass, several hundred shiny rounds of ammunition, wing panelling, and some souvenirs for Lucien. Trophies from his trip were the aileron trim tab wheel and a buckle from the seat harness discarded so hurriedly 44 years earlier when his blessed Mustang went down.

Above *Sharing memories of a dramatic day, Lucien O. Sonnier (left) and Alfred Osborne.*

Right *Lucien Sonnier with a piece of his seat harness, a souvenir of his second, more peaceful visit to the Suffolk village of Monewden.*

16: Corey's stories

VETERAN FIGHTER PILOT Harry R. 'Herky' Corey enlisted on 9 December 1942. One of the lucky ones, Herky survived. From the perfect pinnacle of time, history and, although he might deny it, wisdom, he reviews those days to offer experiences, anecdotes and some serious reflection on strategy:

'Patriotism was not a well-defined concept when you were 19 years old. Competition, winning or losing, and having control were. Being shot at without shooting back was not acceptable. It was known that pilots required excellent co-ordination and perfect eyesight. I was a good athlete and being a fighter pilot would give me the opportunity to shoot first – I spent the next year memorising eye charts unnecessarily.

They failed to tell me about basic training or spending the depth of winter in Atlantic City. I could never recall anything useful that I learned there; the objective seemed to be to prepare you for what lay ahead if you washed out. At formations, in

Harry R. 'Herky' Corey in the cockpit of his P-51. (H. R. Corey)

the black before dawn, it was easy for me to nod off in the rear rank. Frequently, when jolted to attention, I found myself staring, nose-to-nose, into the big, round face of our tormentor, Sergeant Rudzycki.

We had an ocean-front room with a great view from the 12th floor of the Ritz Carlton Hotel, but the only furniture was three double bunks, which I shared with five other guys... The view that brought the war to us came on the night we watched a tanker burn on the horizon, just a few miles offshore...

Nashville, Tennessee, was another roadblock between me and an airplane. We could not leave the site so I never did figure out just where we were; the collection of tar-paper shacks could have been Stalag Luft 1. The mission and activity was designed to separate pilots, bombardiers and navigators through a series of co-ordination and depth perception tests, along with personal interviews. Today, any teenager experienced with video games would ace these tests. I felt in control – it never occurred to me that I might not become a fighter pilot.

Pre-flight was Maxwell Field, Montgomery, Alabama, a permanent installation. We were not flying but this *was* the Air Force and at least we were talking, learning and living aviation... For the first time we had access to an attractive city with beautiful girls. Even without pilot wings, Aviation Cadets had some magnetism. The secret to meeting them was attending church and church functions, a technique that worked well for the balance of our training in the south-east.

We finally moved on to Primary Training at Camden, South Carolina... The field was all grass, and on the tarmac were dozens of biplanes, like those that came to town barnstorming and selling rides. I had a ride in one a few years before; now I would get to fly one. I don't know why we called it the "Stearman" – occasionally it was the PT-17. but never the "Kaydet" ... Stearman was a division of Boeing. The PT-17 had a 32-foot wingspan and was 25 feet long. Maximum take-off weight was 2,700lbs and the 220hp Continental R-670 radial engine provided a maximum speed of 125mph. Its maximum range was just over 4 hours – I was to learn this the hard way. The Stearman endeared itself to all who flew it, because it was designed for aerobatics. Nothing was impossible. The open cockpit elevated the sense of speed, and even modest "g" forces were exhilarating. You were in control and knew that, if necessary, you could aim it between two trees and walk away from any crash landing. It had been done. Every hawk was a potential Me 109, but only in your dreams could you catch him...

The PT-17 'Stearman' endeared itself to all who flew it. (Martin W. Bowman)

My first solo was a near disaster. I was fast on the throttle, but slow on the rudder, and took off at a 45-degree angle. I never felt that much rudder pressure before. My instructor later confirmed that he was always ahead of his students on the rudder because it was so easy to ground loop the PT-17. However, after we parked the plane I bent the trim tab a little as I passed by the rudder. From that time on, after each flight, I bent this fixed tab, if needed, for better trim on take-off. My instructor also always braced both hands just behind the stick when his students turned on to final approach: "There's no room to recover from a snap stall at that height."

Near the end of our tour at Camden, I was scheduled for ground school in the morning and flight time in the afternoon. The game was to beat the mob off the tarmac, otherwise you could waste 10 minutes in line for take-off. I zapped the pre-flight, cranked the inertia starter and fired off. I can't remember a day when we didn't fly, when we couldn't bounce off a cloud, shoot down a PT-17 (provided no one was in the front seat), or just wring it out as if choreographed for some Olympic event.

Then my eye suddenly caught the float for the gas tank in the middle of the upper wing, as it bounced off the bottom of the sight glass. When I took off it must have been stuck at the top, indicating full. I had not taken the time to check the logbook, and now, instead of being the last to land, I had to try to be first. Unfortunately, I hit the peak of traffic and the engine quit before I could get the plane parked. I sat there in front of God and the control tower with no answer when a lieutenant came out to learn the nature of my problem.

The next day I was scheduled for a check ride with Mr Chichester... I aced the check ride, including greasing a severe crosswind landing, the ultimate test in a Stearman. The good news was that this counted as my final check ride and I was the first in my class to qualify for Basic.

It was a short trip to Basic Training and the BT-13 at Bush Field, Augusta, Georgia, one of the few Air Force fields staffed with civilian instructors. The Vultee BT-13 had a Pratt & Whitney R-985 radial of 450hp. The step up in performance and the wide landing gear were welcome, but some of the fun was missing.

Flying became more technical. Night flying was beautiful but boring. Runway lights were preferred because floodlights at the head of a runway tended to make a dust cloud look solid and pilots would drop their planes in from 3 to 6 feet. Formation flying was a new and challenging experience, but it eventually came down to whether your plane had a smooth or sticky throttle linkage. Instrument flying added an intellectual component – it was no longer sufficient to be just a good jock.

Whether under the hood or in the Link, prescribed patterns were executed with the precision of an ice-skater executing his required program. The Link trainer allowed pilots to simulate instrument flight on the ground, under the hood. The results, or "track", would be recorded by a remote control pen on a flat surface. It was called a "crab" and, with a little practice, you could write your initials! Today, computer and video simulation are used.

All turns were required to be shallow, single needle width on the turn and bank instruments. Steeper, banked turns with the ball not centred – unco-ordinated – could result in a spin. Later, during Advanced Training, one could relieve the boredom by doing double needle width turns, which caused the crab to spin like a ballerina! A year or so later, it also became evident from the number of losses we incurred in the weather during combat that the Training Command had failed to provide real-time experience with formation flying in the clouds.

The most dramatic event at Bush Field was a two-plane crash during landing. We were watching the morning squadrons land, waiting our turn. Two planes, one on a high approach, the other dragging it in, were on a collision course over the end of the runway. They succeeded! No Hollywood stunt team could have duplicated the precision. The top plane put his right gear into the rear cockpit of the other plane. His prop cut all the controls near the front seat of the bottom plane. Neither pilot was injured. Fortunately, neither plane had an instructor in the rear seat.

Several cadets had been transferred to bombardier-navigator schools or had washed out; the attrition rate was quite high… The topic that dominated discussions was the choice between single-engine and multi-engine Advanced Training for fighter or bomber pilots respectively. The majority of our small group were dedicated fighter pilots in spite of the significant publicity about the "Memphis Belle" and the "Flying Fortress" "concept". Ploesti and Schweinfurt were recent history, and the Eighth Air Force was just beginning to strive for air superiority, made possible by the P-51 Mustang.

We knew nothing of quotas or how decisions were made, but suspected that many of us would be forced to go to multi-engine because of the increased need for bomber pilots. We had heard about size requirements: two of our boys were at least 6ft 2in and "too big for fighters", while two were certainly "too small to fly a bomber". The question was resolved shortly before graduation in a surprisingly equitable way. We had all been asked to indicate a preference and the whole class (165) was assembled in the mess hall to learn the results. The poll was surprisingly close; only six men would be forced to go to bomber school. Even I knew that this was about 4 per cent, and we all exhaled. The six were determined by lot and each fighter pilot was called forward to choose his lot. Two of the six "x" marks were from our little group, Bernard and myself! I had lost whatever control I thought I had over my future.

Less than a week later the six were called to the Commandant's office. Two men, on a buddy instrument ride, were killed while buzzing. This meant one more opening at fighter school. We were there to draw lots again. This time the "x" was a winner and I had it! Napier Field at Dotham, Alabama, the AT-6, my wings, and a commission lay ahead.

At Napier, the instructors and the atmosphere were Army Air Force, and the level of professionalism improved rapidly… Of course there was the North American AT-6 with its Pratt & Whitney R-1340 radial producing 600hp. It flew like a souped-up Stearman (and the Mustang) and was as graceful as the BT-13 was ugly.'

Having completed his Advanced Training, Herky had just two more phases, Transition and POE (Port of Embarkation) to fulfil before being sent overseas. His story continues:

'We had the wings, the bars, and the uniform, but now there were no girls. We made the transition to P-40s at an auxiliary field near Punta Gorda, Florida. We lived in tents, wore salt-stained flight suits and tried to get into the cockpit without touching hot metal. I was grateful for crosswind landing experience with the Stearman. The P-40 was all nose and had a narrow, spindle-shanked landing gear. It made me uneasy to watch them retract, one at a time, while the wheels rotated 90 degrees – it looked like a wounded crane taking off. However, every increase in performance was welcome and the Allison V-1710 in-line (1,040hp) even sounded reliable; once in the air, everything unpleasant was left below.

It wasn't long before we had to leave all the good things behind. New York City was our Port of Embarkation. We were put up in a third-rate hotel on 33rd Street waiting for transportation, and were required to be in by 10.00 pm. Frank and I decided to see the Broadway show *One Touch of Venus*, but when we got back to the hotel the doors were locked. We tried the fire escape but the MPs had thought of that, so the next day we had to face the resident officer. After he chewed us out, he threatened to send us back to the Training Command, which needed instructors, and was the ultimate threat at the time. However, a few days later I was on a Lockheed Constellation enjoying the view as we headed out over New York harbour. I caught sight of a PBM [Patrol Bomber Marine] approaching at our 2 o'clock level. Shortly thereafter our pilot dumped the stick, then hauled back as the PBM had also nosed down. The faring at the wing root of the "Connie" buckled, banged against the fuselage, then broke off. All except the steward were in their seats with the belts on. The steward hit the ceiling, then broke his ankle when he hit the floor. We returned to the field and took another plane a few days later. I was back in control, at least for the moment.'

Harry Corey's operational career was with the 505FS, 339FG, at Fowlmere, and in the absence of many opportunities to establish a prodigious number of aerial victories, his 505FS gained prominence for destroying 267.5 German aircraft during hazardous strafing sorties, compared to catching 84.5 airborne enemy machines.

Herky eventually became Assistant Operations Officer and, as he later relates, this gave him the opportunity to initiate a strategy for tackling the Me 262. Before then his own contribution to the squadron's performance was 11 ground victories, but Herky still remembers the terrible price paid by the 505FS.

'In my first month at Fowlmere the 505th lost at least eight pilots. In the next month four of our planes strafed an airfield – and none reached the other side. It became

6N-C 'Pauline', 505FS, was Lt Col Joseph L. Thury's aircraft, but was flown on occasion by Herky Corey. (339FG Association)

clear to me in the next few months that strafing well-defended airfields was not cost effective … and history supports this viewpoint. In one year of operation the 339FG lost the equivalent of its total complement of planes. Half of those losses were from the 505FS, and most of these were incurred on strafing missions. Destroying airfields was a job for the bombers.'

Herky also learned to respect 'the other enemy', the capricious cruelty of Britain's unforgiving weather.

'Air combat involves a third dimension because the cloud cover can range from 100 to over 20,000 feet. Winds aloft that can reach 70–90mph are a fourth dimension. We lost 11 pilots and 13 planes due to adverse weather – this was more than we lost to the Luftwaffe… Frequently, missions were flown without ever seeing the ground between take-off and landing. If coupled with the loss of radio contact, this could lead to disaster. We lost two pilots under these circumstances.

It was a long mission, 7 hours, to Posnan, Poland. One element became separated from their squadron during combat and were last heard from in the direction of Southampton. They called for a bearing to our base, which was 40 degrees or north-east. Their transmission was weak and they did not respond. The English Channel is only 110 miles south of our base. A strong wind from the north could easily cause them to drift that far south during a long mission. They went out to sea with very little fuel left…

If we let down over East Anglia we would be competing for space with a few hundred bombers and other fighters. If you happened to go past the base before breaking out, you could meet up with a barrage balloon. The most important key was to establish a rate of descent (or climb) before entering the clouds. This relieved pressure on the controls and helped to avoid the very slow, imperceptible movements that can confuse your inner ear, causing vertigo, and put the seat of your pants in conflict with your instruments. Half of our losses can be attributed to vertigo, which is a disoriented state and can result when fluid in the inner ear responds too slowly, especially if one has a cold (for which pilots could be grounded). Without a visible horizon, the pilot must rely on his instruments and the seat of his pants. If the plane is not trimmed perfectly or doesn't maintain a constant altitude, it is easy to experience vertigo.

During the let-down we would call for a heading from our home station and get an altimeter setting. In addition to correcting for any change in pressure, it provided a slight margin for error because our base was about 50 feet above sea level. It was also a good idea to have an alternative plan in case the radio failed. My system was to pick up the main road from Norwich to London, turn left down the road until I came to my special roundabout, then hang a hard right due west for 2 minutes, let down the gear and flaps, and look for a green flare. On one occasion I had to warn my flight that there was a "Jug" in *our* traffic pattern. Once again we were safely down on that good old grass field, except this time we were at Duxford! Their folks were "kind" enough to point out the direction to Fowlmere, about 4 miles west.

Of course, one could fly 5 minutes in any direction in East Anglia and find an airbase. This was very helpful on one mission when the ceiling was especially low. Captain Richard Olander led Red Flight, and I had White Flight tucked in behind and below so tightly that I was inside Red Four. We came down from 20,000 feet. Shortly after we made landfall, we came over the end of a paved runway. They were shooting up green flares so Olander called for us to take spacing for landing and no one argued. We made one circle, keeping the field off my left wing-tip. When I got back to the flares, we set down. I was enjoying the roll and the cool breeze when I saw something on my left. The other four planes had landed on the second runway and we were headed to the intersection! Fortunately, we had good spacing so that a little throttle allowed us to alternate every other plane at the intersection. It was show time at Wormingford near Colchester, which we subsequently learned was the home of the 55th Fighter Group. After we were inside and the coffee poured, their control tower officer came in with the startling news that we had landed on intersecting runways! Someone in the back of the room said, "We always land that way at a strange field." That together with the hot coffee reduced the adrenaline levels and chased from our minds any thoughts of what might have been or how narrow the margin between success and disaster can be.'

A potential disaster for the Allies was the appearance in 1944 of the Messerschmitt 262 jet fighter. Herky devised a strategy for coping with its superiority and later wrote for the 339FG Newsletter:

'...It is well understood that Hitler was responsible for delays in the production of the Me 262 fighters because he did not consider defence to be an appropriate mission for the Luftwaffe. His Stuka mentality dictated that fighters and bombers were meant to support the Blitzkrieg. The devastation of Poland, the collapse of France and the march to Stalingrad reinforced his mind-set. It is hard for us to believe that Hitler ordered the first Me 262 jets to be equipped as bombers. Some 60 Blitz bombers, introduced on the Western Front in August 1944 after the break-out at St Lo, were destroyed or lost in the Allied advance. It also surprised me to learn there had been a brief but analogous policy disagreement within the USAAF. Thus the first P-51Bs sent to the UK in October 1943 were assigned to a unit of the 9th AF to support our ground armies. It was only after the 8th AAF incurred unacceptable losses that the Mustangs were re-configured and began to escort the bombers on deep penetration missions. There is wide consensus that the Me 262 could have been operational at least 18 months earlier, with obvious implications relative to our superiority, the timing for D-Day and the discomfort of all escort fighter groups.

However, Hitler did have some help from the 8th and 15th AAF. 'Operation Argument' was committed to the destruction of German fighter aircraft factories and airfields prior to D-Day. As part of this operation, the Messerschmitt factories at

The advent of the Me 262 instantly outmoded the Mustang, and new methods of defence and offence had to be devised.
(J. McLachlan)

Augsburg and Regensburg, which also produced the Me 262, were totally destroyed. About 565 jets had been produced by the end of 1944, and, of the total of 1,300 produced, perhaps only 350 saw action. More than 25,000 conventional fighters were also produced in 1944.

In the fall of 1944 we knew very little about the Me 262 except for the scattered reports of jet activity at less than Schwarm (4) levels. Bill Jones, 505FS, was shot down on 9 November 1944 by an Me 262 east of Stuttgart... On 12 December Jim Mankie, 503FS, was also shot down by a jet. I don't recall any intelligence reports or briefings that defined the threat of the Me 262 or what our response should be. However, it was reasonable to expect that the application of the Me 262 would follow the same pattern used with conventional fighters... The probability of even seeing a jet in 1944 was low because there were usually 1,200 bombers and 800 fighters in the string. I doubt that I gave much thought, beyond the conventional wisdom, to alternative tactics until January 1945 when, as Assistant Operations, I was in a position to lead. It was generally accepted at this time that jet activity could be expected on missions to the north along two corridors. One included Wilhelmshaven, Bremen and Hamburg. The other ran from Osnabruck, Hannover and Madgeburg to Berlin. We knew that the range of the Me 262 had to be limited, but all of the targets were within 100 miles of their mid-point. We now know that their range was 60 minutes at full power and 90 minutes at cruising speed.

There were three possible strategies for attacking the jets: 1) intercept at altitude in defence of the bombers; 2) strafe the Me 262 bases; and 3) intercept the jets between their targets and their bases. The official 8th AAF strategy relative to the Me 262 was essentially unchanged, except that we were expected to fly higher and perhaps further in front of the bombers. While this was the only game in town for defending the bombers, it made no sense at all as offensive tactics for attacking the jets. The strategy failed to recognise that our roles were now reversed. The Me 262 had far superior speed and therefore dominated the high ground, while the Mustang was more manoeuvrable and should prevail in a dogfight...

We frequently heard macho statements affirming that jets would break off rather than face a head-on pass. I interpreted this to mean that their pilots were intelligent and simply unwilling to stake their mission unnecessarily on a 3-second kamikaze pass. Their mission clearly was to destroy bombers and demoralise their crews. With their few numbers, they could not afford even the slightest attrition that might result from aggressively engaging our fighters. Their tactics obviously would have been different if the Luftwaffe had the 2,000–3,000 Me 262s that Hitler's intransigence had denied them.

I had never seen a jet at altitude but the speed differential was reported to be 100mph. I did know that the Mustang at 28–30,000 feet was slow and not very manoeuvrable. The stick felt like a paddle in a large pot of mashed potatoes and severe manoeuvres could precipitate a high-speed stall and loss of altitude... . Even with a wall of Mustangs, the jets would simply pick out another box of bombers and avoid engaging our fighters.'

Herky has already described the dangers of strafing, and he realised that bases used by the Me 262 would be afforded maximum protection. In addition, locating them was difficult, but, as he continues:

'... there were a few things I did know about the Me 262. After hitting the bombers, they probably would let down at low speed to conserve fuel. The jet was less efficient at low altitude, while the P-51 performed best at about 15,000 feet. The jets would probably return individually and would not expect to see us; also, at lower speeds the jet could not accelerate as fast as the propeller-driven P-51. All of these factors suggested that the best strategy might be to intercept the jets between their target and their bases. The hope was that, at lower altitude and speed, the Mustang's greater acceleration might provide enough time to shoot the Me 262 down. The validity of this strategy was demonstrated by downing the only two jets we saw on this type of patrol.'

On 20 March 1945 American bombers raided targets in the Hamburg area and Herky introduced his new technique.

'I was leading Upper White Flight in a widely spread line-abreast formation. Lee Steiger, Number Two, was on my left, Bob Irion, Number Three, was on my right and Steve Ananian, Number Four, was off Bob's right wing. I set up a patrol from the Elbe near Boizenburg north-east towards Schwerin Lake, about halfway between Hamburg and the jet base at Parchim... I'm certain that we saw the jet first – he was above, ahead and to the left of me and his wing blocked his view of us. He was letting down on a course about 45 degrees to the right of ours and he crossed about 800 yards in front, between Lee and me. I fired a couple of short bursts as he went by but could see no hits. We dropped tanks, he steepened his descent somewhat and the chase was on.

As the jet crossed in front of Irion, he reported making five or six bursts from dead astern without observing strikes, but we were closing the gap. Bob reported that our airspeed had increased from 300mph to 360mph. I began to think that the pilot had been hit because he never changed his altitude and it looked like he might belly straight in. Several minutes later he did make a shallow turn to his right, apparently correcting his heading. Bob was able to close to 600 yards in the turn and was getting good strikes on the wing and fuselage. The jet then pulled up sharply to the left, trailing a little smoke, and jettisoned his canopy. The pilot baled out but his chute did not deploy. Bob reported that the jet was under power at all times because he had hit his jetwash several times. There was also five-tenths clouds at 4,000 feet, which the jet pilot did not use for cover. I believe this was further indication that he did not see us until I first opened fire. We had encountered the jet at 3,000 feet near Boizenburg on the Elbe and he went down a few miles south of Schwerin. I believe that the pilot was being directed to Parchim airfield and their protective anti-aircraft fire.

We learned three things from this encounter: 1) the strategy worked; 2) we probably should patrol at even higher speeds; and 3) we could have dropped tanks when I first heard that the jets were hitting the bombers, betting on the likelihood that we might find some. If we had run short of fuel, we could have landed on the Continent. What really was needed was a control system ... that could co-ordinate communications between the bombers and the fighters to concentrate our fighters at the jet point of attack and to direct other Mustangs, on patrol, to intercept them before they reached their bases.

My second encounter with jets came on 4 April 1945. The mission was to Hamburg and further north to Kiel. I was leading Upper Blue Section on a sweep ahead of the bombers. There was no report of jet activity. We patrolled in the same general area as on 20 March, but ranging further north because Kiel was also a target... Bob Irion led the second, Green Flight... We patrolled above the clouds, which were estimated at six-tenths to nine-tenths from 6,000 feet down to 1,000 feet.

Here again, I know that we saw him first as he was letting down above us at 10 o'clock and crossed in front at about 30 degrees. I pulled up, turned on to him and got off a short burst, observing only a few hits. He broke down to the right in the clouds. I sent Green Flight above the clouds and we went below. I picked him up again just as he broke left into another cloud. We both broke out into the clear as the jet made a final 180-degree turn to the left. In the turn I closed to about 70 yards and was dead astern for a long burst. He began to break up. I apparently knocked out his left engine because he snap-rolled twice to the left, fell off into a flat spin and went in. His canopy was jettisoned but the pilot went down with his plane somewhere south of Rostock.

On both missions neither jet got off a shot, we maintained the integrity of the section and formed up ready for the next possible encounter. Bob Irion's flight helped box in the Me 262 – it was a team effort...'

Another team to whom Herky characteristically pays tribute is his groundcrew, and he writes in appreciation of their achievements:

'Bless 'em all. The ground crews were the backbone and heart of the Eighth Army Air Force... There were about six non-commissioned officers per pilot on our base, but we were closer to those sergeants who directly supported each pilot in the squadrons. Staff Sergeant 'Honest' John Earnest was my crew chief and George McFarlane was his assistant. We shared armourer George Themascus and a part of all the other specialists. After I was assigned a new P-51D, John said that I should name it. My choice was "Maureen Ann". I did not write it down and left for London and a little R and R. John and George decided to give me a choice of style and

Herky christened his aircraft, then left for London. Confusion over the precise spelling created 'Maureen Ann' on the port side. 'Honest' John Earnest (right) and George McFarlane pose with the nose art. (H. R. Corey)

On the starboard side, 6N-K 44-15467 was 'Maurine Ann'. Herky left this dual personality on his P-51 as a conversation piece. (H. R. Corey)

spelling. However, when I saw the plane, I decided to leave it that way because it was a great conversation piece.

Throughout training, we took for granted that we would fly the best fighter plane in the world. Once operational, we learned to respect the professionals whose technical skills kept our planes maintained for peak performance. "Honest" John and George made sure that 6N-K always got me there and back. Sixty-four missions without having to abort earned a bronze star for them both.

Occasionally a pilot would make it too difficult for his crew to achieve this honour. Radios sometimes failed only at altitude. Engines overheated inexplicably. Group Engineering Officer Harold "Hal" Meyer told me about the most creative scheme and the most innovative solution. The Merlin engine ran rough even at peak performance, a dramatic change from the purr of the Allison engine. The take-off check-list included a test of the dual ignition for a minimum rpm drop on either the right side or the left side. The magneto switch must be returned to the "both" position before take-off. One pilot had more than the expected abortions due to a rough engine. Finally, it was deduced that the pilot had to be running with the mag switch positioned one side only, in order to foul the plugs. The Engineering NCOs rewired his magneto switch so that both banks would also fire when the switch was turned to either "right" or "left" position. There is no report of the pilot's reaction...

There were several accidents on the base. All possibilities were represented. One pilot overshot the runway when his flaps failed to deploy fully. The plane nosed over and a hole had to be dug beneath the cockpit to extract the pilot. One plane chewed up an automobile on the taxi strip. Fortunately, the driver was unhurt. Another plane overshot the runway when the engine faltered on take-off. An empty gas tanker was sliced open by a loose Mustang. An ex-bomber pilot assumed that he was ready for showtime aerobatics. However, when he tried to slow roll a few feet above the runway, he only made it half-way round.

The 505th FS Operations building was on the flight line, about half-way down the runway. We could watch the planes take off from our window. I was the Assistant Operations Officer at the time. As the 505th Squadron took off, one of the wingmen apparently got sucked into the vortex of his element leader's plane. He lost control and ground looped in a cloud of dust as his gear collapsed. However, the pilot walked away. Engineering Line Chief Milo Briggs came in to say that he was going out to the plane to be sure that the switches were off and to arrange for its removal. I asked Sergeant Briggs also to check the trim tabs to be sure that they were set in the take-off position. No cowboy could hold this Mustang on take-off without help from the rudder trim tab. Later, when Milo returned, I asked him if the trim tabs were set for take-off. "They are now," he said. The pilot of this plane had been with the 505FS for less than a month, but he had already wiped out one plane in a similar accident. A summary court-martial was worth $50–75. If his pay had been docked a second time, his wife would have had to send him care packages instead of receiving an allotment each month. This pilot is alive and well today, probably because he gave up flying at an early age.

Missions to Berlin were longer than 5 hours, and it was 7 hours to Poznan, Poland. Even with significant dehydration, use of the relief tube was a certainty; all of the crew chiefs kept a bucket of suds waiting for our return. We had a reasonably effective cockpit heater but the temperature on the other side of the plexiglass could be 25 degrees below zero. Use of the relief tube required significant dexterity, and I recall frequently fumbling through 3 inches of clothing, trying to find something that was only 1 inch long! In order to avoid an embarrassing accident, I developed my

Herky, nearest the camera, borrows 6N-C to lead a formation of 505FS Mustangs. Note the P-51 with Malcolm hood being flown by First Lieutenant Leo H. Becker. (H. R. Corey)

"RTBT" strategy – "Relief Tube Before Target". At best this resulted in a few moments of erratic flying. New pilots would frequently call out, "Herky, check your oxygen, your oxygen!" "Quiet, Blue Two, he's just executing his RTBT strategy!"

Late in the war we were on a search and destroy mission in southern Bavaria. Lt Colonel Joe Thury was leading the 505FS. I led Blue Flight and the second section. Because we were spread out, I was the first to see several planes parked in the woods, just west of the Chiemsee. I called Red Leader to make a 180-degree turn and follow us in. This put my flight on lead and we had a very profitable day. The other two squadrons also found targets of opportunity such that the 339FG destroyed more than 110 planes that day.

However, I became overzealous on one pass. I pulled up a little late and my prop cut off the tops of a few pine trees. Pine needles filled the cockpit like green snow, having been sucked up through the scoop. My first concern was that they might block off part of the radiator, but there was no sign of a temperature increase. My next concern was how to explain this to "Honest" John; he and George would be faced with a substantial clean-up job. Back at the base and parked, I noticed that John had already eyeballed the plane before I climbed out.

"How did you get those 'grass stains' on the leading edge?"

For some reason the only thing we both could do was laugh. I'm certain that John and George enjoyed telling the other chiefs about my "grass stains", but they never complained about having to vacuum out the system. I was also grateful that the news of my screw-up never got back to the Colonel.

339FG groundcrew attend to a Mustang at Fowlmere – the climate was not always so accommodating. Note the bombs 'grazing' in the background. (A. A. C. Jordan)

A crew chief checks his 339FG charge. Herky appreciated the efforts of his groundcrew. (A. A. C. Jordan)

Herky remembers this roomy old Norseman 'Dragon Lady' as the pride of the 339FG fleet. 'It was most useful when Major Archie "Flak" Tower and I ferried nurses and Red Cross ladies from Edinburgh in Scotland to Fowlmere for major parties.' Quite what the guests thought of the undressed lady on the 'door art' is not recorded. (H. R. Corey)

While strafing planes on another occasion, I took a single, small hit somewhere on the right wing. A visual inspection did not turn up any damage. John never gave up looking, however, or showed any suspicion that I might have imagined being hit. When I came back to the line after lunch, my plane was up on jacks with the gear retracted. John had found a single 9mm slug imbedded in the forging at the top of the right strut. It could not be seen with the gear down. Just routine stuff for the groundcrews. The pilots had great respect for all of the groundcrew specialists. I never had any concern about equipment failure. This freed our minds to concentrate on the job that we were trained for.

A period of relaxation followed the

War's end and a chance for Herky (centre) to give George McFarlane (left) and 'Honest' John Earnest some time in the AT-6. (H. R. Corey)

war's end. The weather was beautiful during those few days the English call spring. Routine test and training flights became fun. There were opportunities to jump a Spitfire or another Mustang. I recall bouncing a Lancaster. He banked steeply as the pilots hung the empty plane on its props and flaps. I could see crew members laughing as I turned with them, but could not draw a bead on them to "shoot" it down.

There was also time to offer my crew chiefs a ride in the AT-6 that was available on our base. George McFarlane was in the rear seat, enjoying the experience as we buzzed the perimeter of the field. Fortunately, Arthur Lombardi, radio maintenance Sergeant from the 503FS, was there with his camera to take a great photo. His comment was, "Barely visible below the horizon, this AT-6 mowed the farmer's field along the Base Perimeter fence. The clothing was being dried along the wire fence." I made sure that I did not bring back another plane with "grass stains" on the propeller. However, I believe that we did help to dry out the laundry.

I flew my last and most rewarding mission in this AT-6. I ferried an NCO from Fowlmere to Glasgow, Scotland, where his wife was having a baby. We squeezed into a small grass field full of Tiger Moths. When the British Sergeant Major learned of our trip, he asked if I would take one of his NCOs to Manchester on the way back because his wife was also expecting. It was every pilot's wish to end his tour on a "milk run"!'

A classic 'buzz-job'! Herky feels sure that propwash from this low pass helped to dry the laundry!
(H. R. Corey)

17: Tea Car girl

BETWEEN 1943 AND 1945 there occurred a blending of British and American life that presaged post-war events. Permeating Britain but particularly East Anglia, the Americans caused a cultural shock in many a British backwater. Such was their spirit and evident sacrifice that they left an enduring legacy of friendship lasting for decades and continuing today.

Aspects of life on both sides were affected, and one British custom, amusing to our American Allies, was the habit of drinking tea. To them it was quaint, and we certainly proved unable to produce decent coffee. This feature of British life penetrated American bases in the form of YMCA Tea Cars, some sponsored by American benefactors.

Helen Moore was a dedicated volunteer Tea Car driver, and among other destinations her route included the airfield at East Wretham. Initially operating Wellingtons of 311 (Czech) Bomber Squadron and 1429 Training Flight, there followed a period of Lancaster activity from 115 Squadron and 1678 Heavy Conversion Unit before the airfield became home to the 359FG, USAAF.

YMCA Tea Cars and their crews pictured in bomb-damaged Norwich. (H. Moore)

'In 1941,' Helen recalls, 'my husband of three months departed for the Middle East and the Eighth Army. He joined as a Private and finished up as a Colonel, but I did not see him again for nearly five years. Mrs Vrede Cole, a friend in Thetford (my home town and hers), with a husband also abroad, started the Tea Car service in our area. Several other wives helped – there were two to each car... They dispersed all over Norfolk, a county packed with troops, airfields, battle areas, etc. We also had Wretham airfield to visit. At first the Poles and Czechs who had escaped and come to England were there. Then Commonwealth airmen – Canadians, New Zealanders, Australians. Finally, the Americans.

'On the Tea Cars there was every conceivable everyday article for the men's needs. Shoe polish and laces, soap, toothpaste, razor blades, etc, as well as tea and cakes. Most sought-after was a ration of chocolate.'

During the 359FG's sojourn at East Wretham, the Tea Car became a welcome sight. When Vrede Cole gave up the role, her sister Bonnie worked the run with Helen until she, too, moved on, leaving only Helen to say farewell when the Americans departed in 1945. Invited to write of her experiences for a booklet published at the time, Helen's words provide a different insight on life on an American fighter base.

'Bonnie and I were filled with trepidation when we first learned that we had to work among American troops. We were excited and rather nervous about our reception. We had worked previously with Czechs, Poles, New Zealand, Australian, South African and British troops of all descriptions, but the thought of working with Yanks was ... well, somehow we knew it would be different to say the least. And it was!

Arriving on a day in August 1943 to welcome our Allies with tea and cakes, we were vastly interested in the different variety of clothes they worked in – especially the queer little hats with the turned-up brim, apparently worn anyway on the head but the one it was intended for.

At first sight we noticed how pale and thin all the men looked. In amazement we wondered if these were the United States A-1 men! Since then we discovered that there had been a very rough crossing and a tedious journey to the station. I now constantly tease everyone by saying how much better they look and how much weight they have put on since partaking of YMCA tea and cakes every day. And they do!

When we made our first stop the boys crowded round curiously, looked us over and shook our ego immensely by anxiously asking, "Could you tell us if there are any American girls round here?" They demanded coffee and we persuaded them earnestly that our tea was very good and hot! They found later when the proverbial English winter developed that hot tea was to be appreciated. Soon we were distributing from 30 to 40 gallons daily in our vans, which you will admit is a lot of tea when doled out in cupfuls.

We were cheered when an officer came up on the first day and told us that he was from San Francisco and knew Mr & Mrs Walter A. Haas, who had donated my van to the British War Relief Fund – it was then that we began to feel that "we really belonged".

When at first we arrived in the morning blowing the horn vigorously, the Americans sauntered over slowly. This wasn't the procedure we'd been accustomed to, as the RAF who had been there before made one mad rush when the nose of the van drove into sight.

The GIs soon discovered that they had to run fast if they wanted the best cakes or a morning paper, and now I wish their folks at home could see them when I turn into the field. They come chasing along on bicycles and every conceivable kind of vehicle. They hang on the van and push and pull to obtain the best position in the "queue".

"Queue" was one word they didn't use before – only for a Chinaman's pigtail. Now it's used with great frequency and without ever noticing it.

Of course we had great fun over the differences in the language pronunciation. "Have" was one word that still causes amusement. "Have a cup of tea" is a daily phrase used a thousand times, and I pronounce it with a long "a", which still gets a laugh.

When first told we looked "sharp", we looked at each other in amazement, as "sharp" is an adjective used over here if a person is particularly intelligent. Since then I have absorbed so many American slang expressions that I astound my family by using rather peculiar phrases such as "sweating it out" or "on the Beam" – which just isn't done in polite society and often causes me confusion.

Dealing with the money caused a great deal of fun. The boys handed us out masses of coins of every sort in order to give us, say, tuppence ha'penny, and many always handed us some huge amounts such as 10 shillings or a pound note in order to pay for a one-penny cup of tea. We feel we helped them considerably from the start to learn the value of our system of exchange.

Bonnie and I became big sisters to a whole field of men. After a time we knew most of them by their first or nicknames – knew their life stories, their troubles, their pleasures, their homesickness and their ambitions. I've discussed every conceivable problem with the GIs. Those parted from their wives I can readily understand and sympathise with as my own husband has been away from me in the Army overseas for nearly four years.

As time went on we found our tea wagon activities were only a small part of our efforts to promote Anglo-American relations. All our free time gradually got involved with the life of the field.

Bonnie is a professional dancer and she started a weekly dancing class at the Aero Club. As the class grew I was called in to "be practised on" when she had taught the steps. Bonnie has since left to work with the Y in another area and I found myself doing the incredible by carrying on with about six other girls as partners. These evenings are really fun and are enjoyed immensely by both the girls and the men. Now and again we get a GI to give us a jitterbug lesson – a lease-lend arrangement.

Last year I lent my tennis court four nights a week for the use of the men. This was

Helen Moore made many long-standing friendships with 359FG personnel, including armourer Tony Chardella seen here on the wing of a P-47, with Russ Harrison (right) peering into the ammunition bay. (A. Chardella)

Turning out in all weathers, Helen and Bonnie became big sisters to the men of the 359FG. (A. Chardella)

Helen and her mother with 359FG friends on the family tennis court. (H. Moore)

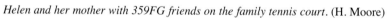

a great success. I hope to repeat them again this year when the grass is induced to grow again on the bare patches!

Almost overnight we found ourselves gradually doing the personal shopping for the whole base. This started in a small way when somebody said, "Helen, can you get me a bicycle tyre or tube in town" – or "Bonnie, can you get my pictures developed for me?" Soon it grew to such dimensions that we spent literally hours each day buying the oddest collection of things imaginable! We've purchased among other things countless tyres and tubes, spokes for wheels, cotter pins, chains, pedals, patches and all the things that go to repair a bicycle. We've bought birthday cards, Easter cards, Christmas cards to be sent to wives, mothers and sweethearts. Those for the girlfriend take the longest time. (I must be sentimental.) Then there's been frying pans, coffee and teapots, a puppy, an electric iron, a mouse trap, cups and mugs, buttons, darning wool, dyes, nails and tacks, brushes, sheets of music, Christmas presents of jewellery and antiques. Photographs to be developed by the hundred. I've never been on such good terms with the local tradesmen. This, incidentally, is good for me.

We've delivered countless messages around the town. Someone rushed up desperately saying, "I'm working tonight, can you tell Doris I sha'n't be in town?", or "Alice is coming down from London or Manchester – is there anywhere in town where she can stay?" Phone calls from all over the country from friends asking me to deliver messages. Telegrams have to be sent, etc.

Of course we've assisted in several weddings. For one we managed at the last minute to obtain a bouquet of scarlet dahlias for a bride who unexpectedly arrived without a bridal outfit! I remember driving a frantic bridegroom into town for this occasion to meet trains. Somehow the bride had set out in the wrong direction and mislaid her outfit en route amidst the confusion of it all. She arrived all right and I attended a very charming ceremony and the bride looked beautiful with the scarlet bouquet!

Our comings and goings soon became known and the boys found they had a regular van service at their disposal. Now we usually find small bunches waiting, coming or going on passes or furloughs. So many interesting incidents happen everyday it's impossible to record them – like serving a bride and groom with tea and cake just before their wedding. We grew to love our life on the field, busy as it was. The boys are always so glad to see us, always so friendly and helpful.

I didn't realise how much we were liked until Bonnie had to go. She was missed very much and I was besieged with enquiries, and still am, as to her whereabouts and when is she coming back. In fact, I began to think it was I who should have gone instead.

If ever we're in trouble with our tea wagon, a puncture or engaging trouble, willing hands are always ready to help out. All sorts of jobs have been done for me too. One regularly mends the tea-strainers when they become the worse for wear. Cake knives are sharpened, even our vacuum cleaner was mended, our poker soldered together, lawn-mower and my watch repaired. These things were all next to impossible to get done in wartime England.

I feel I have so many friends on the base that when I do visit the States, as I threaten to do one day, I sha'n't lack companions to show me around. I feel I belong to the base now so much. The personal loss I shall suffer when eventually they leave will be very acute.

If all Anglo-American friendships prosper as ours has, the world won't need to worry for many a long day.'

Over 50 years later, Helen still corresponds with 359FG veterans and is understandably proud of her role as a Tea Car girl.

18: Wreckage recovered – courage recalled

WITH MOUNTING EXCITEMENT, David Wade watched the needle on his Fisher metal detector register an ever-strengthening signal as he carefully traversed an area of finely tilled soil. Swinging across the scale, the pointer indicated one of the strongest readings he had ever seen, yet the cause of his excitement proffered no visible clues. Even close scrutiny of the rich, brown soil revealed only a few fragments of domestic glass and numerous shards of pottery, probably pre-dating the object of our attention by many decades. After 46 years we were seeking evidence of the wartime tragedy that befell Second Lieutenant William C. Fitch of the 350FS, 353FG, based at Raydon in Suffolk.

Aloft from AAF Station 157 during the afternoon of Sunday 15 April 1945, Fitch was flying a routine training flight. According to the scant records available, he collided with another Mustang, possibly during a mock dog-fight. The other P-51 landed safely, but Fitch's aircraft stalled and fell. Recovering too low, his aircraft clipped the gable end of the farmhouse on Lodge Farm, Thaxted, Essex, not far from

the 4FG base at Debden. Amazingly, his damaged aircraft climbed away and it seemed for a few seconds that he might gain enough height to bale out, but then the P-51 stalled again and nose-dived steeply into a spring meadow 200 yards from the farmhouse. It seems as if his aircraft struck the ground and cartwheeled, killing him instantly. His life with the 353FG had lasted only 11 days since being posted from the 70th Reinforcement Depot.

Pacing out the Fisher reading, David estimated it as some 15 feet square and guided Geoff Barker, driving his digger, to the point where the signal peaked. Gently scraping off the topsoil, we were surprised to find a large wing-section, complete with drop-tank mountings, buried only 18 inches deep. Indicative of

With mounting excitement, David Wade watches the needle on his Fisher detector register an ever-strengthening signal.

A 353FG photographer captures the scene at Lodge Farm on 15 April 1944. (G. Cross)

the state of destruction and, perhaps, the activities of the wartime recovery crew, we found one of the Hamilton-Standard propeller blades beneath the wing together with a set of different-sized dinghy bungs. Working carefully and digging by hand, we eventually lifted the remnants of the wing and discovered a tangle of parachute shroud lines entwined amidst the debris and trailing into deeper wreckage still hidden. Protruding from the soil nearby was the snout of a machine-gun, which was removed to follow the parachute.

Delicately tracing the rigging lines we found the burnt remains of the canopy, presumably made of nylon because heat had melted and welded some of the folds into solid lumps, a reminder of how grim a task it must have been to remove the pilot's remains. By now, we were amongst wreckage predominated by cockpit components and equipment: rudder pedals, remains of the control column, instrumentation, pieces of gunsight, together with numerous controls and switches still unrecognisable. Later, sorting this debris, David discovered items more personal to the pilot: one of his dog-tags and, emphasising his loss even more powerfully, the graduation ring so proudly worn to show the young aviator's achievement.

Having removed the cockpit, we continued excavating by hand until, below soil level, we found a layer of heavy clay still emitting the pungent stench of high octane aviation fuel. It almost became a case of using our noses to follow the path of wreckage. At a depth of about 5 feet we unearthed smashed sections of the Packard Merlin and, nestling neatly alongside, one undercarriage leg and the forlorn remains of a tyre. Chaining the broken engine to the digger bucket, it was easily hoisted clear, allowing the undercarriage leg to be manhandled from the crater. A final sweep with the Fisher concluded excavations before the site was back-filled and restored.

Champagne-cumulus coasted peacefully overhead on a soft September breeze as we loaded the trailer. Once, a lost life-time ago, these mangled pieces had been a

Scraping off the topsoil reveals a section of wing only 18 inches deep.

Fuel boosters, supercharger control and the engine starter switch emerge from the lost fighter's cockpit.

Chaining the broken engine to the digger bucket, it was easily hoisted clear.

Alan McLachlan manhandles an undercarriage leg and the forlorn remains of a tyre from the crater. Wreckage recovered – courage recalled.

splendid machine capable of sipping easily from such clouds and intoxicating the young man who flew it. Less romantically, North American P-51D-20-NA, serial 44-63197, had been coded LH-L in the 350FS. Later cleaning revealed a name in stylish red, edged in black, which had adorned the starboard side of the fighter's nose, 'Maggi'. Evidence of nose art on the port side provided a puzzling and presumably incomplete 'uscul'. Guessing the fighter's full nose art came up with 'Muscular Maggi', but, lacking pictures, this is pure speculation.

Discovering such historical detail would please us and other aviation purists, but, superb as it was, the aircraft is not the point. However interesting parts of a famous wartime fighter may be, the wreckage should only be a vehicle for recognising and remembering the courage of a young pilot who arrived to do his duty so near the war's end but, like so many, never made it home.

Items from the Mustang dig on 7 September 1991 are now displayed in the 93BG Memorial Museum at Hardwick. Wreckage recovered represents courage recalled, a tribute to a young fighter pilot who perished and whose memory will be honoured by exhibiting items from the machine he flew.

Index